CHRISTIAN SHRINKS
Answer ALL Your Questions...

(No Couch Required)

By:
Dr. Ab and Karen Abercrombie

Dedication

This book is lovingly dedicated to our one and only daughter, Sarah. No one we know has a greater God-given gift of relationship and love. You are our greatest earthly blessing, a good and perfect gift from above. We love you!

Acknowledgments

M any have encouraged and trained us through the years and we are grateful for all of the support we have had from colleagues, friends, and Christian brothers and sisters. Yet two primary mentors come to mind who deserve special mention: Rev. Bruce Edwards and Mrs. Jane Mills. We are so very grateful for your leadership and service to our lives. You have discipled us, loved us, and inspired us. Thanks for showing us the beauty of the Kingdom in your lives.

Finally, we must thank the many pastors who have referred to us over the years and the hundreds of clients, from whom these stories and questions arise. Thank you for trusting us and for training us to trust God's wisdom over the teachings of this world.

TABLE OF CONTENTS

INTRODUCTION

We have been family therapists for a long time: twenty-five years (Dr. Ab) and twenty-three years (Karen) respectively. Over the course of our professional career we have seen a great many changes—changes in the psychological profession, changes in our patients, and changes in the world.

About halfway through our journey, we began to realize that things were getting worse instead of better. We recognized that the methods and ideas taught in "mental health" schools were inadequate. The people we saw in therapy were confused, lost, and adrift in the ignorance of the world's wisdom. Increasingly we met with families and individuals who had no moral compass, no spiritual base, and little if any hope.

Even the Christian families who consulted us were confused. Increasingly, the Christian home had come to imitate the methods and choices of the world. The Body of Christ, it seemed, had turned its ear to secular sources of information rather than the absolute truth of God's Word.

Today, the national divorce rate is approaching 50 percent and the Christian divorce rate is alarmingly similar. Forty percent of America's children live in a single-parent home.[1] One third of professed Christians now live together before marriage. Seventy percent of pastors report a history of marital stress, and 40 percent of ministers admit to some form of extramarital involvement. Atheists have a lower divorce rate than Southern Baptists![2] What in the world has happened?

The Apostle Paul wrote in Galatians 5:9: "**A little leaven leavens the whole lump.**" In the Bible leaven is often used as a metaphor for sin. In this example, Paul tells us that it only takes a "little" sin, a small compromise, a tiny concession, and before long the "whole lump," the whole person, the whole family, and the whole church is inundated with ungodly behavior and hurtful choices.

As we watched the trends of the world take life in the patients visiting our office, we began to recognize the futility of our therapeutic approach. We realized that while much of what we learned and now taught our patients had value, its power was lost if it did not find agreement with God's Word. So much of what occurs in the counseling room either minimizes or directly goes against Scripture. Even counselors who claim to be Christian or "spiritual" misunderstand and misuse God's teaching.

About twelve years ago we made a commitment to ground everything done in the consulting room with Scripture. We became determined to learn God's Word and to make certain that we gave no counsel or guidance that violates His principles and standards. Of course, we are not theologians, and we are not perfect administrators of the Scriptures. Yet in a short time, we began to see new life and renewed hope in the patients we treated. We learned very quickly that there is absolute power in the Word of God that cannot be quenched and cannot be overstated.

> **For the word of God is living and powerful, and sharper than any two-edged sword, piercing even to the division of soul and spirit, and of joints and marrow, and is a discerner of the thoughts and intents of the heart. (Heb 4:12)**

The truth and power was right there all along, ready to be applied. God's Word opens areas that are dark and hidden, torn and scared, broken and hurting. God's Word heals with direction, instruction, and hope. Scripture helped us begin to understand that the psychological and family battles, like all battles, are spiritual rather than physical.

For we do not wrestle against flesh and blood, but against principalities, against powers, against the rulers of the darkness of this age, against spiritual hosts of wickedness in the heavenly places. (Eph 6:12)

When we started fighting the right battle with the right weapon, God began to bless and give victory to our practice in a way we had not seen before. We started seeing the unbeliever saved, the backslidden revived, and the oppressed delivered. We saw God answer prayers time and again with His promises fulfilled completely. As families learned the true intent of God, they were relieved to have structure, guidelines, and vision.

You see, the secular world tells us many lies that go counter to God's truth. For example, we are told:

- There are no spiritual and moral absolutes; everything is relative.
- There is no defined structure for marriage, family, and childrearing.
- Emotional and sexual needs should define what is acceptable and normal.
- Attention to one's individual needs (the self) should take priority over commitments to the spouse, children, friends, etc.

Unfortunately, we humans are not capable of running our own lives. We need structure, guidelines, and truth. We crave boundaries and moral restraint. We are wired for monogamy and family life. We were never designed to live unstructured, unconcerned, and unspiritual lives. We were created for the glory of God, to serve His good and perfect will. We were built for submission to our Higher Authority, not the lower animals. God gave us "dominion" over everything on the earth, and we were never intended to be in subjection to the world's order **(Gen 1:28)**.

We have observed that individuals and families thrive when given a strong pillar of support. Our effort in writing this book is to offer the foundation of Christ as that point of reliance. In the work of Jesus we find freedom and redemption that never disappoints. In His sacrifice we are saved from sin and released from all curses that bind and restrict our lives. Jesus said: **"I have come that they may have life, and that they may have it more abundantly" (John 10:10b).**

This book is written to bring you hope: the hope that is in Christ and in the application of His perfect Word. It is our goal to provide you the strong counsel of the Living God, poured out through His inerrant Scriptures. Each topic addressed in this book comes from our experience with patients we have treated, students we have taught, and churches we have served.

Our prayer is that you will see yourself in these pages and that you will identify with the struggles and victories we describe. We hope that you will see yourself in relationship to your personal spiritual dilemma, and that you will embrace God's promise and truth in a literal and purposeful way.

Finally, please do not stop with this book. The Bible is the only true and absolute source of light for a world filled with darkness. Use this text simply as a springboard and dive headlong into Scripture, allowing the Word to take root in your daily life.

Go with us now as we enter the counseling room. Relate to the problems noted; meditate with the solutions God gave; and examine your heart and the needs therein. We know that our God is faithful and He will never disappoint those who truly seek after His will for their lives. God bless you!

CHAPTER 1

WHY A CHRISTIAN SHRINK?

IN NEED OF ANSWERS

Consulting a "shrink" is never easy. The contact is made with much dread and anxiety, usually at a time of severe crisis. For this reason, the selection of "wise counsel" is crucial, especially for the Christian. The Bible teaches:

> **Blessed is the man who walks not in the counsel of the ungodly... (Ps 1:1a)**

Unfortunately, most counseling and support that is available through secular psychology is built upon the wisdom of man and therefore doomed to disaster. There are even "Christian counselors" who fail to honor the integrity of God's Word and unwittingly lead many individuals and families astray with biblically incorrect advice. The influence of the psychological profession is significant. In order to demonstrate the potential danger of a non-biblical orientation, we begin with two case examples:

EXAMPLE ONE
Cliff and Tina are Christians. They have been married seven years and have two young sons. Cliff is a realtor and Tina works

part-time as a tutor but spends the majority of her time raising the children. About two years ago Cliff began "drifting away." He started working more, talking less, and generally appeared angry and frustrated. When asked about this change in his disposition, Cliff's response was always the same: "Everything is fine."

Last week Tina found a note in Cliff's pocket from a female co-worker. While the letter did not offer evidence of a physical affair, it did suggest a developing relationship and movement toward increasingly inappropriate involvement. Boundaries had been broken and the marriage was under fire.

When confronted, Cliff admitted a friendship but denied physical contact. He said he had been unhappy in the marriage for some time but didn't know how to tell Tina about it. He began to confide in the "friend" at work and soon found he had shut Tina out entirely. Cliff admitted he was at risk, confessed he was wrong, and asked Tina to forgive him.

There were a lot of tears, anger, and accusations before the two could come to an agreement about seeing a counselor. There had been much damage to the integrity of the marriage; trust was broken; doubt was rampant. Tina was smart enough to know that this "emotional affair" was only a symptom of a bigger marital problem that needed professional help. Cliff agreed and the two began looking for a therapist.

Cliff and Tina were embarrassed about the problems they were having and felt they could not speak to their pastor. Doing so, they feared, would lessen his respect for them and might threaten their leadership positions in the church. For similar reasons they decided not to speak to friends or family but rather to confront the issue alone. Turning to the Yellow Pages, they looked up Marriage Counselors. Even though they were Christians, they decided credentials were more important than religious background and selected a counselor with plenty of degrees, certifications, and yellow page advertising space.

In the first session, the counselor listened intently to the issues then asked for some time with both Cliff and Tina alone. With Cliff the counselor asked numerous questions about Cliff's sexual history before marriage and about his intimate life with Tina. He learned that Cliff, being a Christian, had been a virgin when he married Tina. He also learned that their intimate life had been "somewhat flat" since the second baby had come.

The counselor proposed a theory that Cliff's attraction to the co-worker was "natural and normal." He went on to say that Cliff's lack of experience with other women had left him sexually repressed and frustrated. The counselor said that by marrying Tina without other sexual experiences, Cliff had "set himself up" to be unhappy sexually and would, most likely, always be searching for opportunities to "express" his longing outside of marriage.

Cliff was confused and speechless. Some of what the doctor said made sense. He had been curious about other women through-out the marriage and had sometimes wondered what it would be like with someone else. The counselor said they would explore it more in the next session and encouraged Cliff to stop feeling guilty. "After all," the worldly-wise counselor said, "man was never meant to be monogamous!" Cliff felt strangely better but left with a number of questions about his marriage and his sexuality.

Next the counselor met with Tina. Taking the same track, he found that she too had been a virgin on her wedding day and that Cliff had been the only man in her life. Quickly the therapist moved to a position of caution, warning Tina that Cliff was "right on the edge." He explained that Cliff was curious sexually and suggested that Tina needed to become "more open" to his needs. Tina felt embarrassed and said she didn't understand. The counselor assured her that many women without "proper sexual training" had similar difficulties, but that he could teach the couple some "creative ways" to spice up the bedroom. As Tina left the office she felt confused and inadequate.

With the benefit of one counseling session, a repentant Christian husband has been encouraged to "normalize" and accept his sin while shifting the blame for his transgression to sexual repression and an inexperienced wife. One session of secular wisdom has fractured the wife's hope and left her feeling even more insecure than when she walked in. She secretly feared that she was inadequate before the session. Now, thanks to the professional, she is sure she is.

EXAMPLE TWO

Thad, a twenty-two-year-old youth minister, has a secret struggle that would shock anyone who knows him. Since being molested by an uncle at the age of 14, he has been confused about his sexuality. In spite of the trauma he experienced, he is strangely attracted to other men. He has never acted on these feelings but fears he might. He tries to date women but feels too nervous. He withdraws, works a lot, and privately turns to homosexual pornography. The imagery of the pornography only deepens his confusion and shame.

As a born-again Christian, Thad has been taught that homosexual involvement is sin and cannot be endorsed by God. This truth is his support as he tries to escape the fantasy and imagery that preoccupies him. Finally, in his desperation, he decides to get professional psychological help. Obviously, as a minister, he is reticent about asking his pastor or friends for advice. Still, he knows the importance of Christian counsel and makes some inquiries, then sets an appointment with a female therapist operating under the title "Christian Psychologist."

The office is nice, the staff warm. The radio in the lobby is tuned to the local Christian station. Thad breathes a sigh of relief, as it seems he has found the right place. The psychologist greets him and makes him feel at ease right away. With great pain and tears, he relates his problem to the very intense listener. He feels accepted as he purges his heart with his confession and states his desire to turn away from pornography and the indulgence of homosexual fantasy.

After a long silence the psychologist leans forward and asks Thad to look her in the eyes. She begins her therapeutic response:

Psychologist: "Thad, why do you feel so guilty. God made all kinds of people, straight and gay. He wouldn't want you to deny or turn away from the way He intended you to be."
Thad: "What are you saying? You think God made me homosexual?"
Psychologist: "Of course I do. We have too much clinical evidence available now to state anything else. Science has identified a gay gene for one thing. Also, we can look at brain scans and see the differences between heterosexual

and homosexual patterns of brain activity. Why would these things exist if God didn't make it so?"

Thad: "I've read about these things, but I thought they were simply theories."

Psychologist: "Not theory; fact!"

Thad: "But what about the Bible? The Bible says, 'If a man lies with a male as he lies with a woman, both of them have committed an abomination' (Lev 20:13)."

Psychologist: (Smiling) "These are antiquated rules that were part of the ancient Hebrew culture and tradition. They are not meant for today. Besides, does that passage mention the words homosexual or sex?"

Thad: "No."

Psychologist: "No, it doesn't. Science and culture have evolved since that time. We are not shackled to archaic notions that fail to reflect God's love for all His creations. Also, I think if you will look to some of the newer translations of the Bible, you will find even the vague prohibitions against homosexual love have been restated. We know so much more about the meaning of the original languages then when some of the earlier English versions were completed."

Thad: "This all goes against everything I have been taught."

Psychologist: "Well Thad, you are not the first to be misled by well-meaning teachers who want to keep God in a box. God is doing new things all the time. His message is love, not exclusion. God wants you the way He made you. There is no need to deny His plan. Our work together has nothing to do with sin or the containment of a natural orientation to sex: our work is to help you out from under the legalism of man that has made you ashamed of who you are in God's kingdom."

Thad left the session confused but excited that maybe, just maybe, God could accept him as a homosexual. Perhaps he had restricted himself to the opinions of a few bigots who really didn't understand God's greater purpose. Thad went home and began to research more liberal views of homosexuality in the church. He found that there were a number of professing Christians who embrace homosexual behavior as normal and acceptable. He discovered websites for homosexual pastors, churches, and even bishops.

With the "help" of a "Christian Psychologist," Thad had thwarted the conviction of the Holy Spirit, denigrated God's authoritative Word, and crippled years of godly teaching that had been his source of perseverance. Now, with all gates removed, he could begin to explore the potential of his "sexual orientation," seemingly without conflict, or so his logical thinking told him. In reality, though, his inner conflict had just begun.

THE IMPORTANCE OF BIBLICAL COUNSELING

These are only two examples of the inherent hazards Christians face when looking for help. There is a great deal that goes on in the therapy office that is not helpful, and can, in fact, be harmful. Any counsel that is in disagreement with God's Word has the potential to undermine one's stability and hope. As we have seen in these scenarios, mental health care, in most cases, has little if anything to do with the principles of God, His order, or His will. As noted, even someone claiming Christian credentials can render a devastating effect on the soul and mind.

This being said, how then do we merge the polar opposites: Christian and Shrink? Sometimes it is a tough fit. We believe there is a need for effective, biblical, and godly counsel. We believe there is a need for mental health care that acknowledges the teachings of God over the notions of man. Christian therapy ought to rely on God's order, treating all individual and family issues within the framework of prayer and biblical study. To be a counselor, family therapist or other professional working from this point of view can be an honorable, ordained work of life.

Since spiritual change is the objective, the biblical counselor must be centered upon God's agenda first and foremost. To simply smooth over a crisis without the delivery of spiritual truth misses God's intent entirely. A period of crisis is often the breaking point that opens a heart to the gospel message. How great an error we risk if we offer only a secular word of encouragement, a communicational technique, or a psychiatric medication instead of Jesus. This is not to say that methods of counseling, help in communication, and even medication are useless, but they are secondary in importance to the biblical truth that allows God's purposes to be realized.

God's Word cuts to the core of the issue and illuminates the spiritual need. Symptoms such as depression, anxiety, and marital struggle must be viewed from a spiritual perspective first and a physical second. Biblical truth becomes our point of contrast, our measuring stick, our plumb line. When our difficulties are held up against the light of the Word, we can move quickly to the base of the problem and address it.

The Bible provides the reader clear, definitive direction that is unambiguous. In most cases, Scripture is black and white, not gray. These cemented positions are the types of guidelines people need to live happy, obedient lifestyles that protect them from conflict, stress, indecision, and angst.

Psychology does not hold to this principle. Most secular therapists are taught to avoid bias, direct opinion, and moral absolutes. There are even respected forms of therapy that promote the abandonment of any idea or framework that is authoritative or rigid in its terminology. Therapists learn quickly that there is no "right and wrong." Instead, there is only the psychological conflict that arises when one is forced into a restricted mindset. "Freedom of choice and expression" is their mantra and they believe that the guidelines of a Divine Authority can't do anything but limit an individual's growth.

Worldly psychology goes further yet. It holds the opinion that the individual or the "self" is primary over spouse, family, or society. Emphasis is placed upon emotion, drive, and attainment rather than responsibility, accountability, sacrifice, and duty. This philosophy of "self above all" is evident in our ongoing societal decline; it is a direct result of the breakdown in family values and the integrity of the home. The worship of the self has become this generation's idolatry, and if unfettered, will continue to lead the world further from the truth and closer to the lie.

Therefore God also gave them up to uncleanness, in the lusts of their hearts, to dishonor their bodies among themselves, who exchanged the truth of God for the lie, and worshiped and served the creature rather than the

Creator, who is blessed forever. Amen. (Rom 1:24-25)

Does this scripture not define our current trend and orientation to life? By worshiping and serving the "creature rather than the Creator," our society has abandoned the truth of God's love and authority, giving preference to any created thing, human or beast, and elevating that creature to a level of deity. This line of thought is evident in so many religious and secular movements, wherein the idea that everything and everyone is God is proudly advanced (i.e. the god of the self). This fallacy is grounded directly in evolutionary theory, the lie taught as the truth for decades. After all, if humans can evolve from monkeys, why can't gods evolve from humans?

Christian shrinks then, should be professionals who respect biblical authority first, giving credence to treatment methods only when they are in concert with God's rules of order. The trouble is that most Christian counselors are trained in the methods of the world, not the methods of the Word.

Effective Christian counselors should be learning God's Word thoroughly and then applying psychological theory that is consistent with biblical teaching. God's Word is not a supplement; it is whole and complete. Anytime we make the written Word a secondary matter, we have already denied its authority and weakened its application.

It is our desire to provide the reader with clear, direct, and biblical answers to many of the tough questions we have been asked over the years. In each problem and every case example, it is obvious that God's Word, when correctly applied, is sufficient for all relationship crises.

CHAPTER 2

THE SINGLE LIFE

INTRODUCTION

It is a difficult time to be single. There are so many temptations that draw us and challenge our obedience. We live in a world where literally anything is available and we are encouraged to have all we want of it.

But as a believer, you know that God ordained every step, every day of your life. He has called you and consecrated you for a good and perfect work. Singles must hold to that truth and search for God's intent in everything they confront. God spoke to the prophet Jeremiah saying:

"Before I formed you in the womb I knew you;
Before you were born I sanctified you..." (Jer 1:5a)

Sanctified means set apart. God set you apart before your birth for a work yet to be fully realized. In our obedience we must wait for God to reveal His full plan, His ultimate goal. That means sometimes waiting when we really want to move ahead. It means listening for Him and tuning out the distortion of others. It means honoring His will in thought and deed so that we can receive His fullest blessing.

**Your eyes saw my substance, being yet unformed.
And in Your book they all were written,
The days fashioned for me,
When as yet there were none of them. (Ps 139:16)**

What a beautiful scripture that reminds us how very precious we are to Him. At the foundation of the world you were known, seen by your Creator. Your "substance" was written in His book and your days were "fashioned" (planned) before you were given life. With so much thought, love, planning, and care devoted to you, do you not think God has just the right place, the right person, the right home for you? Listen and He will define it for you.

NOW FOR YOUR QUESTIONS...

DATING

I am a 22-year-old Christian who has been dating a wonderful man for the past two years of college. How do I know if he is "the one" for me?

The first criterion is often the one most overlooked. If you are a Christian, you must know if your proposed mate is born-again. There can be no worse beginning than the disobedient act of marrying a non-Christian. Unfortunately, Christians are often uncomfortable talking about this issue or accept shallow answers out of a desire to hear the right response.

If we are devoted to having a marriage in accord with God's order, we must give full respect to the pre-marital warning Paul wrote to the Corinthian Church:

Do not be unequally yoked together with unbelievers. For what fellowship has righteousness with lawlessness? And what communion has light with darkness? (2 Cor 6:14)

In other words, we are not to be "joined" in any way, with an unbeliever. It doesn't get much clearer than this. God can only bless a union between likeminded Christians. We must be true to this edict and allow God time to provide the one chosen for us.

As therapists, we have heard all kinds of justifications for dating and even marrying a non-Christian:

"He says he believes in God." (**...but consider James 2:19 where it says "even the demons believe and tremble."**)

"Maybe God placed us together so that over time, she will become a believer."
(**...but in 2 Corinthians 6:17 we are commanded to "come out from among them and be separate..."**)

"I'll remain active in my Christian walk, even if he doesn't share my faith."
(**"Evil company corrupts good habits." 1 Corinthians 15:33**)

"He says he is a believer; he just isn't acting like it right now."
(**...but Jesus said in Matthew 7:20, "by their fruits you will know them."**)

Deal with first things first. Determine early just who this person is that attracts you. Preferably you will know before the first date, but find out soon before the feelings and yearnings of the flesh take root.

I am a young (20-year-old) college student and I'm really not ready to get married. Is it OK to date someone who isn't a Christian, just for fun?

The truth is, not only should we not marry a non-believer, we shouldn't be dating one either. By avoiding this question early in the relationship, we allow feelings and needs to develop that weaken our resolve to be equally joined. Rest assured, you can have feelings, even love someone who is without salvation. The more advanced the dating, the greater the risk of this occurring.

We should make efforts to befriend non-Christians and lead them to the Lord, but dating crosses another line and makes for a very different set of expectations. In fact, most evangelistic efforts should be toward individuals of the same sex. Whether married or single, boundaries get blurred in relating to the opposite sex.

Be clear in your own mind about your motivation and date only those you believe are biblically qualified to be your future mate. Recreational dating opens the door to activities and emotions that have nothing to do with the fulfillment of God's plan for your life and relationships.

> **They are of the world. Therefore they speak as of the world, and the world hears them. We are of God. He who knows God hears us; he who is not of God does not hear us. By this we know the spirit of truth and the spirit of error. (1 John 4:5-6)**

CHOOSING A MATE

Is the presence of salvation the "only" criterion for evaluating a potential mate? Should I settle on a mate just because she is born-again, even if I believe we are not compatible in other areas?

Certainly not! There are many things you need to learn and know about each other. For example, all Christians are not at the same place or level of maturity. This can create problems not unlike marrying a non-Christian. But even if you are similar in this regard, individuals have different needs and different requirements for happiness.

For example couples who move along in the courting process may find that they have *chemistry* for each other. That is, they have a physical attraction that is appealing and affirming. This is a good thing and should be present in all relationships approaching marriage. But don't let it be the only thing. Chemistry is most intense in the first six months of marriage. After that it has an ebb and flow: it comes and goes. There must be other foundational connections that hold and bond you.

When we are dating we tend to lie a lot. We don't mean to, we just want to attract the object of our affection because we have an *"urge to merge."* But some honest communication is essential if you are to know that your mutual expectations are a good match. At the very least, you should explore openly your feelings and needs in the following areas:

Money and finances (**1 Tim 5:8, 6:10, Matt 6:21**).
Children and parenting styles (**Eph 6:4, Col 3:21, Ps 127:3**).
Time together and recreation (**Eccl 5:20**).
Work and career (**Mark 8:36, 1 Cor 10:31, Prov 14:23**).
Extended family (**Gen 2:24, Ex 20:12**).
Denominational or doctrinal differences (**Heb 4:12, Matt 7:15, Ps 133:1**).
Friendships and boundaries (**1 Cor 15:33, Prov 27:17**).
Communication and conflict resolution (**Jas 1:19, 3:1-12, Ps 141:3, Eph 4:26**).

Most will find areas of total compatibility, areas of flexibility and compromise, and areas of absolute disagreement. If you haven't experienced areas of difficulty, then you probably haven't spoken truthfully and openly on some topics. While everything cannot be anticipated and addressed, it is crucial to ferret out any topics of potential strife.

Since we tend to be "blinded" by new love, it is vital to have structured pre-marital counseling with a professional counselor or pastor who can help you look at areas you may avoid discussing when moving toward marriage.

SEXUAL PURITY

I've been engaged to a great Christian girl for over a year. If we love each other and know we are getting married, wouldn't it be a good idea to live together first?

Absolutely not! It is a myth that living together before marriage enhances the future success of the union. In fact, research tells us that couples who cohabitate before marriage are more likely to divorce than couples who wait until after marriage to share sexual intimacy.

To have a marriage that is in keeping with God's order, we must live in concert with His written Word. Paul wrote boldly on this issue:

> **Flee sexual immorality. Every sin that a man does is outside the body, but he who commits sexual immorality sins against his own body. Or do you not know that your body is the temple of the Holy Spirit who is in you, whom you have from God, and you are not your own? For you were bought at a price; therefore glorify God in your body and in your spirit, which are God's. (1 Cor 6:18-20)**

Sexual purity honors God's Word and lays a strong foundation for a committed sexual union when joined in matrimony. Only at the time of marriage does God endorse and bless the physical unification of the couple as evident in the first marital vow:

> **And Adam said: "This is now bone of my bones and flesh of my flesh; She shall be called Woman, because she was taken out of Man." Therefore a man shall leave his father and mother and be joined to his wife, and they shall become one flesh. (Gen 2: 23-24)**

Again, God leaves no ambiguity. We become physically "one flesh" when the man is "joined to his wife," not to his "partner, lover, or significant other."

I'm a Christian and I believe in the Bible, but isn't it unrealistic to expect Christian singles to remain virgins until marriage?

We admit that the expectation is difficult, but it is not unrealistic. Much of what we are called to do as believers goes against our strongest natural desires while also challenging the pressures and trends of our culture. Without Christ as your Savior, and without the Holy Spirit as your guide, it would be impossible. But Jesus reminds us: **"With men this is impossible, but with God all things are possible" (Matt 19:26b).**

The book of Galatians speaks of the transformation that is to take place in the heart AND in the behavior of the believer. As Christians, we must always seek to honor the gift of salvation we have been given. By honoring God, we give Him preference and priority over all attractions of the world. Paul wrote that we should "walk in the Spirit" while spurning the lust of the flesh:

> **I say then: Walk in the Spirit, and you shall not fulfill the lust of the flesh. For the flesh lusts against the Spirit, and the Spirit against the flesh; and these are contrary to one another, so that you do not do the things that you wish. But if you are led by the Spirit, you are not under the law. Now the works of the flesh are evident, which are: adultery, fornication, uncleanness, lewdness, idolatry, sorcery, hatred, contentions, jealousies, outbursts of wrath, selfish ambitions, dissensions, heresies, envy, murders, drunkenness, revelries, and the like; of which I tell you beforehand, just as I also told you in time past, that those who practice such things will not inherit the kingdom of God. (Gal 5:16-21)**

Many Christians, whom we have counseled, have read this scripture and said something like, "I am not a murderer or a drunk!" It is amazing how selective we can be when reading God's Word. Often we have to literally direct them to the key words or phrases we are counseling about at the time. In the case of sexual purity, we address "fornication, selfish ambition, and lewdness." We help the single person see that these activities are listed with murder, and the like, as being incompatible with life in the Spirit.

But the fruit of the Spirit is love, joy, peace, longsuffering, kindness, goodness, faithfulness, gentleness, self-control.

Against such there is no law. And those who are Christ's have crucified the flesh with its passions and desires. (Gal 5:22-24)

The fruit of the Spirit includes "self-control, longsuffering (patience) and faithfulness." Sometimes we are asked, "If I am single, who am I being faithful to by not having sex?" We reply, "To God who saved you." Often the concept of faithfulness to Him is foreign to us. No one can possibly do more for us than was done on the cross, yet we still summon up greater devotion to boyfriends and girlfriends than we do the Creator of the universe.

There are other reasons for living a chaste life in addition to doing so out of faithfulness and obedience. Sex before marriage creates a tear in the fabric of the psyche that is not easily repaired. As we have shown, sex with multiple people is not God's plan. Whenever we go outside of His design, there will be permanent consequences.

Sex opens us to false emotions of love and connection. As a result, we often try to justify the act of lust by building a relationship around it. So many times, individuals end up in a bad situation with the wrong person because they have become sexually intimate. As a result, couples sometimes force a bond that is not godly or healthy. This is especially true for women who feel a deeper association between sexual intimacy and love. Once physically involved the deception is strong and the risk of poor discernment is great.

While an unhealthy relationship is one outcome of premarital sex, the loss of relationship is another. Frequently, when individuals engage in sexual relations prior to marriage, they find that this makes the relationships crumble and fall apart. We have observed that feelings of distrust and jealousy are common among couples engaging in premarital sex, leading to channels of conflict that often become irreconcilable. Another danger is simply the risk that the relationship never becomes anything greater than physical attraction. When sex is the centerpiece of a union, the more substantial elements of relating such as communication, transparency, and problem solving, may fail to mature.

We have counseled many individuals following the break-up of a pre-marital relationship. Whenever the couple has been sexual, recovery is inhibited. Quite commonly there are feelings of shame and guilt and the sense of betrayal is invariably greater. We have also seen increased vulnerability to further sexual involvement once the boundary of purity has been breached.

God created us to relate in an exclusive way: one man, one woman. Any involvement that goes counter to that structure is outside His will, and we will bear spiritual and psychological pain as a result. Endure and flee the seduction of the world so that you can have all that God wants you to have.

If sex is off-limits, what kinds of physical contact are appropriate before marriage?

That is a dangerous question to answer and leads us down a very slippery slope. The issue of sexual purity and self-control is not related to the creation of a legalistic standard of conduct. Your question implies a desire to "go as far as possible" without breaking some rule or guideline. However, if you begin with the search for latitude and room to explore, you will end in compromise.

Instead the Christian must begin with a desire for obedience and honor to the Lord. From this perspective, compromise is not an option. Most Christians will know through the conviction of the Holy Spirit, exactly when they are approaching a line of danger and risk. In speaking of the Holy Spirit, Jesus said: **"And when He has come, He will convict the world of sin, and of righteousness, and of judgment" (John 16:8).**

The Spirit of God removes the need for a list of "dos and don'ts." As a believer, the Discerner of "sin, righteousness, and judgment" lives within us and will direct our choices. The question is, will you yield to His direction? So often one can feel the conviction of the Holy Spirit, but the action chosen comes out of a hardened or rebellious heart.

The more we resist the leading of the Spirit, the more hardened we grow. Eventually, the Christian can become desensitized to the prompting of God. That spiritual deadness often leads us toward action that is of a carnal nature.

As a single Christian, it is vital to keep yourself open and yielded before the Lord. Listen for His voice, search His Word for guidance, and avoid the practice and instruction of your peers. This typically means avoiding the pattern set forth by other Christian singles as well. In many instances, Christian singles have come to justify and act upon the world's model for physical and sexual activity.

There is the opinion floating about that the Bible must be read within a contemporary context. There is the belief that true adherence to biblical instruction on purity is archaic and out of step with what is happening today. But the Bible tells us that our God does not change: **"Jesus Christ is the same yesterday, today, and forever" (Heb 13:8).**

As the Scripture asserts, there is only one constant truth. Be wary of teachings, patterns, or trends that seek to "update" the meaning of God's Word. Scripture means today exactly what it has always meant, and it does not change. Make your choices accordingly and measure your success against Scripture, not against the conduct of others.

CASE EXAMPLE

Andrea and Clark are deeply in love. They have come for pre-marriage counseling to fine tune a few things, hoping to increase their current state of blinded bliss. She is 25 and has never been married; he is 28 and was divorced six months ago from his wife of two years.

Andrea is an up-and-coming stockbroker and has just purchased her first rental property as an investment. Clark is working in retail sales, making only slightly above minimum wage. He attended college but didn't finish. He trained as a nurse, but didn't like "that type of work." On the side, he is working on his dream of becoming a Christian recording artist.

Andrea does most of the talking, most of the planning, and makes all of the decisions. Clark looks like he's been picked up in a twister and can't get down. As family therapists, we couldn't wait to ask: "How did you two get together?" Andrea explained they had met while Clark was going through his divorce. They quickly bonded ("love at first sight!") and have been together ever since.

They also let us know that they were living together due to Clark's financial problems, but had stopped having sex. "Stopped?" we asked. "Well, mostly," Clark replied. He went on to say he was not happy about their current mutual abstinence. "Since we love each other and plan to be married, God doesn't want us to deny ourselves." (This is one of those moments when a Christian shrink has to bite his tongue to keep from screaming and running out of the room!)

"You did say you are both Christians, right?"

Andrea said, "Of course we are; isn't it obvious how much we love God? I work in the nursery and Clark is on the praise team."

Over the course of two very long sessions we found that Clark had a problem with pornography, which he blamed on the "interruption" in their sex life. He owed several thousand dollars that he could not pay to creditors, and had no real plan or goal for his life. Andrea excused him, explained him, and enabled him, while constantly telling him he should do better.

The two would not address the problems between them. They would not address their salvation. They would not tolerate God's Word as a structure for planning this marriage. They would not stop living together and never really stopped having sex together. They found us to be therapists who did not appreciate how special their "kind of love" really is. Gratefully, we were released as their therapists. Thankfully, they never did marry.

This case represents how emotion and need can distort the truth beyond comprehension. We don't know the true spiritual status of Andrea and Clark, meaning, whether they are Christians or not. But we do know that they were flying past all the road signs God had provided about how to live, plan, and prepare for marriage. Like a speeding train, they could not be slowed until the inevitable crash. In this case they divided before marriage and greater catastrophe. In far too many cases, the speed carries them right over the cliff into a marriage that is not of God.

SUMMARY

King Solomon was a man of great wisdom and wealth, yet he fell prey to the seduction of his abundance. Able to build, consume, and take anything he wanted from this world, he eventually learned that all was worthless and vulnerable without God's involvement.

> **Unless the Lord builds the house, they labor in vain who build it;**
> **Unless the Lord guards the city, the watchman stays awake in vain. (Ps 127:1a)**

The period of living single, dating, and waiting on the mate God chooses, can be a wonderful time of anticipation. It is an awesome thing to wake each day knowing that you are primary in God's thoughts **(Ps 40:5)** and that He has a perfect plan written out for your life **(Ps 139:15-16).** When you accepted Christ as your Savior, you handed Him the reins to control and direct your earthly and eternal destinies. You have given Him your life **(Luke 9:24).** Now trust Him to give you what you need in a relationship and do not rush ahead. God is always faithful.

CHAPTER 3

MARRIAGE GOD'S WAY

INTRODUCTION

When it comes to relationships, the ones between men and women are by far the most exciting. This is true in life and also in the therapy office. The most frequent reason for consulting a counselor invariably relates to issues with the opposite sex.

Relating to one another is a challenge as old as creation. Yet, other than our relationship to Him, there is no covenant that God values more than the promise between a husband and wife. We need only look to the first book of the Bible to know that the marital relationship is central to God's plan.

And the LORD God said, "It is not good that man should be alone; I will make him a helper comparable to him." (Gen 2:18)

God forged a partnership right from the beginning, placing in motion a dynamic that has become the fuel of life. Within the Scriptures we see God's perfect design. Our movement outside this prescribed pattern is at the root of almost all marital and relational issues between men and women.

God has a specific structure for marriage that begins with the man and woman. He has defined the roles of each precisely. As therapists we have found that most couples really do not know what God requires. Instead, they are much more familiar with the world's definition of "normal." The answer for today's family requires a deliberate turning away from the world's system, and instead delving into the Word of God.

NOW FOR YOUR QUESTIONS...

THE MAN'S CALL

I've been married for several years but only recently became a Christian. More than ever before, I want to be a godly man for my wife. What does the Bible say about the role of the husband in the home?

Biblically, the man is called to be the priest of his home. He is directed to love, honor, protect, and lead; indeed he is held to a very high standard of accountability. One of the first instructions given to the husband is the most basic, yet the most demanding:

> **Husbands, love your wives, just as Christ also loved the church and gave Himself for her. (Eph 5:25)**

This scripture is a powerful calling. It is an instruction to minister to our home as Christ ministered to the church. If we are to love as Jesus loved, then we are to be close and active, not distant and passive.

There was nothing passive about our Lord's love for us. God could have loved us from the heavens, but instead drew near and demonstrated His love in an active, behavioral expression.

Jesus touched **(Matt 8:1-3)**; He healed **(Matt 14:14)**; He instructed **(Mark 10:1)**; He provided **(Mark 6:37-44)**; He prayed **(John 17:13-21)**; He forgave **(Matt 9:2)**; He resisted temptation **(Heb 4:15)**; He served **(Mark 10:45)**; and finally, He sacrificed all **(John 19:30)**.

Using our Savior as the template of comparison, allow us to inquire:

- Do you touch your wife as Jesus touched? His touch was filled with understanding and compassion. It was a touch that gave but did not take. Touching your wife physically in this way assures her of your commitment and love for her **(2 Cor 7:3)**.

- When your wife is in pain, do you promote healing? Our wives need to know they can bring their injuries and needs to us. They need us to be engaged, interested, and invested in reestablishing their peace **(Gal 6:2)**.

- As the spiritual leader of the home, is your study of God's Word faithful so that you can instruct and encourage your wife? A man cannot feed others unless he is fed. Your fervent attention to learning the Bible will allow you to lead your family from a Christian worldview and will transform not only your message but also your heart **(Heb 4:12, 1 Cor 14:35)**.

- Are you providing for your family's financial needs and security? So many families today are overburdened by debt and commitments beyond their means, creating tremendous stress. Financial problems are cited as the second leading cause of divorce. Fiscal responsibility and leadership from the husband is central to protecting the home **(1 Tim 5:8)**.

- Are you in prayer *for* your wife and *with* your wife? Do you make it a priority to lift her needs to God and to share the intimacy of prayer together? Research tells us that less than 1 percent of couples who regularly pray together get divorced **(Jas 5:16)**.

- Do you forgive as Christ forgave? Can you resolve and release the issues that divide you, or do you harbor them in your heart, allowing anger and sin to take root? Studies tell us that the capacity to forgive is fundamental to the maintenance of good healthy relationships **(Eph 4:26-27)**.

- When temptation comes, what do you do? There is no safe level of thought or deed when it comes to sin. Any compromise or concession made by the man will affect his family **(Gal 5:9)**. Boundaries are essential if we are to preserve the marital covenant. We must actively pursue God's cover and protection for our homes on a daily basis **(Eph 6:10-18)**.

- How do you serve your bride? Whether in small matters or large, serving our wives is one of the foremost ways to demonstrate honor. It expresses consideration, it defines her as valuable, and it produces a climate of mutual respect and loyalty. Do something unexpected that reminds her of her precious place in your life (**John 13:14-15**).

- Finally, is your love sacrificial? Jesus gave everything for those entrusted to His care, and husbands are called to do the same **(Luke 9:23)**. What can you sacrifice today that will bless your wife? Is it time at work, hours watching T.V., attitudes or ambitions, behaviors or habits? If it limits or injures the marriage, it needs to go.

Having observed couples for 25 years, we are convinced that the man is the portal to the family: It is through him that good or evil gains access to the home. When the man is weak in his active love and protection of the family, the family, too, is weak and vulnerable.

This is not to say problems cannot arise from other sources, including the wife. Yet, when there is strength in leadership, there is stability in the system. The man is defined clearly as the leader, no matter what liberal distortion you have been fed.

Second, Scripture teaches us that the husband should lead, but he should lead in the manner of Christ:

For the husband is head of the wife, as also Christ is head of the church; and He is the Savior of the body. (Eph 5:23)

Men love this scripture! But just as we are to love as Christ loved, we are to lead as He led. The Bible is careful to clarify just exactly what being the "head" of something entails. Here, God reminds us that the "headship" of Christ required total sacrifice as the "Savior of the body." If Christ gave Himself for the body of the church, men are to do likewise for the "body" of the home.

Yes, men are to lead, but they are to lead from a submitted, sacrificial position, willing to give anything and everything to the body of his wife and family. We have seen in family after family, that when men lead under this biblical description, the family flourishes.

Third, men are to establish their homes as their first and primary place of ministry. The Apostle Peter wrote:

Husbands, likewise, dwell with them with understanding, giving honor to the wife, as to the weaker vessel, and as being heirs together of the grace of life, that your prayers may not be hindered. (1 Pet 3:7)

This is one of our favorite scriptures because again, God defines the gentle blending of care and strength, of leadership and love. Here men are instructed to "understand" the wife. Now I know this seems impossible, but God never orders what can't be done.

God designed men and women to be different. Our differences are easier to negotiate when we understand that we are this way for God's purpose to be fulfilled. Part of the "understanding" Peter wrote about is grounded in our acceptance of God's plan for the marital home and that our wives are not built to think and act as men. Clearly gender differences are central to God's order:

So God created man in His own image; in the image of God He created him; male and female He created them. (Gen 1:27)

God made us male and female so that we could relate, strengthen, and support each other. Can you imagine the difficulty in the home if God had made us the same? Different is good and it is God's order. By seeking to understand the wife, we give respect to God's design. He made this wife, this helper, for you. Explore the wonder of God's work.

Next the scripture tells us that we should give "honor to the wife as to the weaker vessel." Men like this scripture too. But remember, weaker does not mean "inferior." It means that the man is like a thick crock of pottery, strong and stable; the woman is like a beautiful piece of cut glass. Each has its value in the home, but each has a very different function.

This valuable vessel should be protected, highlighted, supported, and preserved. The pottery (man) can get chipped or cracked and maintain its function. The cut glass (woman) is not to bear the same weight or duty. Care for her and honor her as the one God has given under your care.

This scripture further reminds us that we are "heirs together of the grace of life." God prompts us to remember that our wives are precious to the kingdom of God. Whenever tempted to harm our wives with word or action, we must not forget that as a believer, she has a kingdom inheritance.

Finally, God tells men to do all of this so that your "prayers may not be hindered." The Word tells us that sin divides us from God (**Isa 59:1-2**). Here God makes it known that failure in the home is a sin that limits our access to His throne. While every husband is imperfect, we must be active in knowing what God expects in our marriages and be repentant when we fall. Prayer is essential if we are to live out the biblical standards of a husband.

CASE EXAMPLE

We remember meeting with a minister and his wife from out-of-state. Samuel and Liz were in their early forties and had been married nearly twenty years. Liz had been involved in a brief affair and later confessed her failing to Samuel. The pain and emotion of the first meeting was intense. The wife expressed grief and guilt, the husband anger and deep sadness.

The two had been believers and servants of God for nearly two decades and each had contributed to the kingdom in mighty ways. Yet sitting in our office, they were broken, almost lifeless, under the oppression of this trauma.

Liz was repentant and seeking her husband's forgiveness. He was understandably in shock. For a period of time he was too angry to accept her request. But on the fourth session an amazing thing happened. Samuel said to Liz: "Yes, I forgive you, but can you forgive me?"

Liz was speechless. Samuel continued: "I know what you did, and it is wrong. But long before you fell, I pushed you." He went on to describe his failure to honor and understand her; his avoidance of time with her; his preoccupation with matters of the world rather than the needs of his home. Samuel was clear that he did not excuse her for her action, but he did not excuse himself either.

This minister knew God's Word better than his family therapist. When he began to contrast his life with the instruction he was to follow, he knew he had opened the door for his wife's transgression.

Samuel's acceptance of his failure aided the mending of this home immeasurably. He knew that his wife was his responsibility, and he stood up and accepted his burden as the leader of the home. Liz drew to his side and took refuge in his renewed resolve to honor her and to guard her from future threat.

In her repentance, Liz found grace. In Samuel's repentance, he found strength. Both became accountable and the marriage survived what could easily have been its end. Of course feelings were expressed, trust was challenged, and faith was tested. It all didn't come together overnight. But with time, the marital unit was restored, and believe it or not, improved through this near-fatal crisis.

Men have opportunities long before the boundaries of their home are broken. Each day is an occasion to step forward and fulfill the teachings of God in our marriages. We call it "Preventive Leadership." Just as in the case of car or home maintenance, you either tend to the small things to avoid future catastrophe, or you avoid those small steps and thus face complete breakdown. Which type of man will you be?

THE WOMAN'S CALL

What does the Bible say about the wife's role in the marriage and home?

God's Word tells us that the wife is indeed unique, created in a manner unlike any other creature. Do you realize that God spoke the world and all its creatures into existence? He made man from the dust of the earth brought to life by His very breath. But, God created woman from the rib of man. God didn't do this because he needed a spare part! We see this as the ultimate expression of intimacy between a man and woman, and it reflects the Creator's plan for oneness in the marital bond **(Gen 2:1-25)**.

God could have created woman through any means, but He chose this rendering of life so that man and woman were forever to be "one flesh" **(Gen 2:24)**. This reality does away with the idea that husbands and wives are to be independent of one another. Instead we are to relate in an interdependent way. Each is different, yet each bears gifts and strengths central to the union. Remove the idea from your mind that dependency is bad. God requires our dependency on Him and has joined husband and wife in just such a manner. Early in Genesis, God describes the primary role of woman:

"...I will make him a helper comparable to him." (Gen 2:18b)

Now we know why wives try to *help* their husbands so much; they are simply being biblical! In our world, the idea of being someone's "helper" is often viewed as an inferior position. But according to Scripture, the Christian life is all about service. The Bible gives us numerous examples to reference wherein Jesus served, gave, and yielded. His greatest strength was found in His love to those He tended **(Matt 20:28)**. Since we are instructed to do the same, why should service and support be defined as a lesser calling **(Gal 5:13; John 14:12)**?

We have found in our clinical work that most women secretively long for this position. They desire a place from which they can support and care for their mate, rather than lead out and drive the tempo of the home. Contemporary thinkers will disagree and argue that this conclusion injures or lessens a woman's value. But our value is found in our God-given gifts and calling. When we are in the position God ordained, we are happier and more successful.

So we ask; are you fulfilling your biblical role as "helper comparable to him?" Look into your heart and examine how you encourage, support, and follow your husband. Or do you instead criticize, undermine, and drag him kicking and screaming along *your* chosen path? Don't underestimate the freedom of being in the right place with the right abilities.

Second, wives are encouraged to acknowledge God's spiritual order. As Paul taught the Church at Ephesus:

Wives, submit to your own husbands, as to the Lord. (Eph 5:22)

We know, we know, you hate hearing that one! But if we take God's Word literally, and we do, there is no other way but to seek God's plan on this issue. God's order is hierarchical. Each of us, male and female, is called to humility and submission. We are called to submit to God **(Jas 4:7),** to earthly authority and leaders **(1 Pet 2:13),** to our elders **(1 Pet 5:5),** to our parents **(Deut 5:16),** and to the death of the flesh **(Rom 8:13).** The process of Christian growth is all about the reduction of the self and the yielding to God's objective.

God is saying in His Word that He has equipped the man with the raw material for leadership. But even military greats do not enter the service as five-star generals. Likewise, Christian husbands don't become the Apostle Paul within the first month of marriage. Men must learn to lead; women must learn to honor, respect, and encourage their development.

Submission does not mean passivity. Helpers are gifted, intelligent, and assertive individuals who, out of love, speak truth to the leader they support. What good is a corporate advisor, a political analyst, a coach, or a confidant who is unwilling to speak her mind? Women, your family needs your activity, insight, feedback, and strength.

But in the end, it is the man who is accountable and must make the final call. He will answer to God for himself and for everyone under his care, including his wife. Look into the Garden of Eden for an example. There the woman was left unprotected; falling victim to the devil's deception, she ate of the fruit and opened the door to sin. The man, following her leadership, later ate of the fruit as well, completing the downfall of paradise **(Gen 3:1-7)**. But when God came to the Garden after the commission of sin, whom did He seek?

Then the LORD God called to Adam and said to him, "Where are you?" (Gen 3:9)

God came looking for the *man*, the one He had given "dominion." Yet when Adam answered God, he was already weakened by the subjugation of his authority. When God asked Adam if he had eaten from the forbidden tree, he stood up like a "real man," pointed his finger and said:

"The woman whom You gave to be with me, she gave me of the tree, and I ate." (Gen 3:12b)

Blame, shame, and division entered the marital covenant. If only Adam had been on the point position examining the territory, he would have alerted his wife to the danger of the serpent. He would have reminded her of God's instructions. He would have stepped in between his wife and the threat. He would have wrapped that snake around a tree! And when God called, Adam could have given a good report.

If only Eve had told Adam that the serpent was tempting her and that she needed Adam's help. She could have brought into remembrance God's instruction taught to her by a loving leader. She could have offered counsel on dealing with the threat. If only they had operated as a team, under God's order, they could have conquered sin. If only...

Sometimes there is not a second opportunity to handle a bad situation. Men and women must be on alert and ready to move to their God-defined positions in the battle. Choices in the moment often lead to consequences that are permanent.

Third, God addresses the "inward" qualities of a godly woman:

Do not let your adornment be merely outward—arranging the hair, wearing gold, or putting on fine apparel—rather let it be the hidden person of the heart, with the incorruptible beauty of a gentle and quiet spirit, which is very precious in the sight of God. (1 Pet 3:3-4)

Men do appreciate external beauty, but God reminds us that it is our heart that matters most. Part of the wonder of a long-term relationship lies in the joining of the spirit between two saints. Physical beauty and all of its accessories will fade, but the heart will define us in the end.

God encourages the wife to develop a gentle and quiet spirit that He calls "precious." So often today, women feel the pressure of our sexualized society. The need for physical perfection, fitness, and youth has driven mass numbers of women into plastic surgery, eating disorders, and chronic dieting. The ever-present stress to maintain the "flesh" often leads women to ignore the spirit.

In God's order, the development of the heart will yield the greatest fruit. He isn't saying that you should "let yourself go" physically, but that flesh goes the way of all flesh. Only the life of the spirit endures.

It is hard to trust that the "visually oriented" man can come to adopt this view, but he can. Imagine seeing our spouses in the spiritual, as God sees us. What greater beauty or excitement could there be?

Finally, God defines the value of a virtuous wife:

Who can find a virtuous wife?
For her worth is far above rubies.
The heart of her husband safely trusts her;
So he will have no lack of gain.
She does him good and not evil all the days of her life.
(Prov 31:10-12)

Other words for virtuous include honorable, righteous, and honest. This is perhaps the centerpiece of the wife's call. In many ways, this scripture defines the wife as the ground wire for the husband. The man must know that his home is under the care and management of a helper that is totally trustworthy, "so that he will have no lack of gain." The wife removes the worry from his shoulders and frees him to earn a living, defend the home, and safely carry out the demands of his very challenging life.

She is his friend, his confidante, upon whom his heart can lean. Knowing that the wife does "good and not evil" encourages and gives life to the man. She is positive and uplifting in all she does.

Men grow up in athletics and other competitive situations. They appreciate the loyalty and cheers of fans and supporters that spur them on. Win or lose, a true supporter is always the same, always behind the team. Women are called to this place of encouragement.

Strength and honor are her clothing; she shall rejoice in time to come. She opens her mouth with wisdom, and on her tongue is the law of kindness. She watches over the ways of her household, and does not eat the bread of idleness. Her children rise up and call her blessed; her husband also, and he praises her: "Many daughters have done well, but you excel them all." Charm is deceitful and beauty is passing, but a woman who fears the Lord, she shall be praised. Give her of the fruit of her hands, and let her own works praise her in the gates. (Prov 31:25-31)

If anyone tries to tell you that a godly, submitted woman is weak, devalued, abused, or suppressed, give him or her Proverbs chapter 31 to read. The woman described here is one of strength, honor, and wisdom. She has beauty, character, industry, and love. She is valued and praised for her devotion to her home and her fear and reverence for the Lord.

Respect for God's Word yields patience. Trusting and obeying His commands may bear fruit you cannot see for some time. God is not always an advocate of "immediate gratification," but time and again we see Him bless the obedience of His children. And obedience is something we do out of love, not reward. Hold the course and see what God can do.

Why should I follow God's directives when my spouse doesn't?

We are awfully glad you asked that question. There are no links between God's directives to the husband and wife. Where does it say; "Husbands love your wives as Christ also loved the church, **IF** she submits to you." Did you read anywhere: "Wives submit to your husband **WHEN** he loves you as his own body"?

The commandments are independent. God deals with us individually as His children. We are to love, honor, submit, and obey no matter what our spouses do, so there is no cover in waiting for the "other one" to get it straight. We are called to be men and women of God no matter who shows up at the other side of the dinner table.

CASE EXAMPLE

In our clinical work, we see more women than men. This is due to several reasons: Women are more willing to admit the need for help; women, as a rule, are more expressive; but also women are burdened beyond belief, due in no small part to the strain of living outside God's plan.

One such woman is Arlene. She is 35, married for 13 years with two elementary-aged children. She was saved at 20, married a Christian at 22, and hasn't slowed down since. She works a 45-50 hour-a-week job, commutes 90 minutes a day, picks up her kids from after-school care about 6:30 p.m., and then starts dinner as soon as she gets home. Her husband Bo is a professional, earns a high wage, serves the church as a deacon, and is totally oblivious to his wife's strain.

To the outside world looking in, they have the ideal life: the money, the house, the cars, the kids; but on the inside there are the battle scars of success. So why is Arlene in a shrink's office? She asked herself the same question, along with several others: "Why am I so unhappy? Why don't I feel anything for my husband? What am I supposed to do?"

Arlene was depressed clinically, and for good reason. Her energy, drive, emotion, and spirit were depleted. There was nothing more for her to give, and the sad part was that she had been giving in all the wrong areas. What's more, no one was giving to her, just taking.

Since Arlene is a Christian, we began to contrast her life with the life described for the woman in God's Word. She was saddened to see how far she had drifted from the prescribed course.

Later when Bo joined the sessions, we found that he was lonely, angry, and lost as well. He didn't like the condition of his home either, but contrasting it to the world's order, it looked right.

It was hard, but the couple began to study God's Word and to shape their life choices from a perspective of obedience. They committed themselves to follow the roles God defined for them. Arlene began by yielding the problem to her leader (her husband), and Bo began to devise a plan of action that would lessen her burden by altering the priorities of their home life.

The result: Arlene now works from home as a consultant. She labors fewer hours for less pay. She sees the children off to school and greets them in the afternoon. Her husband finds her with energy and focus in the evening rather than burdened by fatigue.

They traded one of their new cars for an older, less expensive model. Other financial commitments were examined, challenged, and reduced. Hard choices were made and priorities redefined. Arlene is still a hard worker but she works in the areas important to God. She has found that these same areas are important to Bo and the children. God knew what she could not see under the delusion of the world's deceitful ploy. As the fog began to clear, Arlene could sense her purpose and joy returning.

Arlene's love for her husband was refurbished, and Bo's affection for her has soared. She feels protected by him and precious to him. He feels supported, honored, and served by her. Together they reduced the world and increased the Word. Success was measured on God's scale.

COMMUNICATION

It is no surprise that communication problems bring more couples to therapy than any other issue. It is a bit comical when you realize how well couples express themselves during courtship. Yet, when the ceremony is over, the "rules of engagement" change and suddenly they begin to say, "I don't know this person anymore!"

The pursuit and excitement of courtship is easy ground compared to the day-to-day challenge of relating in a meaningful and loving way. Problems change, issues surface, children arrive, bills come, and suddenly we are forced to relate on a different battlefield.

Some athletes are great at practice, but when you put them in the game with able opponents, critical coaches, and expectant fans, they blow it. The standards are suddenly higher and the risk of exposure is greater.

Couples have to learn to relate successfully in all circumstances. When you recognize what your training background has been (your parents), you may realize that you have a lot to learn. Like it or not, we will repeat many of the patterns of our childhood. Breaking that bondage requires replacing the weeds with wheat. God has many things to say about how we are to speak, relate, and treat others, and it is guaranteed to be superior to what you have witnessed in life.

Remember that communication involves far more than what is said. In fact, the largest portion of communication is unspoken. If you don't believe it, watch your husband; he is a master at silent expression. Of course, women have ways of relating through their behavior as well. They just add a few more words to augment the experience.

Words are a powerful source of edification or destruction. Proverbs 18:21a warns: **"Death and life are in the power of the tongue."** The intent of our communication will define our method and our outcome.

Communication should primarily be an effort of understanding. The more we clarify and define opinions, needs, and requests, the greater the likelihood of resourceful conclusions. But when communication becomes a method of control, we lose the opportunity to be understood and move into selfish positions that do not serve the union.

Remember that communication is about listening more than speaking. The better we are able to receive information, the better we can process and respond in a profitable way. As Christians, we must be the purveyors of peace in our homes. This cannot happen within the context of hostility or withdrawal.

NOW FOR YOUR QUESTIONS...

Every time we try to talk about a problem, we end up in a huge argument. In the end we are fighting over something totally unrelated to the issue we first brought up. We often conclude by calling names, threatening divorce, and then stop speaking for a week. How do we get out of this cycle?

First you need to be really honest with yourself. Are you actually so angry with your spouse that you want a divorce? Is that why it gets threatened so often? Or, do you simply lack the proper self-control and skill to communicate effectively?

If the anger and hurt between you is truly deep enough to promote separation, you will require professional help to uncover the root of this pain and pursue a remedy. If your dilemma is control and problem solving, these issues can be improved with education and commitment to change.

First, there must be some absolute rules for fighting that can never be violated. Anytime you break these basic guidelines, you are in danger of hurting one another and will fail to resolve your core conflict.

Never attack the person; attack the issue. Once the argument begins to be about the other person and not the topic of discussion, it is time to pull back and restate what you are trying to resolve. This means no name-calling and no absolute characterizations. Common statements include: "You ALWAYS disappoint me; you NEVER do anything right; you are IMPOSSIBLE!" **(Eph 4:29-32).**

Stop getting off the issue and stay on the point. No matter how tempted, we must stay on the issue and refuse to address unrelated material. Do not get pulled into another direction, and resist following your spouse onto topics that are out of place. This means there can be no use of historical data or past wrongs as a means of diverting the focus of the argument (i.e., your husband asks you about a credit card charge and you attack him for insulting your mother in 1979). Pursuit of this type of material takes you further and further from the truth (**Eph 4:25**).

Avoid blaming. Look for areas that you can take responsibility for and that you can personally change. Search for areas of agreement. Be willing to seek a solution rather than debate about who is "wrong" (**Matt 7:3-5**).

Stop shutting down and retreating into your anger. Feelings that are driven underground will find expression in our moods, emotions, and behavior. Emotions do not simply evaporate. Instead they take root and easily become a poison to the spirit and to the relationship (**Eph 4:26-27**).

For you, brethren, have been called to liberty; only do not use liberty as an opportunity for the flesh, but through love serve one another. For all the law is fulfilled in one word, even in this: "You shall love your neighbor as yourself." But if you bite and devour one another, beware lest you be consumed by one another! (Gal 5:13-15)

Here Paul defines the cost of angry communication: the consumption of one another. As Christians we must not give liberty to the flesh, but live according to the Spirit and its fruit (**Gal 5:22-23**).

Confronting a negative communication cycle will require discipline and devotion to change. It requires taking on the responsibility of personal movement first, no matter what the response of the partner. Any married person who is waiting for his or her spouse to make the first move is not doing enough to improve their plight.

Chances are, your spouse doesn't like this process any more than you do. Make a contract together to remove these murderous attacks and distortions. Never ever threaten to do what you really don't want (divorce). And if you do want it, then pray for God to change your heart and to give you control enough to speak of the issues and not rush to a conclusion.

My husband is a good Christian man, but he just doesn't talk to me. He shows me in a number of ways that he loves me, but I just want to hear it from his lips. How do I get my husband to communicate his feelings for me?

Certainly you need to be told of your importance. Thankfully, you know through your husband's behavior that you are loved and valued. That's a good sign that he is willing to learn how to better please you.

People have very different needs regarding the expression of love. Very often, our spouses simply do not understand our particular preferences because they are so different from their own. Many times we do not relate our needs because we have the false notion that asking for something in some way lessens its value. No doubt it would be wonderful if he simply knew what to do. But the real expression of love has to do with his willingness more than with his skill. Skills can be learned, but a willing heart is more difficult to cultivate.

You are ahead of the game by knowing of your husband's desire to please you. We recommend you do the following:

1. Explain to your husband just how much he pleases you with his behavioral expressions of love. Let him know that his efforts are noticed and valued.

2. Now tell him what would make his efforts even more effective. If he is showing you affection through action, it's a good sign that your happiness is important to him. Help him to understand how key words can move you, draw you closer, and strengthen your bond.

3. Tell him specifically what you want to hear and ask him to make these expressions a priority.

4. When he later does what you have asked, don't discount it because he didn't do it sooner. Instead, encourage him that this is exactly what you wanted and let him feel how much it

matters to you. Ask him to "keep it up!"

5. Ask if there are ways you can convey the same feelings to him. Help him talk about what really "hits the spot" for him, and give it to him. Responding to positive change in a reciprocal manner is a powerful reinforcement.

Since you have a positive relationship that is expressive, focus on the enhancement of what is good rather than the inadequacy of it. Learn also to appreciate his more natural efforts as a true and faithful conveyance of his devotion to you. Let him be constantly reminded of the gift God has given us in our wives **(Prov 5:18-19)**.

CASE EXAMPLE
The first day we met with Sherman and Angie, we almost had to clear the office building. From the moment they sat down, there was a barrage of insults, attacks, name-calling and cursing. Thank the Lord they were Christians or it might have gotten really bad!

Initially we felt more like security guards on the Jerry Springer show than family therapists. Eventually we helped them contain their emotions enough to ask them some questions. The dialogue went like this:

Shrink: "Why are you two together?"
Angie: "Are you suggesting we shouldn't be?"
Shrink: "I would never suggest such a thing. But you just called Sherman a really foul name, told him you hated him, and suggested he move out."
Angie: "I didn't mean all that."
Shrink: "You had us convinced. What about you Sherman?"
Sherman: "I think she hates me and I don't understand it. She knows she means the whole world to me."
Shrink: "You must have told her that in the parking lot. Because since you've been here Sherman, you have attacked her family, her weight, and her character. You called her some very harsh names and accused her of being unfaithful."
Sherman: "You make it sound worse than it is. She knows

that I don't really think she's cheating on me."
Angie: "How would I know that? You accuse me of it all the time!"
Shrink: "So if you don't really mean these hateful things, why on earth do you say them?"
Sherman and Angie: [Silence]

Sherman and Angie had been fighting for so long, they were on automatic pilot. Whenever conflict arose, they simply went to war. Both were products of angry, hostile childhoods. Both had parents who controlled their families through threats and attacks. Each felt ashamed that their marriage had taken on a similar tone. Each really did want to change.

In subsequent sessions, Sherman and Angie came to realize that their war was internal more than relational. In other words, the greatest volume of anger and insecurity came from their individual experiences in life, not from their marriage. They were limited by the unresolved emotions of childhood and by the absence of appropriate training on how to communicate with someone you love.

The first thing Sherman and Angie had to learn was the capacity to discern between internal states of emotion (self-generated) and emotions that were generated within the context of the marriage. Probably 80 percent of the time, the anger that was vented was already simmering underneath on a low flame. Sherman and Angie both were chronically angry people and had been so since their youth. In finding each other, they found a spouse that was familiar with "war zone" living. In a strange way, this kind of fighting felt familiar, if not normal.

Breaking that set of expectations is hard and it requires a willingness to confront and cast off the self-imposed curses of our past. The curse of past injury is found in our repetition of what was done to us. But Christ broke the stronghold of past failures with His sacrifice on the cross. Our failures, and the failures of our ancestors, no longer bind us as He took on the curse for us all.

Christ has redeemed us from the curse of the law, having become a curse for us (for it is written, "Cursed

is everyone who hangs on a tree"), that the blessing of Abraham might come upon the Gentiles in Christ Jesus, that we might receive the promise of the Spirit through faith. (Gal 3:13-14)

As believers, we are not predestined to duplicate or relive the past. Instead we must act with the resolve of freedom and seek God's help in rebuking these patterns. Sherman and Angie have done that. Now instead of "automatically" reproducing past trauma, they exercise control and examine their impulses.

When anger or disappointment *is* related to the marriage, they express it, but the emotions are voiced with clear boundaries and restriction of language and force. If, however, self-examination reveals a patterned response from an old feeling unrelated to the marriage, each addresses it quietly and privately rather than pouring it out on the spouse. The two report not only peace in their marriage, but inner tranquility and freedom from their past.

INTIMACY

The intimacy expressed between husband and wife is sacred. That means it is holy, blessed and sanctified. It should not be taken for granted, nor should it be perverted or defiled in any way. True intimacy, God's intimacy, is so much more than sexuality. When respected and nurtured it can become one of the highest forms of marital expression. When dishonored, the breakdown of intimacy can be one of the most painful aspects of marital life.

Marriage is honorable among all, and the bed undefiled; but fornicators and adulterers God will judge. Let your conduct be without covetousness; be content with such things as you have. For He Himself has said, "I will never leave you nor forsake you." (Heb 13:4-5)

Intimacy begins with a promise. The promise is essential because trust is essential. No human can fully yield and extend him/herself to another if that bond of assurance is not present. Just as we draw assurance from God's promise to "never leave nor forsake" us, so does our partner find comfort in our promises to him or her. Our heavenly Father is a covenant God. His faithfulness to us is our example to follow within our marriage. The author of Hebrews records God's promise to the nation of Israel:

"For this is the covenant that I will make with the house of Israel after those days, says the Lord: I will put My laws in their mind and write them on their hearts; and I will be their God, and they shall be My people." (Heb 8:10)

What a promise: "I will be their God, and they shall be My people." God offers Himself fully and accepts us fully. We may break our promise, but He does not. It is impossible for God to lie **(Heb 6:17-18).**

This is the reason that true intimacy cannot happen outside of marriage. Since there is no promise, there is no faith; and if there is no faith, there is no security. Without that confidence, it may be possible to bare the body, but never the soul, to one another.

Beyond the covenant there must be communication. Relating to each other is how we ratify the promise. The manner in which we express our love, in word and deed, brings continual endorsement of the covenant relationship. Each time we express our affection, restate our faithfulness, or affirm our commitment, we add an additional paragraph to the marital contract.

Sex is possible without communication, but intimacy is not. The greater our capacity to relate, edify, support, resolve conflict, forgive and protect, the lesser the barriers to complete submission to one another.

NOW FOR YOUR QUESTIONS...

My wife does not understand how important sex is to me. I have tried everything to increase her libido, but nothing works. As a Christian man, am I supposed to simply accept this and stay faithful? What about what I want?

First let us say that God created man and He created sex. Anatomically, we are constructed to experience pleasure when intimate. It is our belief that God created the joy of sexual gratification because it is to be a unique and exclusive experience between husband and wife.

So to answer your question, God does indeed expect you to be faithful, but He does not suggest that we should simply "endure" sexual problems. Instead, we are called to resolve such issues because failure to do so threatens the covenant. It is possible, however, that you are addressing the wrong issue.

True sexual dysfunction is not frequent in its occurrence. More often, sexual difficulty is a symptom that alerts us to other problems. As an example, chronic thirst is a symptom of diabetes, but you cannot cure the disease by drinking more water. Instead the insulin production must be regulated so as to stabilize all aspects of bodily function.

Similarly, more sex will not correct what is unstable in the body of your marriage. More frequent and/or improved sexual relations will be an outcome of better overall health in the relationship, not the reverse.

To be fair, some individuals do have medical or psychological issues that reduce libido. Depending upon your wife's age, general health, sexual history, etc., it is possible, but unlikely, that other factors are involved. Be very careful about portraying your wife as "the problem." The sexual relationship is something that requires mutual effort if it is to improve.

Men sometimes fail to realize that declining sexual interest and loss of intimacy affects the wife too. Women, like men, enjoy and need good sexual relations. It is very likely that your wife is grieving and confused and needs your support rather than your criticism.

Usually a general medical exam can answer most questions on this issue. Assuming that the exam reveals no medical problems we are back to the relationship between the two of you. If you want your sex life to improve, you must take the initiative to improve your intimate life.

In order for men to be aroused sexually they need only the

thought or image that is physically appealing. For women there needs to be an emotional connection. Women simply do not turn on or off with the suggestion of sexual activity.

When there is a problem in the relationship, men and women tend to approach it from polarized positions. Men push harder for sex, thinking that sex gives confirmation of connection and love. Women tend to withdraw from sex and seek emotional affirmation through communication. Once emotional security is reestablished, she is more likely to regain interest in physical engagement.

We suggest you do the following:

1. Confess to your wife that you have taken the wrong approach to the problem. Reassure her that you are interested in working things out and that you are willing to be patient. Ask your wife to pray with you that God will heal whatever is broken. James gives us the order of confession and prayer that leads to healing:

Confess your trespasses to one another, and pray for one another, that you may be healed. The effective, fervent prayer of a righteous man avails much. (Jas 5:16)

2. Remove the pressure you've put on your wife to engage physically. This will lessen the defensive posture she has taken that is pushing the two of you farther apart. You must search your heart for forgiveness, knowing that sexual problems involve both parties. Work to approach your wife without anger. Colossians 3:19 states: **"Husbands, love your wives and do not be bitter toward them."**

3. Ask your wife to talk with you about your relationship. Find out what is lacking for her. You may discover that your wife needs some very basic, simple behaviors from you. Work at listening and agree to give what is needed with no expectation of reciprocity.

Therefore, as the elect of God, holy and beloved, put on

tender mercies, kindness, humility, meekness, longsuffering; bearing with one another, and forgiving one another, if anyone has a complaint against another; even as Christ forgave you, so you also must do. But above all these things put on love, which is the bond of perfection. (Col 3:12-14)

4. It is important that you learn to touch your wife in a non-sexual way. Devote yourself to holding her hand, sitting close to her, kissing her, making eye contact with her. This type of confirmation helps reawaken the trust and assurance she needs to be closer to you.

5. As you talk, be willing to address problem areas. It could be that there are unresolved injuries or issues that have become a roadblock. Sex will not improve until these matters are addressed one by one.

During this time of work and reparation, you must not let yourself drift outside the marital boundary. Remain focused on your wife, your marriage, and your promise. When intimate relations are derailed, it is easy to toy with temptation. Bring your wife to mind frequently throughout the day, calling into remembrance the covenant that exists between you. Flee from all enticing material, whether it is suggestive T.V. shows, conversations with other women, pornography, or the Internet. Remember the words of Christ:

"The lamp of the body is the eye. Therefore, when your eye is good, your whole body also is full of light. But when your eye is bad, your body also is full of darkness." (Luke 11:34)

Men sometimes feel slighted by our advice on this matter. Many feel they have waited long enough and that the wife should do more. But leaders must carry the lion's share of responsibility when problems arise. The other reality is this: you simply cannot get what you are seeking any other way. No attempt to focus on frequency or intensity of sex will fix a sexual problem. The heart must be tended, emotions exchanged, and resolution of conflict achieved. Then, and only then, the walls that divide you will come down.

My husband wants sex all the time. I like sex, but he is obsessed. Is it a good idea to withhold my pleasures until he learns to treat me right?

Withholding food from a starving man will not quiet his hunger. This type of "indirect" communication will only serve to worsen the problem. Also, the Bible discourages this type of resistance as it opens the door to temptation and loss of control:

Let the husband render to his wife the affection due her, and likewise also the wife to her husband. The wife does not have authority over her own body, but the husband does. And likewise the husband does not have authority over his own body, but the wife does. Do not deprive one another except with consent for a time, that you may give yourselves to fasting and prayer; and come together again so that Satan does not tempt you because of your lack of self-control. (1 Cor 7:3-5)

We have a godly responsibility to our spouse physically. Sexual intimacy is a vital part of sexual purity because when we are engaged happily with our partner, the risk of sexual immortality is lessened. Thus, we do not recommend you withdraw from your husband sexually to make a point.

You say that you do enjoy sex. It could be that the real issue between you is not so much related to sexual incompatibility but communication problems. Couples can have different sexual tempos and your husband may have a generally greater drive for sex. But it appears that you are unhappy with his preoccupation with sex. Your need is for a more compete expression that includes connection and relationship outside the bedroom.

Instead of focusing on the reduction of sex, focus on the increase of behaviors that make you feel affirmed and valued by him. What do you need? We suggest you do the following:

1. Let your husband know that you do indeed like sex. Men like to be affirmed too. Let him know how nice it is to be wanted and desired by your husband. Assure him there are no technical or performance issues in bed.

2. Help him understand that while sex is good, his way of relating about it makes you feel discounted. Explain to him the importance of behaviors that help you to feel comfortable and connected with him. Let him know that you need more conversation about non-sexual material. Show him the importance of time spent together, and teach him how to touch you in a way that feels loving but not lascivious.

3. Let him see the potential benefit of creating respectful exchanges with you. Show him that this will lead to greater comfort, security, and confirmation of his love. These behaviors draw you closer, build trust, and enhance the intimate life.

In the event your husband is truly obsessed with sex, he also will benefit from better, more assuring communication between the two of you. Men who become overly focused on sex are often insecure about the relationship as well. Improved capacity to relate should bring a renewed confidence for him and you may see a reduction in his preoccupation.

Direct communication is key. Whatever you do, don't let behavior become your method of relating. Instead approach the challenge as a relationship issue that you share as a couple. Try not to characterize your husband as having a problem, and seek to express your needs in a way that gives him a chance to respond. Paul provides a structure for godly communication:

Let no corrupt word proceed out of your mouth, but what is good for necessary edification, that it may impart grace to the hearers. (Eph 4:29)

CASE EXAMPLE

Gary and Emma are quiet and shy as they talk about intimacy in their marriage. They blush when describing their reasons for seeking therapy: Gary wants sex "all the time" and Emma "never wants sex." In this case personal responsibility is not the issue. Emma feels like a failure and Gary believes he is a sex-crazed freak. Neither is the truth.

We eventually translated Gary's desire for sex to mean, two to three times a week, not "all the time." However, when sex didn't occur at the expected frequency, he felt anxious, insecure and feared he wasn't "good enough." As a result, he would push for sex everyday, thinking that if Emma agreed to have sex that often, it would make him feel reassured that she loved him and that he was sexually competent.

We also found out that Emma did want to have sex because she was very anxious and insecure about her abilities in the bedroom. Emma was a virgin when they married, while Gary had had one previous sexual partner. The knowledge of this provoked a fear of comparison in Emma's mind. Although very attracted to Gary, she found herself withdrawing out of anxiety. The more she withdrew physically, the more he complained and asked for sex. In a cyclical manner each reinforced the other one's fears.

Just this level of communication made a world of difference. When Gary realized that Emma was attracted to him and longed for sexual intimacy, he was very relieved. Gary expressed his regret that he had not waited for his bride before having sex the first time, and asked her to forgive him. He reassured her that the previous encounter with the past girlfriend was a mistake and not a special memory or a source of reference.

As their anxiety diminished, greater intimacy became the natural byproduct. When Gary's history was confronted and reassurance was given to Emma, the two easily fell into a more relaxed, comfortable, and safe sexual relationship. They also learned to talk about sex with less embarrassment and could communicate needs and requests more easily.

At last report, the couple no longer kept a count of how often they were intimate as evidence of how well they were doing. Instead they became invested in keeping honest with each other and working out feelings that were anxious or insecure. A little honesty and a lot of validation went a long way in this case.

This example speaks to the importance of abstinence before marriage. Even a single choice can do harm to one's sexual identity and security. With Gary and Emma it was a silent poison that could have easily tainted their sexual union indefinitely. God wants us to find our expression of sexuality only with the one He gives us as a spouse.

> **Let your fountain be blessed,**
> **And rejoice with the wife of your youth.**
> **As a loving deer and a graceful doe,**
> **Let her breasts satisfy you at all times;**
> **And always be enraptured with her love.**
> **For why should you, my son, be enraptured by an immoral woman,**
> **And be embraced in the arms of a seductress?**
> **(Prov 5:18-20)**

One man, one woman, joined as husband and wife: that is His design. This passage demonstrates just how special God intends it to be. Enraptured literally means to be filled with delight. God has created an intimacy for us that is so powerful that He questions why we would look anywhere else.

BECOMING A SPIRITUAL TEAM

As a marriage matures functionally, it should also mature spiritually. It is crucial to become a "spiritual team" that approaches everything in life from a biblical worldview. A truly spiritual relationship involves so much more than feelings, impulses, drive, and determination. The Christian home requires preparation and continual building-up in the Word of God. By engulfing the home in God's teachings, we train our minds and our hearts to recall His methods when making decisions, instead of the methods of the world.

> **Your word I have hidden in my heart, that I might not sin against You. (Psalm 119:11)**

A spiritual team will make time each day to fortify its position and connection with God. For the married couple this means daily Bible study and prayer. And here's the kicker: the study and prayer should be done TOGETHER! Yes, we hear your objections; there is no time, we are too tired, it's too awkward to pray together, I'm already in a Bible study on Wednesdays, etc.

Unfortunately, most of our focus and distraction comes from the world. We must remember that the world can add nothing to our spiritual account. Everything we do for the order of the flesh is akin to making life-long deposits into a savings account that is zeroed-out upon our death. It is only the work and wisdom of the Kingdom that will have eternal value **(1 Cor 3:11-15).**

Men are to be the spiritual guides in their homes. They are responsible for teaching and leading the family in spiritual truth. Failure to do so leaves the man and his family exposed to attack. Daily Bible study gives the home clear guidelines for living that can be found through no other source.

Hearing the Word of God over and over reinforces our hope, joy, and perseverance. It gives us vision that sustains our obedience. And, as we have said many times, distance from the truth brings us closer to the lie. Be willing to share Scripture daily as a basis for your home's foundation.

Why pray together? Because Jesus taught us to do so:

"Again I say to you that if two of you agree on earth concerning anything that they ask, it will be done for them by My Father in heaven. For where two or three are gathered together in My name, I am there in the midst of them." (Matt 18:19-20)

Agreement and unity is important for a family and, as Jesus asserts, it is a key component of prayer. Agreement on earth creates agreement in Heaven. When spouses pray together, they create a climate of agreement even if they have been in conflict previously. Joint prayer allows the couple to put aside their earthly strivings and allows God to reveal His will and purpose. Even when struggling over some issue, the married couple can kneel before the Lord and find agreement in the request that He intercede where their efforts toward resolution have failed.

It is important also to pray with our children and with the whole family present. But these times of prayer ought to never replace the married couple's private joint prayers each day. Praying together can be one of the most intimate and fulfilling activities in a Christian marriage. We urge you to seize its power and experience the depth and harmony it builds.

In addition to home study and prayer, take advantage of opportunities in the community or church for additional instruction. We recommend groups that study the Bible in complete context, verse-by-verse. Locate godly teachers who can provide strong discipleship.

Finally, the spiritual team must have supporting members. Fellowship with other believers is a great source of encouragement and keeps you plugged into families that share your Christian worldview. Be very cautious about deep association and reliance on unbelievers **(2 Cor 6:14)**. Yes, we should witness and minister to the non-Christian, but we are instructed to stay away from activities and patterns that are unholy and unclean. Find association with families who can reinforce and support your walk with Christ.

In summary, the emotional and relational elements of your life will be a reflection of your spiritual life. Study, prayer, discipleship, and fellowship are keys to your growth and maturity as a Christian, keeping you connected and active in your relationship with Christ. Take every opportunity to advance your family's time and focus with Jesus.

CHAPTER 4

RELATIONSHIP CRISIS

INTRODUCTION

Merriam-Webster defines crisis as: a turning point for better or worse. In the course of married life it is likely that some form of crisis, some "turning point", will come. The Bible offers many examples of moments like these, when the human spirit can turn either way. We are given examples of both perseverance and of failure. While many issues will surface that we cannot control, our survival of a crisis largely depends upon our choice to turn one way or another.

Abraham faced a crisis of faith when told to sacrifice his son Isaac as a burnt offering to the Lord:

Now it came to pass after these things that God tested Abraham, and said to him, "Abraham!" And he said, "Here I am." Then He said, "Take now your son, your only son Isaac, whom you love, and go to the land of Moriah, and offer him there as a burnt offering on one of the mountains of which I shall tell you." (Gen 22:1-2)

Abraham chose obedience, and his faith was rewarded with the life of his son being preserved. God then promised to bless and multiply his descendents:

> **Then the Angel of the Lord called to Abraham a second time out of heaven, and said: "By Myself I have sworn, says the Lord, because you have done this thing, and have not withheld your son, your only son— blessing I will bless you, and multiplying I will multiply your descendants as the stars of the heaven and as the sand which is on the seashore; and your descendants shall possess the gate of their enemies. In your seed all the nations of the earth shall be blessed, because you have obeyed My voice." (Gen 22:15-18)**

Again God relates His economy: obedience receives blessing. Too often we find ourselves taking an easier path, incorrectly thinking that the relief from burden is the blessing. We divorce, give up, run away, or act-out in order to avoid the choice of obedience. But time and time again we see that temporary relief is shallow indeed compared to the depth of blessing that God provides for perseverance.

An example of this occurred in Judah during the days of Jeremiah the prophet. The people of Judah were facing imminent captivity into the hands of the Babylonians. They wanted to escape to Egypt but first sent the prophet to "inquire of the Lord."

> **Now all the captains of the forces, Johanan the son of Kareah, Jezaniah the son of Hoshaiah, and all the people, from the least to the greatest, came near and said to Jeremiah the prophet, "Please, let our petition be acceptable to you, and pray for us to the Lord your God, for all this remnant (since we are left but a few of many, as you can see), that the Lord your God may show us the way in which we should walk and the thing we should do." (Jer 42:1-3)**

> **"...Whether it is pleasing or displeasing, we will obey the voice of the Lord our God to whom we send you, that**

it may be well with us when we obey the voice of the Lord our God." (Jer 42:6)

Have you ever prayed to God, knowing already what you planned to do? Often our prayers and petitions seek validation of our impulse rather than revelation of His plan. The leaders of Judah were determined to go to Egypt but wanted God to sign off on the plan. In this case, Jeremiah heard from the Lord and related the prophetic word to the leaders of Judah:

> **Thus says the Lord, the God of Israel, to whom you sent me to present your petition before Him: "If you will still remain in this land, then I will build you and not pull you down, and I will plant you and not pluck you up. For I relent concerning the disaster that I have brought upon you. Do not be afraid of the king of Babylon, of whom you are afraid; do not be afraid of him," says the Lord, "for I am with you, to save you and deliver you from his hand. And I will show you mercy, that he may have mercy on you and cause you to return to your own land." (Jer 42:9-12)**

God tells the remnant to stay in their current land and not "run away." In return for their obedience and endurance, He promises to build them up and deliver them from the threat of destruction at the hand of the Babylonian king. Blessing is promised; submission is required. But knowing their wayward hearts, God also warned them:

> **Then hear now the word of the Lord, O remnant of Judah! Thus says the Lord of hosts, the God of Israel: "If you wholly set your faces to enter Egypt, and go to dwell there, then it shall be that the sword which you feared shall overtake you there in the land of Egypt; the famine of which you were afraid shall follow close after you there in Egypt; and there you shall die. So shall it be with all the men who set their faces to go to Egypt to dwell there. They shall die by the sword, by**

famine, and by pestilence. And none of them shall remain or escape from the disaster that I will bring upon them." (Jer 42:15-17)

But the leaders accused the prophet of lying to them, and they disobediently went to Egypt, where God did fulfill His promise of calamity. In the land of Egypt, they faced famine, war, pestilence and severe loss of life and freedom at the hands of the Babylonian king who attacked and overthrew Egypt. Judah could not say it wasn't warned! **(Jer 42, 43, and 44).**

To Christians, the fear of threat often distorts our willingness to adhere to God's Word and His principles. Sometimes our fear concerns a very real threat such as illness, death, or divorce. Other times our fear is little more than the anxiety of losing an opportunity for pleasure. We create in our minds a sense of urgency, concerned that if we deny ourselves a certain opportunity, we will never have this chance again. We apply this logic to extra-marital affairs, inappropriate financial decisions, and other behaviors that involve some level of acting on an impulsive desire.

Our focus here is not to portray God as punitive. Rather, He is omniscient: He possesses universal and complete knowledge. God sees the entirety of our situation and wants to direct us in the way that is best. He always has a plan, always has a method, and always has our greatest interest in mind. His warnings in Scripture bring evidence of His capacity to see beyond our field of vision. He cautions us in advance concerning the outcomes we cannot see. Ultimately, He wants us in His will, obedient to His overall objective.

In all circumstances, we are called to obey God's word, even when it is so difficult to do so. Paul was obedient and submitted, even in his suffering:

I know how to be abased, and I know how to abound. Everywhere and in all things I have learned both to be full and to be hungry, both to abound and to suffer need. I can do all things through Christ who strengthens me. (Phil 4:12-13)

NOW FOR YOUR QUESTIONS...

INFIDELITY

I have become close to a woman at work. She's a great friend and I can tell her anything. My wife is so jealous and insecure that she wants me to stop seeing my friend. Is there anything wrong with me having good Christian friends of the opposite sex?

There certainly is something wrong! We know that the contemporary world advances the idea that we are a genderless culture and that we should be free to interact with whomever we please without sexual overtones, but that just isn't the way it is. Men are still men and women are still women. This "great friend" is a huge threat to your marriage and to your walk as a Christian man. Your wife is correct to sound the alarm and require proper boundaries with this other woman.

Most affairs do not begin with immediate attraction and a drive to the local motel. They begin with gradual drifts into increasingly inappropriate areas. Situations such as private conversations, using each other as confidants, having lunch together alone, and working late, are all signs that you are moving in the wrong direction. The more isolated you become, the greater the attraction and the higher the risk of inappropriate action.

Each time you confide in another female you dishonor your wife. You are taking your private thoughts and needs to another. That level of intimacy is reserved for your spouse only. The fact that you are annoyed with your wife speaks of your growing disharmony with her and your increasing bond to another.

It may be that you have no current intent to cheat on your wife physically, but if this process continues, you will in time. And even if you keep it at the current level of involvement, it can be almost as hurtful to your marriage as the physical act of sex. Remember that what you do with your heart is just as important as what you do with your body.

No temptation has overtaken you except such as is

common to man; but God is faithful, who will not allow you to be tempted beyond what you are able, but with the temptation will also make the way of escape, that you may be able to bear it. (1 Cor 10:13)

You are at a turning point. God has given you "the way of escape" through your wife and her demand for boundaries. We encourage you to accept the doorway offered. Once untangled from the friend, you can begin to examine what may need attention in your marriage. As long as you are carrying your feelings elsewhere, you are acting disobediently and you are violating the promise of fidelity made to your wife.

My husband is faithful physically, but often enjoys pornography on the Internet. I am uncomfortable with it, but he feels there is no harm done since he uses it only for fantasy material. Is this type of activity safe, or am I right to be concerned?

You are indeed right to be concerned. There is no safe level of involvement in pornography and its resulting fantasy life. God's Word is clear that the behavioral action of sin begins in our mind and in our heart: **"For as he thinks in his heart, so is he" (Prov 23:7a).** By flooding our mind with pornographic images, we expose our heart to great threat. As our mind and heart go, so go our bodies, our emotions, and our commitment.

Many will argue that pornography on the Web is "victimless" and that no one gets hurt. Clinical experience tells us quite the opposite. Once a person gets involved, there begins a systematic erosion in their personal and family life. For many it becomes a trap of ever increasing bondage.

Once a person is a regular user of pornography, regrettably, fantasy acted out with their spouse usually no longer suffices. Instead we have seen the deliberate movement to activity outside the home such as extra-marital affairs, hiring of prostitutes, sexual addiction, homosexuality, and other dysfunctional expressions.

Remember, the homeless alcoholic did not begin his addiction homeless and living on the street. Likely he had a family, a home, and a job at one time too. Addiction is progressive, debilitating, and often deadly. We cannot afford to ignore the early warning signs if we are to combat the problem.

Hard as it may be to accept, your husband has already committed the act of adultery. Jesus sets the definition: **"But I say to you that whoever looks at a woman to lust for her has already committed adultery with her in his heart"** (Matt 5:28).

You must address the issue in a serious and firm manner. First, fervently pray for God to give you wisdom and direction. Seek the prayers of trusted friends and your pastor. Pray that your husband will be convicted of his sin and turn back to you. Make your husband aware of your feelings, and ask him to pray with you for deliverance.

Second, you must not allow yourself to be drawn into sharing pornography with him, or acting out fantasies that have been inspired by the pornography he's seen. Many women fear that by doing so they will open the door to behavioral infidelity on their husband's part. In reality, there is an increased risk of escalated involvement in pornography and sexual acting-out by your husband as you foster and enable his craving for this medium. You cannot give validation and acceptance to sin. Instead you must be resolute in your position so that your marital bed will remain undefiled **(Heb 13:4).**

Be prepared. Holding a firm position and confronting an addiction like pornography may provoke anger and threat from your husband. The grip of pornographic material can be powerful, and it creates a strong delusion in the mind of the user. You will need the support and ongoing prayers of others if you are to endure.

Next you must insist that all use of pornography, including Internet service, be interrupted. A friend who is a recovering alcoholic told me once, "You don't go into a barbershop unless you are getting a haircut, and you don't go to a bar except to drink." The Internet is your husband's bar. He may plan to surf the Net, shop at eBay, and check his stocks, but the accessibility of the "drug" is too great. He will need a long season disconnected from the lure of that box.

You must address this with all the seriousness of any infidelity.

Hold to your boundaries and do not yield. The problem will only grow worse, otherwise. If your husband is unwilling to adhere to your requests, then a separation may be in order. He may need to live elsewhere until he is willing to honor the marital covenant.

My wife and I are both Christians, but she has had several affairs over the past 10 years. They don't last long and she always confesses to me what she has done. I think she is truly repentant and wants to do better, but Satan seems to have her in his grip. Shouldn't I continue to forgive her and pray that God will rescue her from this bondage to sex?

We respect your devotion to your wife and the commitment to honor your covenant. Your willingness to forgive when your wife repents is biblical. Jesus said:

"Take heed to yourselves. If your brother sins against you, rebuke him; and if he repents, forgive him. And if he sins against you seven times in a day, and seven times in a day returns to you, saying, 'I repent,' you shall forgive him." (Luke 17:3-4)

Jesus sets a high bar, no doubt. Right after this instruction, the disciples said, **"Increase our faith!" (Luke 17:5).** But Jesus also knew that "sexual immorality" in a marriage is perhaps the hardest thing to endure, and so He gave us permission to divorce under this situation if a resolution cannot be found **(Matt 5:32).**

In your case, some questions arise. First, forgiveness does not necessarily preclude divorce. In other words, you may forgive your wife's multiple transgressions yet believe it is not safe or healthy for you to continue to live with her. As we have discussed throughout this chapter, sin produces both earthly consequences and God's discipline.

Second, while we do not know your wife's heart, we question the depth of her repentance. Repentance is more than confession of sin; it is a turning away from sin. For example, what has your wife done to actively break this "bondage" you describe?

Is she in prayer with you about her sin, seeking God's strength where she is weak? Does she have a female accountability advisor with whom she is working to avoid temptation? Have the two of you counseled with your pastor or with a Christian counselor? Are you in study of God's Word? Is she working with you to establish boundaries that limit her temptation and vulnerability to other men? Has she begun to examine the root of her problem, the reason she acts in this manner?

Hebrews 10:26 states: **"For if we sin willfully after we have received the knowledge of the truth, there no longer remains a sacrifice for sin."** Unless she is actively pursuing freedom from this bondage, it will continue to enslave her.

We believe this type of repetitive sin may not be a "stronghold of Satan" so much as a willful act of disobedience. Sometimes we are so yielded to the flesh that Satan and his entourage don't really have to provoke us. We are willing to take ourselves down all on our own. If your wife has your forgiveness without the requirement of change, then she has no level of accountability and little motivation to do anything different.

Consequence is not the same as condemnation. If your wife is truly a believer, she will inherit the Kingdom. But she may have to accept the consequence of repeatedly violating the sanctity of your marriage. As it stands, you are subject to emotional pain, the risk of her getting pregnant, the risk of disease, and even death.

Yes, forgive your wife. Have mercy as you were given mercy **(Jas 2:13).** But mercy and forgiveness can be given in concert with boundary and the requirement of change. You are not subject to her sin, and you are permitted to require true and lasting modification of her behavior if she is to remain your wife. We encourage you to seek God on this matter and to consider a firmer position with your wife that demands respect for you and for God's order.

INFERTILITY

My husband and I have been trying to get pregnant for several years. We have been through every medical test and procedure available and have spent thousands of dollars, but to no avail.

Medically, I am the one with the problem. Children are so important to my husband. I am afraid he will eventually leave me if I am unable to give him an heir. What do I do next?

Infertility is very painful, especially when you are the point of focus. Many we have counseled feel incomplete or even cursed. Some have expressed their problem as a "punishment from God" for past sins. But truly it is none of these things.

We will never know exactly why God does what He does. The Bible gives us examples of women burdened by infertility and God's response to them. Very often these are the women through whom God did a special work. Sarah, at a very advanced age and following a lifetime of infertility, became the mother of Isaac and of the entire Hebrew nation **(Gen 21)**. Hannah grieved her barren condition and committed her yet un-conceived son to God's special service. Soon after, she conceived Samuel, who became a mighty prophet, priest, and judge **(1 Sam 2 and 3)**. Elizabeth was late in life when God blessed her with the birth of John the Baptist, the one who was to "prepare the way of the Lord" **(Luke 1, Matt 3:3)**.

Trusting God in this matter is difficult because we sense there is so much at stake. We feel a burden of time, identity, and relationship bearing down on us. And while medical options are much improved, they are imperfect at best and stressful and disappointing at worst. In the end, we must stay focused on the reality that God has a good and perfect will for us all:

Rejoice always, pray without ceasing, in everything give thanks; for this is the will of God in Christ Jesus for you. (1 Thess 5:16-18)

The world suggests that we must have children to be considered a normal married couple. Yet God made each of us for His glory and purpose. While we believe one should pursue all options available, ultimately we must remember that the final decision is God's. At some point we must yield to prayer and seek His peace if we are to understand His goal.

God uses another medical condition to express this point in His

Word. Jesus makes it clear that whatever infirmity we bear, it can be used for the work of God to find expression:

Now as Jesus passed by, He saw a man who was blind from birth. And His disciples asked Him, saying, "Rabbi, who sinned, this man or his parents, that he was born blind?" Jesus answered, "Neither this man nor his parents sinned, but that the works of God should be revealed in him." (John 9:1-3)

God may yet provide you a child, and the struggle of your process becomes your testimony. He may have selected a child for you to adopt who will be a special child with great purpose. Or God may have other works to be revealed. Allow your prayer to ask that "His will be done." **(Luke 22:42).**

Finally, do not confuse your husband's desire and potential disappointment as a threat to your marriage. Silence on the issue increases the potential for problems. Find a way to tell him your fears and allow him to express his sadness. Should a child not be in your future, each one of you will be affected. Do not avoid discussion, letting fear and resentment take root. Remain obedient partners in this process, be willing to accept God's decision, and then reap the blessing of where He takes you.

FINANCIAL CRISIS

My wife and I are way over our heads in debt. With a mortgage, car loans, student loans and credit cards, we are drowning! Is bankruptcy an option for Christians?

Generally speaking, it is not a godly option. In Romans 13:8 Paul reminds the believer: **"Owe no one anything except to love one another, for he who loves another has fulfilled the law."** And in the Old Testament we find an absolute prohibition: **"You shall not steal" (Deut 5:19).**

Although the world teaches otherwise, the accumulation of debt is not a good practice, and the failure to pay debt is stealing. We understand that in certain situations filing bankruptcy is unavoidable. But your question did not mention a long-term illness, loss of job, catastrophic event, or natural disaster. Instead you speak of personal debt that has allowed you to have a nice house, cars, education, and whatever you purchased on credit cards. Failure to pay these debts forces others to pay them for you. The debt doesn't just disappear like smoke when you file bankruptcy. Your escape of burden creates burden for another.

Assuming you have no legitimate crisis other than discomfort and stress, it is time to settle in and confront your sin of overindulgence. You are faced with digging yourself out of debt through sacrifice and accountability. There are many reputable credit-counseling organizations that can help restructure your debt and build discipline to pay it.

Eventually you must also address the cause of your dilemma. Credit is easy to obtain and hard to pay. You have become focused on the immediate and not the long term. Very often we transfer emotional issues to spending, finding some temporary refuge in dining out, buying new shoes, or a faster car. The short-term relief then leads to ever-increasing stress and anxiety as the bills come in. This anxiety may cause you to go out and spend more to gain temporary relief, which then leads to more stress and more spending. Round and round we go...

You cannot buy your way out of discomfort or stress. Whether this is an individual or marital issue, it needs your full attention. Find a good course on biblical money management and confront this need for spending and accumulation.

CASE EXAMPLE
Hal and Agnes are Christians in their mid-thirties who entered therapy in serious financial trouble. Recently Agnes admitted a serious problem with spending and credit card debt that she had kept from her husband. When she could no longer make the minimum credit card payments or stop the creditors from calling, she confessed a debt of nearly $50,000 distributed over eight credit cards. This debt, on top of other obligations such as the mortgage

and car loans, threatened to throw the family into bankruptcy.

Hal was very angry with Agnes for spending "all this money." He relates that he had "no idea" the problem was this deep. He even threatened divorce. Agnes expressed much guilt and responsibility for the problem.

> *Shrink:* "Hal, how did $50,000 of spending occur without your knowledge?"
>
> *Hal:* "I wish I knew!"
>
> *Shrink:* "Agnes, what did you buy?"
>
> *Agnes:* "Mostly stuff for Hal and the kids. I got Hal a big screen T.V. last Christmas and some new fishing rods for his birthday. I buy lots of toys for the children, almost every week. We also eat out a lot and put the meals on the credit cards. Eventually I got in the habit of buying many basics on the cards like groceries and household items because I couldn't keep up the payments on our income. It seemed like the more upset I got about our debt, the more I would spend. I know it sounds crazy, but sometimes I just couldn't stop."
>
> *Hal:* "That is crazy. In fact, you have ruined us!"
>
> *Shrink:* "Hal, you told me that you are a Christian family…"
>
> *Hal:* "Right."
>
> *Shrink:* "As the leader of the home, how were you oblivious to the family's spending habits?"
>
> *Hal:* "Are you suggesting this is my fault?"
>
> *Shrink:* "I am suggesting the problem is bigger than your wife's impulsive buying. I wonder how you didn't notice the toys coming into the house. I wonder how you thought the family would pay for the big screen TV and the fishing equipment. Did you question the amount spent on dining out?"
>
> *Hal:* "I assumed she was saving money from our budget or that she had gotten some zero interest deal on the TV."
>
> *Shrink:* "You assumed…but didn't ask. Maybe your denial was as great as Agnes'."
>
> *Hal:* "Maybe."

Shrink: "Agnes, why do you think there has been so much spending?"
Agnes: "I think we are just unhappy. I try to fix things with Hal and the children by purchasing gifts, going out to eat, and surprising everybody."
Shrink: "Does it work?"
Agnes: "Yes, for a little while. Then the fun of it passes and I feel scared about the bill that I know is coming next month. I try to block it out of my mind, but mostly I am terrified all the time."
Shrink: "So you do the worrying for both Hal and yourself. You both get the TV and the fun, but you alone get the ulcer. Now the threat is so big you both have to deal with your choices."

Excessive spending, like most compulsive behaviors, begins as an effort to relieve pain or anxiety. Like a drug, its effect is short-term and requires constant feeding. Over time the issue grows into a catastrophe. Usually issues like these are "shared" within the family. In the case of Hal and Agnes, both were in denial, and both were trying to fill some emotional void through spending and the acquisition of material things.

As the therapy advanced we found significant marital dissatisfaction that played out in the compulsive spending. As the issues of communication and intimacy were resolved, the two were then able to negotiate and set proper limits on spending. It took a long time, but Hal and Agnes worked their way out of debt without filing bankruptcy. In addition to their therapy, they consulted a Christian credit-counseling group that worked with their creditors to restructure their loans and interest rates.

Hal and Agnes are learning to be good stewards of their money; to communicate responsibly, and to serve one another's emotional needs through new, non-material expressions. They have worked to strengthen their spiritual lives by adding prayer and Bible study to their daily routine, and they now seek God's help in controlling urges and impulses that are unhealthy and threatening to their spiritual and emotional well-being.

Jesus asks us to consider the following quandary: **"For what will it profit a man if he gains the whole world, and loses his own soul?" (Mark 8:36)**

MEDICAL OR MENTAL ILLNESS

My husband has severe bi-polar disorder and is very unstable. He cannot work and generally is not functional in the home. This has been going on for 20 years with no improvement. I don't want to divorce him, but I may not be able to cope much longer. What should I do?

As you probably know, Bi-Polar Disorder is a chronic medical condition with psychiatric symptoms of severe mood swings, depression, agitation, and manic behavior. We have made great strides in treating the condition with medication and counseling, and patients are realizing longer periods of stability and functioning normally. Unfortunately, success is not always absolute.

People with this condition can be very unpredictable and sometimes are non-compliant with treatment. In other words, due to the nature of their illness, they don't take their medication properly or follow up with their doctor's recommendations. This creates a unique burden for the caregiver who is left to monitor all aspects of his/her therapy and treatment.

We respect your many years of commitment to your husband and encourage you that you are doing the correct thing by remaining in the marriage. God made us "one flesh" and therefore we are to share the afflictions of our union. This condition is not something your husband is doing to you. Most likely he has little control over his behavior.

So often the Bible compares marriage to the relationship between Christ and the church **(Eph 5:23-32)**. As such, we are bound with the bond of sacrifice, just as the Lamb of God was sacrificed for the world.

Your calling to this marriage is most difficult and distinctive; yet for God's purpose you are placed here, and we believe He will bless your attention to your covenant. In the present time you must also address your needs.

Have you noticed when you board a plane that you are given instructions on using the oxygen should the cabin lose pressure? We are told, "If traveling with small children or elderly persons, the caretaker should breathe the oxygen first." Why is this? Simply put, if you are incapacitated, the one relying on you doesn't have a chance!

You are very near that point of incapacitation, and you mustn't feel guilty about it. Instead, design a way to get some air into your lungs or you won't be able to continue at this pace. These suggestions may seem elementary, but we tend to avoid the basics of self-survival as our needs build toward a crash.

First, you should see a doctor and have a physical. You must be in good health to maintain this pace of care. Second, examine your diet and activity to see if improvements can be made that will optimize your fitness and health. Next, find a support group of family members dealing with mental illness. These groups often are a good source of support and ideas, and many times they help one another by providing in-home support.

Ask your local mental health association about programs or sources of support. Speak to your husband's doctor about his care and the possibility of more aggressive treatment. Contact another doctor and get a second opinion.

Speak openly to your extended family about the need for support. Frequently there is an aura of shame or embarrassment that promotes isolation. Try to seek the encouragement of other Christians who are willing to understand and share your burden.

And those members of the body which we think to be less honorable, on these we bestow greater honor; and our unpresentable parts have greater modesty, but our presentable parts have no need. But God composed the body, having given greater honor to that part which lacks it, that there should be no schism in the body, but that the members should have the same care for one another. And if one member suffers, all the members suffer with it; or if one member is honored, all the members rejoice with it. (1 Cor 12:23-26)

MID-LIFE CRISIS

My husband of 23 years just asked for a divorce with no reason given. He said he is moving out of state and I can have "every-thing." He said the money doesn't matter, he just wants "out of here." I feel like I have awakened in the middle of a dream! He said if I resist, then he will fight and I won't get anything! What should I do?

Although we hate the cliché of mid-life crisis, that is exactly what your husband is having. Mid-life used to be a time of reflection, assessment and planning for the next phase of living. Often we are at the peak of our career, the children are almost grown, and the chance of personal time together is great.

However, over the past several decades men have been bombarded with the notion that they should "have it all." They are encouraged to go for the things they have always wanted and forsake the "restriction" of home, wife, and children. As a result, mid-life has become a time of panic with many having the sense that; "If I don't go now, I'll never go." It is a crisis of identity and self-esteem and usually has little, if anything, to do with the marriage itself.

That is exactly why your husband is pressing so hard for this to happen right away. He is afraid to hesitate and would rather the momentum of his decision carry him out the door. Most men in this situation are in a rush, willing to give it all away. Unfortunately, many already have an emotional or sexual involvement elsewhere. The outside involvement with another usually is the catalyst or force that produces this erratic movement.

Time is your greatest ally. Find some support and hunker down to wait. Your husband will pressure you, threaten you, bribe you, and manipulate you to "make this easy." Do not do it! Consider your husband as being in a temporary state of insanity and give him nothing he asks for regarding a separation or divorce. Let time do its work to undermine the fantasy life he is running toward.

Hard though it may be, do not focus on the possible affair at this time. Confessions are not likely to come until he makes a turn back home. Focus instead on your resolve to remain married, telling him this in as few words as possible. Although it is difficult, try to maintain a flat and unemotional demeanor. It is your firm, unchanging resolve that may put the brakes on his escape.

As time slows his movement, there is a good chance he will take another look at his decision. Protect yourself emotionally with friends and possibly a counselor. You will need help as your husband tries to force your compliance.

Honestly, the chances of his return are 50/50. However, if you sign the divorce settlement and let him go easily, you have virtually no chance. Solicit prayer from your friends and your pastor. If your husband is a Christian, ask one of his Christian brothers to visit him and to address this matter **(Gal 6:1)**.

Try not to be frightened about hurting him or making him angry. Your husband needs all the reality he can get right now. Waiting with an uncertain outcome is not easy. Now, more than ever, you must draw your strength from God who never has an identity crisis. Psalm 46:1 proclaims that: **"God is our refuge and strength, a very present help in trouble."** God is always God and He never changes.

CASE EXAMPLE

Mike gave Irene her first computer for Christmas. She loved surfing the Web, meeting Christian friends online, and sharing Scripture. Even her cooking improved with all the great recipes she was finding.

July 4th of the next summer, Irene announced that she needed some time alone and would not attend the family vacation at the beach. Instead, she was going to "take a few days" for prayer and fasting in the mountains. Mike was confused but accepted the plan. After all, her journey was for spiritual reasons. What harm could there be?

The next week, when all returned home, Irene stated a "revelation" that she was to leave Mike and move to North Carolina. She said it would be better if the two teenage boys stayed with Mike as they were nearing the end of high school. Irene suggested this decision had been building for a long time although Mike had no idea she was unhappy.

Mike came for therapy asking what to do. After our first session, he went to Irene's computer and found a history of frequent visits to chat rooms and emails from other men. She also had been to some websites on divorce. When confronted, Irene confessed she had met Jerome "online" and that she had spent the weekend with him in the mountains. Irene and Jerome were "in love" and intended to make a life together.

As planned in therapy, Mike remained as calm as possible and told Irene he would not divorce her. Instead he asked her to enter therapy with him to work out the problem. She refused and left immediately to join Jerome.

Mike took care of the children and the home and did not pursue Irene. He didn't call her or look for her. Soon she began to call and asked if she could visit. Mike told her firmly that she could come home when the other relationship was ended, and not a minute before. He said he had no interest in sharing time with another man. Mike said: "When you are finished with this craziness, call me. We will see if there is anything worth saving of this marriage."

On the phone he was bold, but in private Mike was broken. He was depressed, angry, and terrified that his marriage was over. At the same time, he knew this woman on the phone was not the "same person" as his wife of 20 years. Mike made the resolve to "hold fort" and demand all of her, or accept none of her. He held on to Christian brothers who cared for him and prayed with him. He stayed in God's Word for truth and remained grounded.

Another two weeks passed before Irene called again, crying and begging to come home. When Mike asked why, Irene said she had made an awful mistake and that she needed her family back. Mike told her he was not ready to reconcile, and that in order for him to do so, she would have to come home under his terms:

1. Mike said he did not want the children hurt again by her confusion or the possibility that she might leave again. Irene was to stay at her mother's home, 15 miles away.

2. Irene was to have no contact of any kind with Jerome (the boyfriend) and would agree to whatever methods of validation

Mike required. She would have no Internet access or long-distance phone capability. Any contact with Jerome would terminate the process of reconciliation immediately.

3. Mike and Irene were to enter therapy together and remain in treatment until their issues could be completely resolved.

4. Irene would meet daily with Mike for prayer and Bible study.

5. Irene would have contact with the kids only after Mike believed she was free of Jerome and only when the two believed she was ready to return to the home.

Irene accepted the terms, honored them over a three-month period, and returned home before the next Christmas. It was a horrific year, and much was still needed in the work of restoration. However, the marriage was mending, normalcy was returning with the children, and hope was restored.

Success came in Mike's determined position and willingness to lose his wife rather than compromise God's principles. Irene had to find out that her home could only remain hers if she lived under God's rule of order, respecting the boundaries of the covenant. Of course, forgiveness and trust came slowly, but they did come.

Most crises of marriage can find resolution if God is allowed to work. God's Spirit can heal and change hearts that ordinarily would be broken forever. This is why secular marriages have such difficulty working through crises like these. Without the power of salvation, our hope is lost. As we can see, Christian homes are not immune from trauma and we are tempted by the same temptations as non-Christians. The difference is the strength of regeneration that is alive in the believer.

DEATH OF A SPOUSE

My Christian husband of 35 years died recently after a long illness. How can I cope with his loss and my loneliness?

Coping with death is a painful and slow process. Regrettably there is no way to avoid or eliminate the feelings of loss and loneliness. Instead you will have to confront these and other emotions as understandable reactions to losing a life-partner.

Living and growing with someone for many years creates a reliance and familiarity that cannot be fully replaced. Chances are you will feel lost and disoriented at times as you try to picture life without your mate. Family members will not completely understand your feelings, though they may try. Often those around you are so eager to see you feeling better; they will unwittingly ignore the indicators of your pain.

Many times family and friends may confuse activity with coping. In other words, they believe that if they can get you involved with life again, you will get back to normal. They will encourage you to go back to church, have lunch with a girlfriend, get your hair done, etc. By keeping you moving they believe you will have less time to think about your husband and therefore less time to feel depressed.

While engagement with life is important, you also will need time alone to process your thoughts and feelings. You actually need time to remember and ponder your life together. Doing so does not convey an absence of coping; rather, it is an expected response after 35 years of marriage.

Allow yourself time to look at pictures, videos, old letters and cards. Remembering brings validation to the marriage and allows you to feel and express emotions that need attention. Ask those close to you to reminisce with you. Often people are afraid even to mention the name of the deceased for fear they will stir uncomfortable feelings. Encourage them instead to talk about and acknowledge your husband so that he remains alive in the family's heart and memory.

There is no method known for coping with grief that will allow you to escape feelings of depression and even anger at times. Don't see these as a failure to cope but again as normal reactions to a painful reality. Feelings like these will continue for a minimum of a year or more, as you experience life without him for the first time. Special events like birthdays, anniversaries, and holidays are ripe with emotion. It is important to have support and involvement with others as these days approach.

You should only be concerned if the feelings continue to worsen over time, or if the duration of the emotions seems excessive (lasting beyond 18 to 24 months). Grief can become complicated if improvement is not noted over time.

But remember that the passage of time is not the only healer. It is necessary and healthy to talk about your husband and to express your feelings, positive and negative, as they occur. Suppression of feelings will do far more damage and often will prolong the recovery process.

Jesus experienced and expressed grief over the death of His friend Lazarus:

Therefore, when Jesus saw her weeping, and the Jews who came with her weeping, He groaned in the spirit and was troubled. And He said, "Where have you laid him?" They said to Him, "Lord, come and see." Jesus wept. Then the Jews said, "See how He loved him!" (John 11:33-36)

You see, our Savior who lived in human form, can relate to your loss and pain. Here Jesus attends to the grief of Mary and Martha, while expressing His own suffering. Notice in the Scripture that He "groaned in the spirit and was troubled." Later the Jews acknowledge Jesus' love for Lazarus because they saw Him weeping.

Jesus, acting as our example, demonstrates that emotions are natural and their expression needed. Even Jesus, who knew He would raise Lazarus from the dead, felt the pain of loss and suffering for His friend. Shouldn't we then be afforded the same expression of love that manifests in our grief and sadness?

Thankfully, those of us who are believers have the further assurance of reunion with our loved ones in Heaven. Paul taught:

But I do not want you to be ignorant, brethren, concerning those who have fallen asleep, lest you sorrow as others who have no hope. For if we believe that Jesus died and rose again, even so God will bring with Him

those who sleep in Jesus. (1 Thess 4:13-14)

"God will bring with Him those who sleep in Jesus." This is a beautiful promise of our hope and belief that should sustain us until our scheduled meeting in eternity. But in that hope we must acknowledge God's providence and carry forth until we are called. That means that while our grief should continue for a season, ultimately we have work to continue until our death, or the rapture of the church.

Eventually, we must find our way back to our God-given path and proceed as the independent servant we were called to be. But as believers we can anticipate a great reunion with all the saints in our life. It is a great comfort to know your husband waits for you in heaven.

And God will wipe away every tear from their eyes; there shall be no more death, nor sorrow, nor crying. There shall be no more pain, for the former things have passed away. (Rev 21:4)

SUMMARY

Crisis is part of life, and trials will inevitably come. When grounded solidly in a relationship with Christ, our hope is not in the resources of the world, but in the infinite resources of the Creator. The Apostle John wrote that when the world challenges us, we have a strength that cannot be overtaken:

You are of God, little children, and have overcome them, because He who is in you is greater than he who is in the world. (1 John 4:4)

Call daily upon the power and promise that is afforded every believer. Your help and protection is supernatural, against which no one can stand.

I will lift up my eyes to the hills—From whence comes

my help? My help comes from the Lord, Who made heaven and earth. He will not allow your foot to be moved; He who keeps you will not slumber. Behold, He who keeps Israel shall neither slumber nor sleep. The Lord is your keeper; The Lord is your shade at your right hand. The sun shall not strike you by day, nor the moon by night. The Lord shall preserve you from all evil; He shall preserve your soul. The Lord shall preserve your going out and your coming in from this time forth, and even forevermore. (Ps 121:1-8)

CHAPTER 5

DIVORCE

INTRODUCTION

As Christian therapists, it is never our province to counsel divorce. Our work is to preserve the marital union if at all possible. Many secular therapists believe they have the right and the wisdom to tell a couple they should not be together. We commonly hear from patients that other professionals proclaimed their marriage "hopeless."

Our society is one of emotion and impulse. The world's wisdom is to take whatever action makes you feel good in the moment. But this is not God's way. If it were, He would have gotten rid of us sinners long ago and started over. Instead He is patient and longsuffering in His relationship with us and He encourages us to do likewise when pressure comes. We are to protect the covenant, the promise we made with our spouse, just as God honors His covenant with us **(2 Pet 3:9).**

> **"For the Lord God of Israel says That He hates divorce,**
> **For it covers one's garment with violence,"**
> **Says the Lord of hosts.**
> **"Therefore take heed to your spirit,**
> **That you do not deal treacherously." (Mal 2:16)**

NOW FOR YOUR QUESTIONS...

MARITAL AMBIVALENCE

Even though I've been married nearly 20 years, I believe my marriage was a mistake. I know I love her, but I'm not "in love" with her. I don't think God wants me to be unhappy, do you?

Boy, we wish we had a nickel for every time we have heard that one! So many times we base the evaluation of our marriage totally upon feelings. God gave us emotions, and the sensation of love is one of the greatest. But there is so much more to marriage and commitment than how we feel on a day-to-day basis. According to Scripture, we cannot trust our feelings alone: **"The heart is deceitful above all things, and desperately wicked; who can know it" (Jer 17:9).**

If we listen to our heart only, we will spend a great amount of our time in confusion. Anyone who has been married for more than a few days can attest to the reality that negative feelings will come. The question is, how we will respond?

God does want us to be happy, but He knows more than we will ever know. He knows every single day of our lives **(Ps 139:16)**. Very often we can see only the momentary attraction or repulsion of a situation. We want to have what we want in the moment, or avoid what makes us unhappy.

Our Creator can see the whole movie from start to finish. He doesn't want us to settle for short-term pleasure or time-limited relief. He wants us to have everything that obedience and spiritual growth can bring.

Understandably, we will not prosper outside of God's will. So to answer your question, no, God does not want you to disavow the covenant relationship He gave you so that you can pursue the temporal pleasures you seek. Jesus reminds us to desire "righteousness" first, and His blessings will follow:

"But seek first the kingdom of God and His righteousness, and all these things shall be added to you." (Matt 6:33)

Very often when someone no longer feels "in love," it is due to the boundary of the marriage having already been breached. It doesn't mean you are necessarily having a physical affair, but you should consider whether there is some attachment that has become a threat to the marital bond. The threat may be a confidant of the opposite sex, a friendship that has become too intimate, or a work relationship that is too close. Nothing can improve as long as there is an intimate resource outside the marriage.

GOD AND DIVORCE

Does God allow divorce under any circumstances?

God does not *encourage* divorce under any circumstance. Jesus said: **"Therefore what God has joined together, let not man separate" (Mark 10:9).** Once two have become one flesh, it is impossible to divide without significant pain and sorrow. But our Father has defined two occasions under which divorce is *allowed*. According to Jesus, the first is sexual immorality:

> **"And I say to you, whoever divorces his wife, except for sexual immorality, and marries another, commits adultery; and whoever marries her who is divorced commits adultery." (Matt 19:9)**

Here sexual immorality is given as an *exception*, not a *command*. In other words, even in the case of infidelity, we are to seek resolution and forgiveness whenever possible. It is important that we not leap into divorce simply because we have met the biblical criteria. Acting impulsively on the grief and hurt of the situation may produce life-long consequences that, if given time, possibly could be resolved. This is especially important when children are involved in the home.

This does not mean that a spouse should subject him/herself to repeated immorality and philandering. Working toward resolution requires that the individual involved in infidelity is repentant and willing to turn from his/her sin. Crises of this type almost always require professional attention and should be addressed over an appropriate period of time.

Paul addresses the second scenario under which divorce can occur:

> **But to the rest I, not the Lord, say: If any brother has a wife who does not believe, and she is willing to live with him, let him not divorce her. And a woman who has a husband who does not believe, if he is willing to live with her, let her not divorce him. For the unbelieving husband is sanctified by the wife, and the unbelieving wife is sanctified by the husband; otherwise your children would be unclean, but now they are holy. But if the unbeliever departs, let him depart; a brother or a sister is not under bondage in such cases. But God has called us to peace. (1 Cor 7:12-15)**

The second condition for divorce is also plain. If the Christian is married to an unbeliever and the unbeliever wants to go, let him leave. The Christian "brother or sister is not under bondage" at that point.

But also notice that while we are not to marry a non-Christian, when we do, we are bound together as long as he/she wants to stay. As in the case of sexual immorality, the same principle applies: all effort should be exhausted to save the marriage, even if the biblical criterion is met. 1 Corinthians 7 continues:

> **For how do you know, O wife, whether you will save your husband? Or how do you know, O husband, whether you will save your wife? (v. 16)**

The example set by the Christian in the home may influence the decision by the spouse to accept Christ. This by no means suggests that we should marry non-Christians in an attempt to save them. Most often this situation occurs when two non-Christians marry, and later in the marriage one of the two comes to know the Lord.

Isn't abuse an acceptable reason to divorce?

The Bible does not directly address the issue of abuse within marriage. Certainly every instruction to the husband and wife reflects honor, love, care, and support. In no way does God's Word endorse or encourage the harming of others, mentally, physically, or spiritually.

So often the scriptures related to the wife's submission are misused **(Eph 5:22, Col 3:18, 1 Pet 3:1)**. Submission to the husband in no way requires the tolerance of abuse. At the same time, God does not provide permission to divorce for this reason.

While it is possible for a born-again person to abuse, it is unlikely. True believers will seek to bring all things into subjection **(1 Cor 9:27)**. Like other areas of sin, true repentance should yield a change in heart and a change in behavior. Yet patterns of abuse often stem from childhood injury and can be deeply engrained.

As in dealing with other forms of repetitive sin, the one being abused may have to create boundaries if the sin is to be extinguished. While we cannot advise divorce, we have often encouraged separation for the safety of the one being hurt. Very often distance from the abuser is a matter of life and death.

Separation can be difficult as the abusing spouse may become aggressive in his attempt to control and restrict the departure. While a sense of shame and embarrassment is common, the abused victim must reach out to family, friends, or authorities to help. Your life, and the life of your children, must take priority.

Once apart, conditions must be placed on the abuser and he must agree to seek help, spiritually and psychologically. You cannot return home on the "promise" that things will be different. The separation will be lengthy and must allow time for some measurement of change to occur.

If the abuser happens to be a Christian, then he or she should accept a Christian brother or sister as a point of accountability. A pastor, deacon, or mature friend can and should work to help restore the believer **(Gal 6:1)**.

If the abuser is not a Christian and chooses to leave rather than meet your requirement to stop the abuse, then you are "not under bondage in such cases" (**1 Cor 7:15**). If the abuser *does* meet your requirements for restoration, just make certain to have plenty of support so that you do not fall prey to manipulation and lies. Your boundary must remain firm and absolute, or no change will occur.

CASE EXAMPLE:

While situations like these can feel hopeless, we recall the case of Frank, a church elder, who had an intermittent pattern of physically hurting his wife. By all accounts, and upon interview, it appeared that Frank was born-again. In fact, most areas of his life yielded good fruit, but his marriage was in shambles.

His wife Kimberly sought therapy after avoiding help for nearly 15 years. She agreed to go directly to her parent's home in another town and took the children. I (Dr. Ab) phoned the husband and asked to meet with him. Once we worked through the shock and anger of the wife's decision, he began to soften and accept responsibility for his actions.

Over time, Frank submitted to a process of Christian therapy, attended an anger management group, and established himself with an accountability partner, a mature brother in church. As he became more open and honest about his actions, God used the opportunity to break his pride and help him come into fuller submission.

While Frank attended therapy, Kimberly and the children received spiritual counsel elsewhere. We required several weeks before the family could visit, then several months before a full reconciliation took place. In the process, the abusive man began to deal with the childhood abuse he suffered, his anger and grief, his shame for his actions, and his physical control.

The entire time was wrought with ambivalence, periods of regression, renewed anger and threats of divorce. Kimberly, with encouragement, was able to hold the established boundaries until there was nowhere for Frank to look except toward himself. Eventually, there came a change in his spirit and one could sense that a true surrender had occurred. From that point, the process moved quicker and today the family is still intact.

The key to the entire program was Kimberly's resolve to do two things: 1) Forgive her husband; and, 2) wait for his recovery while maintaining an absolute boundary of distance until he demonstrated the fruit of change over a long period of time.

Was it hard being apart? You bet it was. Was it difficult financially? Without a doubt. Were there times when divorce seemed imminent? Certainly. Was it worth it? Just ask their children and hear the testimony of the couple. They know how powerful and faithful God is.

The spirit of violence that penetrated this home and limited its light in the world was defeated by the power of applying God's Word to the situation. **"Do not be overcome by evil, but overcome evil with good" (Rom 12:21).**

My husband is a severe alcoholic who also abuses other drugs. Doesn't the Bible permit divorce under such dire circumstances?

Again, the Bible does not address this point directly as it relates to marriage and/or divorce. There are instructions regarding the abuse of substances, and God's Word does not endorse it any way **(1 Cor 6:9-12).** But, as in the case of physical abuse, it is not listed as reason for divorce.

We recommend a very similar process as the one described for physical abuse. Boundaries and insistence on treatment and change must be made. Substance abusers will certainly promise to stop, and often they mean it at the time. But addiction is a powerful force that will often render the promise a lie.

As with abuse, personal safety is often an issue when drugs and alcohol are present. Separation may be needed if the addicted individual is to receive the help he needs. Strong boundaries that require behavioral evidence of change and participation in treatment are absolutely necessary. There is no safe level of involvement with drugs and alcohol once someone has developed a problem. Total abstinence is the only solution.

You may have to prepare yourself for a lengthy division while your husband pursues proper spiritual and professional help. You will have to measure success by the evidence of what is done, not what is said or promised. When he is in weekly therapy; when he is in some form of weekly Bible study and church; when he is involved regularly with Alcoholic's Anonymous or Christian support group; and when he has been sober and drug free for a minimum of six-months, reunification of the marriage can be considered.

Remember too that addiction can have dramatic physical ramifications due to withdrawal from the substance. It is strongly advised that the person seek medical support before stopping the drugs or alcohol "cold turkey."

COPING WITH DIVORCE

Divorce for the Christian is a complicated and painful situation. Not only do we have the ordinary feelings of anger, loss, fear, and depression, but we also know that divorce is not part of God's plan for marriage. This often creates feelings of guilt and shame that prolong the recovery process.

The divorce rate among evangelical Christians is about the same as the general population. Many Christians were divorced one or more times before salvation. Others have biblical grounds for separation. Some are divorced because the spouse left them against their protest.

But many are born-again believers who simply end a marriage for all the same reasons the secular world walks away. Christians site feelings of discontentment and unhappiness, boredom and incompatibility, unresolved anger and conflict. While we should know better, we often yield to the same impulses, sin, and failings as the world.

Very often, divorced Christians come to regret the decision they made but find it is too late to repair the marriage. As a result, Christians find themselves having to cope with the fallout just like everyone else. Fallout includes all the feelings mentioned above plus financial changes and problems, custody and child rearing issues, restoration of their spiritual walk, etc. Churches must be sensitive to the needs of divorced Christians and provide programs that support and encourage their recovery.

NOW FOR YOUR QUESTIONS...

I am a Christian but left my wife and children about two years ago. I thought I was unhappy and unfulfilled. After some time, I wanted to reconcile but my wife had remarried. Now I see my children only a couple times a month and even that is strained. How can I cope with the pain of my decision and its effect on so may others?

As a born-again believer, you know that you are spared eternal death for your sins, but you should also know that the earthly consequences of our choices are real, painful, and inevitable. There is no doubt that God will forgive your sin if you repent, but you are still subject to His discipline and to the day-to-day fallout of your actions.

Because of your actions, you are now at a point in life where your needs are secondary. You cannot begin to repair your loss until you have addressed the needs of the innocent victims of your behavior. While your pain and acknowledgement of error are important, you will only find resolution by first caring for those most affected.

If you have repented honestly and sincerely to God, you should also seek forgiveness from your former wife and children. They need to hear your willingness to take responsibility for your sin, and for the reverberations you sent through their respective lives. Jesus taught the importance of reconciliation:

> **"Therefore if you bring your gift to the altar, and there remember that your brother has something against you, leave your gift there before the altar, and go your way. First be reconciled to your brother, and then come and offer your gift." (Matt 5:23-24)**

Going to your former wife may be difficult now that she is remarried. Remember not to interfere with her current relationship. You cannot be reunited with another man's wife. Instead send a card or letter asking for her forgiveness and require nothing of her by way of response. Remember, however, that she has been greatly hurt and that her entire world has been rearranged because of your earlier position. Be realistic about her reaction. It may be a long time before forgiveness can be conveyed to you. You job here is simply to take the burden of responsibility and let her know you are sorry for destroying the marriage.

With your children you must meet directly and seek reconciliation. It is not wise to burden children with a lot of detail about your reasons for divorce or your activities in the process. It is simply enough to confess your sin, relate that your actions were wrong, and take full accountability for hurting them and their mother. A word of caution: your task is to confess your sins and ask for their forgiveness, not to force feelings of forgiveness or affection they may not yet have. Forgiveness and recovery take time. Asking for understanding may be only the first step in a long reparative process. Allow your children time to digest and respond. This meeting is for them, not you.

Over time, if you continue to show repentance and if you are consistent in keeping the children your priority, they are likely to respond favorably. Repairing these relationships will be central to your own recovery.

Beyond these actions, begin to seek God and ask Him to restore you. In the restoration process, ask God to reveal the basis and the reasons for your sin. Examine how you allowed these things to happen. It is crucial that you come to terms with the personal struggles that led you to make the wrong decisions.

Be cautious about starting any new, romantic relationships. Now is not the time to repair your hurt through another person. Spend time alone and with groups, but avoid dating or relationships until you have a better understanding of yourself and your choices.

Going slow in this arena is also important for your children. In the past two years they have already encountered your departure and the loss of daily contact; they have seen their mother hurt; they have been forced to adjust to living with a stepfather; and they are not even sure what happened. They do not need another adjustment right now. Just simply staying available for them is enough at this point.

Throughout Scripture we see evidence of a merciful and restorative God. He is fully aware of your failure, your motivations, and the resulting consequences. In spite of this, He eagerly awaits your return to His open arms. Only God could administer this much mercy and love. Even at our worst, God calls us and seeks to restore our relationship with Him. As we are reconciled to God, we can begin to restore connection and unity in our earthly relationships.

Repentance, however, is more than a prayer and a promise. True repentance means we turn away from the actions and decisions that have created so much pain and loss. God wants to see evidence of a changed heart manifested not only in words, but also in our behavior. Frankly, this will be difficult without a totally submitted return to the Lord's strength and protection. You must remember how broken you feel right now and stay mindful of the damage that is wrought through sinful, rebellious activity.

Sometimes, as the pain lessens and lives take on an "image" of recovery, we can block out the true effect of past errors. God wants you to use this broken time as a reference point that reminds you to stay in submission to Him and to benefit from His wealth and shelter. But be assured, when you have returned to Him, broken and open to do anything He requires, He is faithful and will welcome you home, just as the prodigal son was reclaimed joyfully by his father. Jesus relates the parable:

"And the son said to him, 'Father, I have sinned against heaven and in your sight, and am no longer worthy to be called your son.' But the father said to his servants, 'Bring out the best robe and put it on him, and put a ring on his hand and sandals on his feet. And bring the fatted calf here and kill it, and let us eat and be merry; for this my son was dead and is alive again; he was lost and is found.' And they began to be merry." (Luke 15:21-24)

You will find forgiveness for yourself as you confront each of the tasks outlined. Your peace will be found in this pattern for Christian restoration. Your life and the life of your family is forever changed, but God can use whatever trauma we bring to the table. Let Him work to heal your family's pain.

CASE EXAMPLE

Franklin was 47 when he entered therapy. He was a successful businessman and Christian leader. He had led multiple men's ministries, taught seminars on marriage, gave generously to those in need, and he had led many to salvation. Yet he came to therapy confessing a desire to divorce his wife of 20 years on the grounds that she had been "emotionally unavailable" to him for some time. He was firm about his decision and said that he planned to move out by the end of the week. Franklin said he didn't want any attempt to dissuade him from the course he had selected. The session then proceeded in this manner:

Shrink: "If your mind is made up, then why are you here?"

Franklin: "I just want to feel better about my decision, and I want to know how to help my children adjust."

Shrink: "If you are certain about your choice, and if you feel your choice is justified because your wife is "emotionally unavailable," then why do you need to feel better? It seems you have worked everything out just the way you think it should be."

Franklin: "I told you I didn't want anyone trying to talk me out of this decision. Why are you trying to make me feel guilty?"

Shrink: "Let me speak to you, brother to brother. I am not responsible for your guilt. As a believer, you have the Spirit of God within yourself. Among other things, He is there to convict us of our sin. Your guilt is a response to His leading, not mine."

Franklin: "I told you not to pressure me with this "spiritual" crap!"

Shrink: "There are over 100 shrinks in the county, but you chose a Christian shrink. You knew perfectly well when you came in here that I would speak of spiritual things. Maybe you are not as settled with your decision as you would have me believe. You're the one who said you needed to feel better, remember? If you are doing the right thing, you ought to feel great. Don't you agree?"

Franklin: "Ok, we know it's the wrong thing to do. We know it isn't biblical. But you know what? I'm going to do it anyway. No matter what you say; no matter how much my wife cries; no matter what the Word says; I am going to do what I want to do!"

Shrink: "Well, Franklin, God gave us all the free will we can handle, and then some. You can do whatever you choose, but I don't think you can do it comfortably. In other words, I can't help you feel better when you are knowingly and willfully in sin. You know the truth as well as I do."

Over the next few sessions, Franklin revealed that he had been in sexual sin for years, engaged with pornography and prostitutes. He said his wife knew some of his struggle and had stayed with him through it all. Hearing this, the wife's "emotional unavailability" made sense to me. Under the pressure of repetitive sin, everyone in the family is hurt. Her withdrawal was understandable as she tried to cope with her husband's double life. She tried earnestly to support him and remain loyal to him, but emotionally and spiritually, she was broken. After her years of faithfulness, Franklin now intended to desert her.

Franklin went on to admit that he was in love with a woman he first met as a prostitute. This "love" had become the fuel for his departure. As he confessed his long-standing sin, he became increasingly angry and rebellious, seemingly hardening his resolve to leave his wife with each of our meetings. He was like stone when we looked into Scripture. He was especially angry when I read a passage from Hebrews concerning repetitive, willful sin:

For if we sin willfully after we have received the knowledge of the truth, there no longer remains a sacrifice for sins, but a certain fearful expectation of judgment, and fiery indignation which will devour the adversaries. Anyone who has rejected Moses' law dies without mercy on the testimony of two or three witnesses. Of how much worse punishment, do you suppose, will he be thought worthy who has trampled the Son of God underfoot,

counted the blood of the covenant by which he was sanctified a common thing, and insulted the Spirit of grace? For we know Him who said, "Vengeance is Mine, I will repay," says the Lord. And again, "The Lord will judge His people." It is a fearful thing to fall into the hands of the living God. (Heb 10: 26-31)

Franklin: "So it's your opinion that man can lose his salvation?"
Shrink: "First of all, this passage of Scripture isn't MY opinion, it's God's Word. But to answer your question, I do not believe a "true believer" can lose his salvation. However, being in repetitive sin divides us from God and provokes His discipline. I don't think you can continue down this path of activity and escape God's correction. He cannot endorse or bless this decision, or your new relationship, under these circumstances. Franklin, you are not even repentant. You continue to justify your actions as an outcome of your wife's coldness. As long as you remain in willful sin, you are going to suffer."
Franklin: "That's your Baptist opinion."
Shrink: "That's God's Word. The rest is up to you."
Franklin: "I'm out of here!" (Exits the office)

In spite of his anger and rebellious heart, Franklin did return to therapy a few months later. By this time his divorce was final, his children had withdrawn completely, and the girlfriend had abandoned him. His Christian friends had set boundaries with him because he wouldn't turn from his sin. His business was in trouble. Franklin was severely depressed, suicidal, and alone.

Franklin: "Ab, I can't believe I gave up my family for a prostitute."
Shrink: [no response] (Sometimes even a shrink has to fight the desire to say "I told you so...")
Franklin: "I don't know what to do. I am angry with everyone. I hate Susan (the wife) because she won't talk with me

about reconciliation. My children won't visit me. Anne (the girlfriend) just used me and took my money. And God isn't listening!"

Shrink: "Franklin, God can't associate with evil."

Franklin: "Oh, so now I'm evil...is that it?!"

Shrink: "No, you aren't evil, but your heart is hardened with evil that won't let you submit. God will save you, but only when you have confessed your sin to Him and repented of it **(Isa 59:1-2)**. God hasn't forsaken you, but He has turned His face from you. He has allowed you to have the consequences of your rebellion **(Heb. 12:8)**. You cannot begin to recover, nor can your family recover, until you surrender to God's order. Even then, the road back isn't pretty. You have a lot of mess to clean up. But if your heart truly turns from this sinful conduct, God will join you in the reconstruction of your life."

Franklin: (Crying and expressing true regret for the first time) "I hate myself. I can't live with what I have done. God help me!"

Finally, Franklin lay on the floor of my office, broken and crying out to God. We prayed together, asking God to hear him and forgive his sin. This was the beginning of real change, but it came at great expense. Repentance came after the loss of his home, his wife, his children, his friends, and much of his business.

Franklin stayed in therapy for an extended time. He recovered from his depression and is no longer suicidal. His wife has moved on to a new relationship. After 18 months, his children are only now beginning to spend limited time with him again. All continue to work through the shear destruction brought about by Franklin's actions.

Franklin has remained celibate and recently began to date a very nice, attractive, and appropriate woman from church. He no longer uses pornography nor does he hire prostitutes. Sometimes he is angry with God. Sometimes he has trouble forgiving himself.

God's discipline is stronger than our rebellion. If we continue headstrong down a course of our own choosing, we will go alone **(Deut 8:5)**. God will not chase after an obstinate child, but He will receive this child immediately upon his submitted return. Alas, God's love is even stronger than His discipline.

Recovery from self-induced pain is difficult. When we are the initiator of divorce through sinful conduct, recovery means repentance, brokenness, loss, anger, and guilt. It means rebuilding others before rebuilding ourselves. It requires sacrifice and self-control that should have been employed earlier. In essence, we are forced to slowly climb out of the pit we have created. Left to our own resources, we cannot recover; God's regenerative power is our only hope.

While this is a very sad example, filled with much destruction and pain, it is a presentation of reality that we must see. Throughout every crisis, within every temptation, there are opportunities to turn around and do the right thing.

My husband of 17 years divorced me and moved away to another state. I was taken completely by shock. Now he is remarried and expecting a child. I am left to raise our daughter alone with little contact or support from him. This all happened against my will. How will I ever recover?

Divorce is always difficult, but it is especially so when it is unwanted. The injustice can seem too great to bear. The life of the abandoned spouse is turned upside down and there is nothing that can be done about it. This loss of control produces a range of emotions including fear, anxiety, anger, and misplaced guilt (self-blame). Along with the loss of a husband, family, and home, you have lost your sense of security and direction.

We humans believe we can control most circumstances. When something like this hits with no explanation, no acceptable solution, and no recourse, the reality of our limited influence can be overwhelming. Similar to coping with death, you will grieve a loss brought on by an uncontrollable circumstance.

Many describe the grief associated with divorce as being even harder to bear than when someone dies. It is extremely challenging to deal with your painful emotions of loss, when all the while you're witnessing the life of your ex-spouse going on, seemingly unaffected. While you are hurting, you still must make a living, care for your daughter, and speculate about life beyond marriage. This is certainly a daunting prospect.

First, you must realize that your reaction is normal. There is no reason to assume that you should feel otherwise at this time. In fact, emotion will be stirred at many junctures along the way as challenges rise up. Just when you feel you are recovering, your ex-husband remarries; just when you are feeling more hopeful, your daughter gets into trouble; just as you feel your confidence returning, you meet the "new wife" who is 10 years younger, beautiful, and who seems effortlessly capable.

Grief experts[3] tell us that you will go through several stages in your recovery. First you will be in denial. We all experience a refusal to accept reality at times, especially when nothing can be done to change it. That fog of avoidance can last for some time, as we convince ourselves "this can't happen." When in fact it does "happen" and our denial did not prevent its progression, we enter into a bargaining stage.

When bargaining, we are willing to give up "anything" in order to stop the event in question. We beg our spouses to stay. We offer no expectations if only they won't leave. Some even promise to tolerate other sexual partners as long as the spouse remains in the home. In short we agree to do whatever it takes, even if it goes against our principles and our needs.

Sometimes we try and bargain with God, begging Him to intervene on our behalf. Prayer is profitable, but bargaining with God is not. Our Father does not negotiate help on a *quid pro quo* basis. Please don't misunderstand: we can, and should, come to God for anything we need, but a trade is not necessary. Promising to change in exchange for a miracle is seeking God from the wrong position. James wrote of this very thing: **"You ask and do not receive, because you ask amiss, that you may spend it on your pleasures"** (Jas 4:3).

When bargaining with God and/or our spouse fails to produce the desired result, anger is often the next emotion. Anger is provoked by the futility of the situation and the reality that you cannot change what is happening. Often this type of anger turns inward and can become chronically debilitating.

Most likely you have seen many divorced persons fixed in this position. They are rigid, self-protective, negative, and distrustful. They have an understandable struggle with closeness and intimacy. Sometimes they become sarcastic and hateful, leaking their hurt on their children, friends, family and others. If not addressed, the anger often is internalized, leading to depression.

Depression is almost always a phase of grief. When denial, bargaining, and anger have yielded no break in the pain, depression becomes a cover of surrender. For many, the depression is simply a back-breaking fatigue that sets in, an exhausted state of defeat.

While depression is an expected phase of working through grief, it can become dangerous. There is a fine line between depression as a transitional stage versus depression that becomes clinically significant, even life-threatening. Be attentive to factors such as daily functioning, personal hygiene, sleep and appetite patterns, and suicidal thoughts. Should you begin to miss work; sleep part of the day; have trouble sleeping due to racing thoughts, anxiety, and worry; eat excessively or lose your appetite entirely; or, think in any form about dying or hurting yourself, seek professional help.

The final phase of coping is acceptance. At the end of our depression there is a realty that we are alive and that life calls us to continue. Acceptance is not immediate, nor is it a constant state. There will be short-lived movement between the five stages from time to time as we attempt to settle our lives. But once acceptance is underway, recovery is within reach.

In the end, recovery is a long-term process. It is important that you not try to hurry or avoid the inevitable process. Certainly the question *WHY?* will surface time and again. It is so hard when a suitable answer cannot be found. Sometimes there simply is not an explanation that is adequate.

While self-examination and honesty are vital, it is equally crucial that you not over-analyze your actions, thus creating self-incrimination. Most likely, you will find areas of your marriage that you could have impacted positively. Still, failings on your part are no justification for a spouse's infidelity and/or a divorce that you didn't want. Problems need attention, communication, and commitment to resolve. Divorce, outside of biblical parameters, simply is self-serving avoidance of the hard work marriage requires at times. Do not burden yourself with excessive guilt and blame.

Time alone does not heal, but healing takes time. Be honest about your feelings and try very much not to isolate yourself. Understandably, there will be periods of withdrawal, but seek out fellowship with other believers whenever possible. Many churches now provide support for its divorced members. Be open to opportunities that provide biblical answers and likeminded response to this disappointment.

Ultimately, God is the source of all comfort and peace. In our earthly relations, we often forget that reality and place more hope on the people around us than on our Savior and Lord. This is a time to submit yourself totally to His care, allowing His peace to transcend the comprehension of the world. As Peter wrote:

Therefore humble yourselves under the mighty hand of God, that He may exalt you in due time, casting all your care upon Him, for He cares for you. (1 Pet 5:6-7)

SUMMARY

Divorce has become an all too frequent reality of our society. Today nearly half of marriages (Christian and non-Christian) will end due to infidelity, disappointment, and/or "irreconcilable differences." The standard for divorce is getting lower and lower.

We must return to God's Word and to His covenant-based perspective of marriage. Even if we have broken a marriage previously, it is critical that we repent and reclaim God's perfect design and direction.

It is not wise to languish in our guilt and shame over past sin, but it is important to recognize that divorce is not God's way. If it is a part of your history, then like all sin, it can be healed. But in our healing we are called to a new standard, a renewed obedience that should radiate throughout any new relationships that form.

If you have been a victim of an unwanted divorce, then you too are entitled to restoration. As you grieve and recover, set your sight upon the vision God has for your life. With adversity there is opportunity for God to use and bless us in a new and fresh way.

CHAPTER 6

REMARRIAGE

INTRODUCTION

God is a God of second chances. Whether you are alone due to divorce or the death of a spouse, God can still provide for your relational needs. In seeking God about the prospect of remarriage, we must come openly and willingly before Him, ready to accept His will, whatever it is. God will place some people in new marriages, others He will not. The test will be our obedience and acceptance of whatever He provides.

For many, there is a tendency to rush toward a new relationship in order to ease the pain of loss and/or the guilt of past decisions. Be cognizant of the fact that God first deals with us on a spiritual basis. Yes He will care for our physical and emotional needs; but He desires our submitted, repentant, and willing posture before Him. In order for God to restore us, we have to seek out and accept His plan for rebuilding our lives; a plan that begins with confession, correction, discipline, and waiting on His timing.

NOW FOR YOUR QUESTONS...

REMARRIAGE AFTER DIVORCE

I am a Christian, but I divorced two years ago without a biblical reason. I would change it if I could, but it has been too long. Can God bless a marriage to someone new?

This question is difficult because Jesus made it clear that to remarry without a biblical divorce is adultery:

> **So He said to them, "Whoever divorces his wife and marries commits adultery against her. And if a woman divorces her husband and marries another, she commits adultery." (Mark 10:11-2)**

In advising others, we lean on the completed work of Jesus on the cross. He died for *all* our sins and we have been redeemed as believers. King David knew the mercy of God very well. He wrote: **"As far as the east is from the west, so far has He removed our transgressions from us" (Ps 103:12).**

God forgives and heals a repentant heart. However, the act of His sacrifice brings us freedom from hell, not necessarily freedom from God's correction and discipline nor from the consequences of earthly error.

Anytime we chart our own course and leave God's will, we are "on our own" until we repent and call upon His mercy. But even when we repent, our prior acts stay with us for some time, and we are faced with an undefined process of repair. After all, any good father knows that he must allow his children to work through the consequences of their actions. It has never been good parental practice to "buy" a child's way out of trouble. Our heavenly Father also knows the value of learning through experience and does not always remove the hurdles of recovery for us.

> **"For whom the Lord loves He chastens, and scourges every son whom He receives."** If you endure chastening,

God deals with you as with sons; for what son is there whom a father does not chasten? But if you are without chastening, of which all have become partakers, then you are illegitimate and not sons. Furthermore, we have had human fathers who corrected us, and we paid them respect. Shall we not much more readily be in subjection to the Father of spirits and live? (Heb 12:6-9)

We find hope in the story of Kind David who committed adultery and murder to have the woman of his desires, Bathsheba. David had sex with her and she became pregnant. He then sent her husband to war where he was killed **(2 Sam 11 and 12)**. As a result, the Lord was displeased and told David through his prophet Nathan:

Thus says the Lord: "Behold, I will raise up adversity against you from your own house; and I will take your wives before your eyes and give them to your neighbor, and he shall lie with your wives in the sight of this sun. For you did it secretly, but I will do this thing before all Israel, before the sun." So David said to Nathan, "I have sinned against the Lord." And Nathan said to David, "The Lord also has put away your sin; you shall not die. However, because by this deed you have given great occasion to the enemies of the Lord to blaspheme, the child also who is born to you shall surely die." (2 Sam 12:11-14)

Here we see the strong discipline of the Lord who did not ignore David's sin. He promised "adversity" on the house of David, giving his wives to his neighbor. He exposed what had been done in secret "before all Israel." And, he took the illegitimate son, the product of the adultery. But the Lord did not take David's life, stating: "The Lord has put away your sin."

David was sorrowful and laid himself before God. Listen to the heart of David as he sought the Lord's forgiveness:

Create in me a clean heart, O God,
And renew a steadfast spirit within me.
Do not cast me away from Your presence,
And do not take Your Holy Spirit from me.
Restore to me the joy of Your salvation,
And uphold me by Your generous Spirit.
Then I will teach transgressors Your ways,
And sinners shall be converted to You. (Ps 51:10-13)

David was forgiven, but his earthly trouble was great as a consequence. In subsequent years, David and his kingdom were constantly at war and many hardships fell upon his family. David's sin had generated a long and costly legacy of pain. Yet God allowed David to marry Bathsheba, and they had another son, Solomon, and the "Lord loved him" **(2 Sam 12:24).** To Solomon God entrusted the building of the Temple; he became the king of greatest wealth and wisdom **(1 Kings 3 and 4);** and, our Savior, Jesus Christ came from the lineage of David and Bathsheba, through Solomon **(Matt 1:1-17).**

God renewed David because his heart was truly repentant. Although they suffered God's discipline and paid a high price for their sins, God blessed David and Bathsheba's marriage, giving them Solomon and appointing him the successor to David's throne. And from this genesis of sin, God restored and consecrated the generations to follow, leading to the birth of His only begotten Son, Jesus Christ.

We take from this remarriage of David and Bathsheba the truth that God can restore all things. The restoration doesn't come without pain or loss. Yet it seems from this biblical example that God is willing to bless us again, should we truly humble ourselves and turn permanently from the nature of our sinful conduct.

Ultimately, the decision to remarry is between you and God. God knows your heart and will convict you of sin yet to be answered. We know several Christians who, after divorcing for biblical reasons, felt God's call on their life to remain single. We know others that God has blessed with a powerful second union.

Consider the conditions of your divorce. Pray for forgiveness and give yourself plenty of time before pursuing new relationships. This is not only to heal emotionally, but also to allow God to address His will for your future.

CASE EXAMPLE

Denny was saved at 17 and married a non-Christian at 23. By the time of their nuptials, he was living without any fruit of a Christian life. In fact, he and his wife never discussed salvation, religion, or anything of the sort. Four years later, living very much in the world, they divorced, at his initiation. Although his wife had been unfaithful, Denny did not know of the infidelity until later. In his heart, he had divorced without biblical grounds.

Some years later while still single, Denny recommitted his life to the Lord and began to live in a more obedient manner. He began to study God's Word and realized the pattern of mistakes he had made in his spiritual and relational life. He met another believer, Susan, who had been divorced two years earlier due to her husband's infidelity. Susan and Denny were well suited for each other, unified in their faith, maturing and searching. But Denny couldn't escape the grief of his first marriage and the unresolved disappointment he felt for marrying a non-believer and later initiating divorce. Both acts violated God's teachings.

When we first saw Denny in therapy, he was on the verge of losing Susan because he could not commit himself to her. With time Denny came to forgive himself and accepted that God, through the blood of Jesus, had already forgiven him. His heart was truly repentant. He even wrote his former wife and expressed his sorrow for hurting her, asking her to forgive him. That's when he learned she had been unfaithful, as she expressed this fact in vengeance.

Through much prayer, Denny was able to put his sin, his ignorance, and his poor judgment behind him. As he did so, he was able to open himself to Susan more completely and the two married a few months later.

The keys to Denny's recovery and acceptance of a new mate rested upon:

- His accountability. Denny shouldered the burden for his choices and never once retreated into blaming others. Even after learning of his former wife's indiscretion, Denny maintained that his divorce was disobedient and non-biblical because he had initiated it with no knowledge of her adultery.

- His repentant heart. Denny came before the Lord on numerous occasions, confronting not only his marital decisions but also other areas of sin. He begged God for cleansing and purity and offered to do whatever God required of him.
- His willingness to work through the earthly consequences of his sin and accept the cost due him.
- His capacity to wait for God and His timing. As Denny's life began to change, he could have easily moved ahead of God. Instead he paused and let God convict him and chasten him, so as to correct his erred past. By letting God reshape him, Denny dealt with issues that might have weakened his new marriage.

Denny and Susan are happily married Christians with a new baby. God's hand has restored what was broken and has made good out of what Satan intended for evil.

Indeed we count them blessed who endure. You have heard of the perseverance of Job and seen the end intended by the Lord—that the Lord is very compassionate and merciful. (Jas 5:11)

I DO...AGAIN

My wife and I divorced a year ago at her request. She had a brief affair with a man from work that ended about the time our divorce was final. Since that time we have seen each other regularly and I believe she has truly repented and turned her life back to God. We have talked about remarrying but I am cautious. It is possible that we could reestablish our home?

Yes, it is possible and desirable that you reestablish your home. But a word of caution: do not be naïve about the amount of work and restoration involved. Your union and covenant has been torn apart, and the sexual breach is especially difficult to repair. This perhaps is the reason the Lord gave infidelity as the one allowance for divorce **(Matt 5:32).**

Although you were biblically justified in getting divorced, reconciliation is preferable when possible. It is encouraging to know that your wife has repented and turned from her sin. Likewise, it is encouraging to know that you are working to forgive. Repentance and forgiveness are at the foundation of the Christian existence. When we are successful in these areas, we keep our slate free of corruption that can defile our walk with Jesus and our relations with each other.

Assuming that your wife's infidelity was an isolated occurrence and not a pattern, and assuming her repentance is true, you must face the reality that this piece of history cannot be brought up again. It must become an element of your past that has been resolved and settled. Often this is easier said than done.

If you are not at that level of resolve, then more work should occur before remarriage. While therapy is not necessary for all things, it may be important to work through the remnants of this injury with a counselor and/or pastor. Remember, your hurt and sense of betrayal is real and understandable. These feelings can come to completion, but you must not deny the influence they bear.

A second consideration is the question of what went wrong in the first place. Did your wife's affair happen simply as a result of her sin, or was it a manifestation of other problems in the marriage? Please understand, we do not believe infidelity is a justifiable response to any marital problem, but marital problems do sometimes play a part in a person's vulnerability to act-out sexually.

Whatever weakened the boundary of your home must be addressed thoroughly. If it was a personal issue expressed through your wife's actions, she should get professional and spiritual help to resolve it. If the issue is a product of a communicational or spiritual issue in the union, then marriage counseling is crucial.

Far too often, couples try to reconcile following the passing of a crisis, without earnestly trying to get the bottom of what created the crisis in the first place. As humans we simply want the pain to pass, and we certainly do not like digging into a wound. But in this case, a deeply honest review of your marriage is necessary in order to ensure your future success.

Even though it has been a year since your divorce, don't be rushed into a premature action. Diligently reexamine all key components of this injury including the reality of your wife's repentance and the depth of your forgiveness. Work to meet the following criteria before saying, "I do...again."

- Identify the fruit or evidence of your wife's repentance. Accept not only her words but test the spirit she conveys **(Rom 8:16)**. A repentant spirit is humble, accountable, and peaceful.
- Honestly inspect the nature and extent of your forgiveness. Remember too that forgiving your wife does not necessarily mean you should resume marriage with her. Forgiveness should bring you resolution and peace while starting you on the path of renewed trust **(Matt 6:14)**. If emotions are yet unsettled, be honest and work toward expression and discussion of your continued injury so that these feelings do not give rise to problems later **(Eph 4:26-27)**.
- If you have not done so, have a frank discussion regarding the "reasons" for the affair. This is not to attach blame, nor is it to provide rationalization for your wife's indiscretion. Rather, it is to make certain that the core of the issue is not ignored or hidden, only to reopen later as a threat to your new marriage. As issues of her personal struggle or of your marital problems arise, be realistic about what you can handle on your own versus what needs professional assistance.
- If any of these three areas present a roadblock of incompletion, slow down and express concern. It certainly would not be unusual nor would it be entirely negative to find that some points need more work. This reality should provoke a genuine and deliberate effort on your part to bring completion to these unresolved issues.

When thinking of forgiveness and restoration, we are often reminded of Joseph in the Old Testament. After being sold into slavery by his brothers, and then suffering the many trials that followed, including imprisonment under a false accusation, Joseph is confronted with the opportunity to either forgive or condemn his family **(Gen 37-50)**.

After the death of his father Jacob, and empowered as the Prime Minister of Egypt, Joseph could have punished his brothers with great wrath for their evil deeds against him. Instead, we find a biblical leader filled with God's grace and wisdom, as he said to his brothers:

But Joseph said to them, "Do not be afraid, for am I in the place of God? But as for you, you meant evil against me; but God meant it for good, in order to bring it about as it is this day, to save many people alive. Now therefore, do not be afraid; I will provide for you and your little ones." And he comforted them and spoke kindly to them. (Gen 50:19-21)

What his brothers had meant for evil, God meant for good. This perspective is vital to your reconciliation. This affair, divorce, and remarriage can become a great testimony of your faith and reliance on God. He has a wonderful track record for making good use of our sin and frailty. Let Him work to make good out of this tragedy too.

CASE EXAMPLE

J.P. was a deacon in the church, Bettie a Sunday school teacher. They were married 15 years when J.P. suddenly asked for a divorce. There had been marital problems, but Bettie did not expect divorce to be an option. J.P. offered no reason beyond his frustration that the two could not communicate, and he couldn't deal with it anymore.

There was no evidence of infidelity, nor did any surface in subsequent months. Still, he was resolute in his decision. He rejected counsel from his pastor and from fellow deacons and refused to talk about it any further. After enduring his unwillingness to relent, Bettie signed the divorce papers following a six-month separation and moved to another state to be near family. The couple had no children.

As soon as Bettie relocated, J.P. began to phone her and talk with her as if nothing had happened. Each night he would call, talk about his day, and encourage her in her new job. Bettie felt like she was living in "The Twilight Zone!" After a few months, J.P. suggested he come north for a visit. When he arrived, he tried to initiate a physical relationship with Bettie. Vulnerable and hopeful, she consented. The next day, the cloud had returned and J.P. was sullen and quiet. When pressed for conversation, he became angry and told Bettie, "This is exactly why we can't live together." Then he packed and returned to Florida.

Confused and hurt, Bettie assumed this was the end....again. But within a week the same pattern of phone calls started, leading to the suggestion of a second visit. As a Christian, Bettie wanted her marriage restored, but she wasn't willing to ride this roller-coaster, feeling used and mistreated. Still, J.P. wouldn't talk about anything substantial, avoiding any discussion of the divorce or his future intentions.

This ambivalent pattern is common in divorce situations. Often it is a product of sexual infidelity and the guilt and confusion it creates. In this case, there never was any admission or evidence of extra-marital involvement. Instead, J.P. was simply unstable, depressed, and incapable of confronting the needs of his marriage. Whenever Bettie would receive J.P. on his terms, he seemed comfortable. But if she made any request or expressed any level of affection (other than sexual), J.P. would quickly retreat again.

With the help of a good counselor in Tennessee and through reading James Dobson's book, *Love Must Be Tough*[4], Bettie began to set boundaries with J.P. While she needed him and was fearful of losing her marriage forever, she knew she would get nowhere by allowing him to continue in this "one-sided" interchange. Feeling certain that she was willing to accept whatever consequence came about, Bettie gave J.P. the following ultimatums:

- J.P. was not to phone her again until he had met with his pastor and completed one appointment with a Christian therapist.
- Then, J.P. could call once a day as long as he continued regular contact with the pastor and counselor. If he stopped

either, the phone contact would end.

- There would be no further visits to Tennessee until the two of them could meet with a counselor together to discuss the problems that led to the divorce.
- There would be no further sexual relations unless and until they remarried.

With these boundaries, Bettie adopted a somewhat "flat" non-committal tone with J.P. She worked to contain her enthusiasm and her need for her husband. In short, she was more reserved. By withdrawing and reducing her availability, she began to see a change in J.P. More of his emotion began to surface, including his dependency and sadness over the divorce. His depression became more pronounced now that Bettie wasn't providing him relief for his loneliness and regret.

I (Dr. Ab) began to see J.P. for therapy while Bettie continued in counseling in Tennessee. J.P. was very cautious and guarded about therapy and clearly did not want to attend. Bettie's boundaries were crucial. Had she not forced the situation, the two might still be stuck in that quagmire of indecision. Because of her resolve, her husband was forced to take action and consequently, began to look into the multiple problems that had prompted his departure from the marriage in the first place.

As it turned out, J.P. had a long-standing depression that had colored his perception of the marriage. In his desperation to "feel better" he had discarded his wife. That of course changed nothing except to worsen the depression and increase his desperation. As his depression improved, he began to deal with some spiritual issues that needed attention as well.

J.P. sought Bettie's forgiveness for his sin and worked to strengthen his commitment to Christ. With time, the two were able to have marriage therapy, improving some serious communication problems. It turned out that neither J.P. nor Bettie had much ability to relate positively and affectionately toward one another.

After about a year, the two were happily remarried and have remained together several years after. Bettie's resolve to end the ambivalence was key to salvaging this union. The couple could have danced this dance for years, only deepening their hurt and sorrow. Instead, Bettie required evidence of real change: a process of effort that was measurable and purposeful. She had to leave J.P. with his sorrow long enough for him to hear God's convicting call.

The Word instructs us that sorrow is sometimes a useful tool in the hand of the Master:

For the sorrow that is according to the will of God produces a repentance without regret, leading to salvation, but the sorrow of the world produces death. (2 Cor 7:10 NASB)

Through her boundary and resolve, Bettie allowed God to move in the manner that only He can. J.P.'s sorrow became the salvation of this home.

REMARRIAGE AFTER THE DEATH OF A SPOUSE

My Christian wife died two years ago. We had a wonderful life together for 25 years. I am only 50 and would like to date, possibly marry again. How can I do so without harming my adult children and without injuring my memories of her?

Biblically, there is no reason not to remarry (**1 Tim 5:14**). But as with all things, you must examine your readiness spiritually and emotionally. The success and product of your first union was godly and powerful. Coping with that loss is our first concern.

Whether age 20 or 50, the preparation for relationship is the same. You know well, and have lived out, the biblical structure of marriage. In no way should you settle for anything less as you consider a new relationship. Unfortunately, emotion can affect even the most mature among us. In your loneliness, you must be careful to monitor your feelings and hold to the requirements of a godly association.

Refer to the counsel offered in Chapter Two on "The Single Life." Just because you've been around the block successfully doesn't mean you can't get lost. Be honest in your assessment of yourself and your readiness to proceed. Be honest with your children and allow them to express their feelings. Give them time to adjust to the idea of a new person in your life. (Although ultimately, the children will not decide what is best for you. This is simply an expression of respect and love to them, allowing time for their acceptance, if it can be achieved.)

When a person has enjoyed a positive marriage, grief is less complicated and shorter in duration than when the marriage was troubled. You have few if any regrets. This will help you move forward. But just as God gave you your mate the first time, He must be the one to establish the second. Seek His hand to be in everything you do in this regard.

STEPCHILDREN

My new husband and I are both 35 years old, and this is the second marriage for each of us. Neither of us were Christians at the time of our divorce, but now we are both born-again. I have known the Lord for three years, my husband for six. We have a good relationship and we are very active in our Christian walk, but I can't stand his 12-year-old daughter. She lives with us half the time and she is a constant interference. I think she needs more discipline, but my husband gives in to everything she wants. Shouldn't my husband honor me above his child?

Wow, that's a loaded question if we ever heard one! Remarried families are always challenged by the relationships between children and stepparents. When you think about it, it is only natural that some level of tension arises. Let's look at the facts:

- We have a child who is the product of a divorced home. Based on the information you gave regarding your husband's salvation, I assume she was six or younger when her parents separated.
- The child lives in a "divided" world, spending half her time in one home, the other half in another. She probably has two sets of rules, two sets of standards.
- We have a father who probably has some level of guilt about

his past actions, and this guilt may influence his parenting style. He only has part-time custody and thereby, partial influence on her behavior, values, and personality.

- We have a mother of this child with feelings and influences that affect the child as well. She may be a great mother, a limited mother, an angry, bitter mother; but, whatever type of mother she is, she is a factor that you cannot control.

- We have a stepmother who has no children, who wants to help parent a child that is not her own. Yet since you are not the biological parent, your scope of influence is at best limited, and at worse, escalates the problems.

- We have a relatively new marriage with two people trying to learn about each other and create a life together, but with a hormonal pre-adolescent who brings more "action" than you probably counted on.

- Oh and did we mention that the child is at a crucial age of development and prone to be difficult even in the best of circumstances? This is a time when she needs her father's authority and encouragement desperately. Plus there is an innate rivalry that is to some degree natural between two females in this situation.

Now that we know the facts, let us give a qualified answer to your question. God's order does indeed require honor to the wife. In fact, the marital relationship is second only in importance to the husband's relationship with God himself. That being said, it is important to realize that a blended family has some very different challenges compared to a traditional family unit. While God's order is the same, we must not err too much on the side of rigidity. Sometimes we can become so rigid in our application of absolutes that we become brittle and thus fragile.

There is a way for God's order to prevail, but with empathy and flexibility within a given circumstance. Flexibility is not the same as compromise. Instead your family must learn to express understanding while holding to certain absolutes.

The key to this issue lies in the communication between you and your husband. Most likely, the daughter is acting a lot like other

12-year-olds girls. Add to this the other complications outlined earlier and your marriage can truly be compromised if the two of you don't become an empathetic, uplifting team. You cannot be unified on all things in private, but you had better be together 100 percent of the time in public. That means with children, you "never let them see you sweat." Whatever your problems, they must be worked out behind closed doors.

That alone will begin to advance the cause of honor to the wife. When you are treated respectfully and consistently in front of the daughter, then her capacity to "divide and conquer" is weakened. Deal with your anger, your husband's guilt, and your differing philosophies in seclusion. But with the daughter, the two of you should appear indistinguishable in your ideals and applications.

Work to strengthen your husband and don't attack him for having struggles. Raising a child half-time is tough. Encourage conversation, express empathy, and allow him to work through his fears. He possibly is afraid of losing one or both of you. What a terrible choice to be faced with. Ask him to tell you openly what he needs.

In private, be assertive about your needs. Rather than criticize him for his failures with you, teach him how to do better. Let him know how he can bless you and support you in this challenge. Remind him of your need for time, touch, recreation, etc. Be specific and work out a clear plan to see to it that these needs are addressed.

Part of the problem comes from operating on empty emotional tanks. Twelve-year-old daughters take a lot of work and energy. They take much more than they give. You must look to each other for your emotional support and restoration. Never go into battle hungry and empty.

Your husband must come to understand that one of the greatest gifts we offer our children is the example of a loving, respectful, and functional marriage. Our kids need to see husbands and wives as committed, unified partners. This is the example they will carry into adult life and into their relationships therein. If we demonstrate weakness, instability, and disunity, we are establishing a pattern that will cripple them for life. No matter the daughter's conflict with you, anger with her father, or developmental angst, she needs to experience true balance in the marital unit so that she too, can achieve balance one day.

As a Christian couple you are the example of God's order and plan for the family. Remember that God joined man and woman because there is strength in the union that sustains us. Solomon's counsel is strong evidence of what two, bonded with Christ, can achieve:

> **Two are better than one,**
> **Because they have a good reward for their labor.**
> **For if they fall, one will lift up his companion.**
> **But woe to him who is alone when he falls,**
> **For he has no one to help him up.**
> **Again, if two lie down together, they will keep warm;**
> **But how can one be warm alone?**
> **Though one may be overpowered by another, two can**
> **withstand him.**
> **And a threefold cord is not quickly broken. (Eccl 4:9-12)**

SUMMARY

If marriage is a challenge, remarriage is doubly so. Remarriage often comes out of sin, loss, pain, and suffering. It comes with a history and emotion that is unique and requires attention and grooming daily. Sometimes remarriage comes with children, fragile and broken in their own right.

Remarriage sometimes requires us to repent of our sin, to make restitution and repair, to grieve and resolve emotion, and to take our time. Preparation for a new union is critical and must not be taken lightly. Yet we have shown that for those willing to stay before God and do what is needed, there can be new life, new joy, and new relations.

CHAPTER 7

THE EXTENDED FAMILY

INTRODUCTION

There are two kinds of relationships that we maintain with the extended family. The first is the actual, present-day relationship. It involves the way we interact with relatives in our current family situation. Relating to extended family can be affirming, supportive, and productive, or it can be invasive, complicated, and negative. Overall, contact and relationship with the larger family system can be important. As we have seen in Chapter 2, God places great importance on our family history. There are times in the Old Testament where God calls the ancestry of a family to remembrance **(Ex 3:6)**. Other times He counsels division from the actions of our "fathers" **(Num 14:18)**. But throughout He calls for honor to the generations.

The second type of relationship we maintain with our extended family is mental in nature. Even when living on our own, or after we are married with children, the influence of our family's teaching and character is very much at the core of how we view ourselves and others. Positive character and uplifting experiences tend to beget the same within our homes. A corrupt nature, injury, and pain also tend to be recreated. While faith in Christ makes us a "new creation" **(2 Cor 5:17),** the transformation away from old, imbedded patterns can be a challenge.

Current life relations with parents and siblings can be a true blessing to any home. There is a great source of friendship, continuity, and wisdom available in a healthy family system. Even as adults we can benefit from support, counsel, and fellowship with those who shaped us and cared for us through our youth.

However, all relations with the extended family are not so productive. Even in solid, functional homes, certain patterns and trends can become problematic. When serious issues have been the theme of a family, the potential negative impact is even greater.

Sometimes the "internalized family" is present, even when you have moved across the country. The subtle and blatant influence of our parents and other significant relationships is deeply implanted. Remember the times you have been horrified to realize you lost your temper "just like" Dad? Or maybe you withdrew and sulked "just like" Mom.

There are tapes and videos that are released in our head as we cross certain milestones in our lives. When we leave home, get our first job, finish college, marry, or have children, we find a whole reservoir of resources, helpful and detrimental, to draw from. All the things we swore we would do "differently" are not really so different after all. Often we feel we have been given a script to follow, just like an actor playing a role. It can seem that all the lines are already written and the outcome of the play (our lives), is pre-established.

Of course nothing is as absolute as this. As Christians we are given liberty from sin and from the generational dogma passed down through our families. But often we cannot fully confront a pattern until life provides a platform for its expression. In other words, we may have to become a spouse or a parent before we realize that certain ideas and patterns lurk within us. This doesn't mean we should anticipate or dread the future, but we should see life as an opportunity for transformation, tackling issues and struggles head on as they surface.

This chapter will address real and internalized issues that are related to our family of origin. Through it all we must remember that God instructed man to "leave" his father and mother and merge with his wife, forming a new, symbiotic unit **(Gen 2:24)**. As important as our family's influence may be, our new home, our new responsibility, must remain our primary concern.

NOW FOR YOUR QUESTIONS...

THE EXTERNAL FAMILY

My husband and I have been married about two years and have a new son, our first child. Since our wedding we have been living next door to my husband's parents and in the same small town with the rest of his relatives. I love the town and I am close to his family, but sometimes I feel smothered. His family is always around, and we rarely have any real time alone. Am I wrong to expect a little breathing room now that we're building our own family?

Breathing room? We were going to give you the phone number for U-Haul! Living next door to your in-laws can be a delicate and difficult thing to do. Fortunately you like where you live and you are close to the family. That being said, you will need some degree of division and autonomy in order to feel like a mature and independent family in your own right. This will become all the more important now that your son has been born. Everybody loves a baby, and everybody has advice for a new mother.

Even when family relations are basically healthy, reasonable boundaries are in order. Your need for appropriate space is not grounded in dysfunction and anger, nor does it in any way dishonor the extended family. However, the longer they have "free access" without limits, the harder it will be to implement structure without hurting someone's feelings.

This process must begin with your husband and you. Difficult as it may be, you should speak honestly to him about your concerns. This issue may have more to do with your marriage and less to do with the in-laws. For example, the proximity and involvement of the extended family may not bother you so much if you feel truly connected and honored by your husband and if you know that you, not they, are his priority.

Talk to your husband about your needs as a young wife and a new mother. Explain your desire for time, conversation, and help with the baby. Speak about the actions he can take to support you and to demonstrate his devotion to you. By doing this, you are keeping the focus where it needs to be: on *your* home and family. As the two of you come to agreement about the type of marriage and home life you intend to have, external matters of all varieties are easier to address.

Having a clear vision and set of expectations are keys to creating good boundaries. So often, marriage partners move in different directions thinking they are in harmony, only to find themselves in conflict as a result of incorrect assumptions. Believe it or not, men often think that if they are happy, everybody must be happy. It may shock him somewhat to find out that you don't love "mamma" quite the same way he does, but we are certain he will survive.

It is vital to operate on the basis of request and clarity, not criticism. After all, you seem to respect and care for the in-laws, and living in close surroundings seems to be part of the family culture, not an effort to control or hurt your home. Speak respectfully of his parents, yet ask for what you need.

Ultimately, your husband is the one to deal with his family. Even when he agrees with you and shares your need for breathing room, communicating with parents and extended family can be tough. It is vital that your husband speak for himself and not for you. He must not imply that you are the problem or the reason for the boundary. Instead, he must act as a leader and take full responsibility for choices made in your home. Any reference to you as the driving force in this matter will only create undue tension between the family and yourself. Encourage your husband and show your appreciation for his efforts to honor your marital needs. Don't expect perfection, especially in the beginning, as some of this may take some time to settle.

As you begin to create some boundaries, remember to focus on the positive elements of your situation. You are happy in your home, and you also seem to appreciate the relatives. Find a way to maintain the close ties that are so often absent in today's home. It can be a great asset having "healthy" family close by. Their support with children, their wise counsel, and the sense of security they provide are valuable commodities. As you make some changes and build some fences, it is important to reassure them with good communication that affirms their importance to your home.

Our transient culture has changed traditional family association. Quite often young couples live great distances from family support systems. With good boundaries, respectful communication, and a clear set of expectations, you can have the best of both worlds: an autonomous, independent home, and the wisdom, love, and presence of a larger family structure.

Some scriptures to review and pray about include:

God's order for the home... (**Gen 2:24, 1 Pet 3:7**).
Honor to parents... (**Ex 20:12**).
The importance of truth and clarity... (**Matt 5:37, Eph 4:25, 5:9**).
The importance of empathy and directness... (**Jas 3:5-10**).

My wife grew up in a home where she was always the caretaker. Her father was absent from the family and her mother relied on her to meet her emotional needs. We have been married 10 years and have two kids. In spite of this, my wife speaks to her mother five or six times a day by phone, sometimes as much as an hour at a time. Our weekends are spent tending to the requests of my mother-in-law. My wife feels burdened, but guilty, if she doesn't help her mother. How can I help her?

Your wife is in a very difficult bind, working to fulfill the role given her in childhood while trying to establish a productive adult life. The result may be a sense of failure in both places. It is encouraging to learn that you have empathy for her plight and that you want to help her. Unfortunately, you may not be able to.

You too are in a double bind. If you passively allow her to answer her mother's every call, you reinforce the unhealthy attachment and unwittingly give the mother permission to continue her irrational emotional demands. On the other hand, any attempt to help your wife gain insight and separate from the parental burden, may be experienced as pressure that only increases her stress and feelings of guilt.

Shrinks refer to this type of parent-child relationship as "symbiotic." In biology this term refers to two organisms living as one. In this case, your dependent mother-in-law has convinced your wife that she cannot survive without her. Intellectually, your wife knows better, but this belief has been forged through years and years of pressure and caretaking. Emotionally, your wife cannot separate herself from her mother's dependency due to a very deep fear that doing so may cause her mother's demise.

We assume your wife has made efforts to create boundaries, only to fall prey to the mother's manipulation. At some point, she probably made something of a mental compromise, accepting her fate as her mother's protector along with the assumption that her marital and family life would be limited as a result.

Very often we confuse boundaries with anger or rejection. This is due in part to the buildup of emotion that comes over months and years of boundary violations that we either were unable or unwilling to change. Boundaries are not hostile but productive limits that protect and honor an individual's rights. For example, it is not considered aggressive for a rancher to build a fence on his property line. The fence simply separates his property from his neighbor's in an accepted, customary manner. The fence doesn't attack anyone, but it keeps the rancher's livestock on his ground and protects his land from the violations of others.

God gave human beings boundaries as part of His love. Nowhere does the Bible suggest that love is absent of correct, respectful actions. Instead God gave boundaries in the form of the Ten Commandments **(Deut 5)** and in the teachings of Jesus **(John 15:10)** and the Apostles **(1 John 3:6)**. There were times that even our Savior, Jesus, would retreat from the multitudes to rest and pray **(Matt 14:22-23)**.

Another example of boundary established in the Old Testament involved Moses and his father-in-law Jethro. Jethro had taken note of the burden Moses was under, as he was the sole counsel to all of the Israelites.

And so it was, on the next day, that Moses sat to judge the people; and the people stood before Moses from morning until evening. So when Moses' father-in-law saw all that he did for the people, he said, "What is this thing that you are doing for the people? Why do you alone sit, and all the people stand before you from morning until evening?" And Moses said to his father-in-law, "Because the people come to me to inquire of God. When they have a difficulty, they come to me, and I judge between one and another; and I make known the statutes of God and His laws." So Moses' father-in-law said to him, "The thing that you do is not good. Both you and these people who are with you will surely wear yourselves out. For this thing is too much for you; you are not able to perform it by yourself." (Ex 18:13-18)

Notice Jethro's counsel to Moses: "The thing that you do is not good ... you will surely wear yourselves out." He went on to advise Moses to establish "rulers" or elders who could execute help and judgment for the people, unburdening Moses from the full weight of his excessive responsibility **(Ex 18:19-27).**

Your mother-in-law is exploiting your wife under the banners of love and responsibility. But God's love is balanced, structured, just, and righteous. We are not called to martyrdom for humans. Our sacrifice is to Christ alone. Showing honor, love, and care toward a parent does not require the loss of one's life, literally or figuratively.

Even though you will create pressure for your wife, we believe you should speak to her assertively and lovingly about this matter. In doing so, it is important to express concern for her without criticizing or complaining. While you deserve a wife who is more engaged with your family, now is not the time to attack that issue. Instead, it is the time to pursue answers that will help her attain some level of emotional division from her mother. As she benefits emotionally, so will your home life.

While we do not always recommend therapy, this case may call for external, professional guidance. Deeply ingrained issues like these sometimes require some objectivity and structure to find resolution.

CASE EXAMPLE

Jeff and Kara came for counseling after eight years of marriage. Kara complained that Jeff was a "mama's boy" who spent too much time and energy taking care of his mother. Jeff acknowledged that he did spend a lot of time with his mother but indicated that the attention he gave her was necessary. He said his mother was "fragile" and literally could not take care of herself if he didn't help her. Jeff was frustrated that his wife didn't see this fact and give him more support.

> *Shrink:* "How is your mother 'fragile?'"
> *Jeff:* "What do you mean?"
> *Shrink:* "Well, what makes her 'need' you so much?"
> *Jeff:* "Ever since my father left, she has relied on me to look after her."
> *Shrink:* "Tell me more about her. How old is she, what is her health like, does she work, etc..."
> *Jeff:* "She's 50 years old and seems to be in good health. She's a little overweight. She has a good job as a secretary for the government. She owns a townhouse about a mile from us."
> *Shrink:* "When did your father leave the family?"
> *Jeff:* "When I was eight years old...about 20 years ago. Mom has never recovered."
> *Shrink:* "So she is still quite young, in good health, has a good job, and owns a nice home. How is it she is so functional yet so "fragile?"
> *Jeff:* "She is fragile emotionally. She doesn't date, never remarried, and doesn't have a lot of friends. I'm the one she counts on. Without me, I don't think she would have anybody."

For two decades, Jeff had worried unnecessarily about his mother. He had built a perception of her as fragile based upon a tragic but temporary point in their family history: the departure of Jeff's father. Jeff's sense of excessive obligation, teamed with his mother's exaggerated need, formed an unhealthy unit that restricted

Jeff's growth and individuation from the family. As an only child, having already lost his father, he truly believed that if he didn't take care of his mother, he would lose her too. This type of exaggerated fear is common when one parent is lost through divorce or death.

> *Kara:* "He stops to see her every night after work. Sometimes I hold dinner for him only to find out he ate with her before coming home. When I complain, he acts like I am attacking this defenseless, frail, old woman and that I should be ashamed. His mother is healthy, attractive, and very capable. But whenever Jeff's around, she turns into this sad, weak little creature, and that behavior just reels him in like a big fish!"
>
> *Jeff:* "That's not true. You don't know her the way I do. I saw how hurt she was when Dad left her for that other woman. I don't know what will happen to her if I leave her too!"

Again we see the pressure of this childhood perception come into conflict with reality. The reality is that Jeff's wife needs him to be her husband. She isn't asking Jeff to dishonor his mother but to place his family life in proper order. Whenever this message was conveyed, Jeff became visually anxious if not panicked. One could see that he truly believed his mother was in grave danger if he did not perpetuate this childhood theme of rescue and nurture.

We encouraged Jeff and Kara to divide their therapy and continue in individual sessions. We did this because the pressure to deal with his mother was so difficult for Jeff that he couldn't work on anything else. In solo counseling, Jeff was able to talk more about his irrational fear that his mother would literally "die" without his constant attention. With time Jeff was able to recognize that as a child, he was terrified that something would happen to her and that he would be either alone or forced to live with his father and step-mother. His anger was so intense with the father that he had never reconciled that relationship. Jeff confessed that he longed for some contact with his father, but again, he was fearful that doing so would be "the end" of his mother.

Jeff's irrational anxiety was heightened by the marital stress and his fear of losing his wife. From his viewpoint, someone would be lost, either his mother or wife. This resurrected the childhood fears of abandonment that created his over-attachment to mother in the first place.

With time Jeff was able to modify his view of his mother and to give himself credit for supporting her emotionally when she really needed it. He also came to realize that by rescuing his mother, he was unwittingly holding her back. She would never take a risk or venture out in her own life, as long as he met all of her emotional needs.

Eventually, the decisions Jeff made in therapy had to be placed in motion. In other words, he had to gently but firmly establish some boundaries with his mother. Because of their 20-year collusion, he had to separate with some sensitivity to her needs and the likelihood that she would be confused about his actions.

While it was difficult for Jeff, his greatest fears did not come to pass. His mother did survive the redefinition of their relationship and has actually begun to make some new inroads in her own life. If fact, she now has had a few dates with a nice man from her neighborhood and has had some recreational time with other women friends. She is more respectful of Jeff's time and more accepting of Kara.

Jeff has been amazed at his wife's response. As he has made Kara his priority, she has accepted him gladly. The pressure and conflict he felt with Kara has passed and he no longer believes he is at risk of losing his wife. The two are expecting their first child soon. Previously, Jeff was never "ready" for children. This was due largely to his delayed development. It's hard to see yourself as a father when you are still feeling like a child. As Jeff has separated from the delusion of the past, he is far more focused on the present ant the future blessings of adult life.

Scenarios like Jeff's don't always work out so cleanly. When an adult child is faced with creating boundaries with a parent they must face the risk that the parent may not respond well. In Jeff's case, the mother came to accept the change and actually added new relational aspects to her life. However, parents will sometimes work even harder to hold onto the dysfunctional merger with adult children.

Accordingly, anyone facing this type of dilemma must accept the possibility of an unhealthy response to a healthy action. Setting a limit in such a relationship could lead to anger, provocation of guilt and shame, distorted renditions of reality, and direct attempts to manipulate. As long as the adult child is assertive, consistent, and respectful, then he/she has done nothing wrong by creating proper boundaries. But be prepared, the distortions will most likely come and these can recreate old childhood feelings. Stand firm and derive your support from your adult relationships rather than the approval for perpetuating a negative cycle with a parent.

Remember that we were designed by God to honor our parents (**Deut 5:16**) but also to leave them (**Eph 5:31**). God's order and plan requires the creation and development of new family units that generate a tradition of spiritual and upright living. Look to the future and do not hold on to the past. The past has had its day and served its purpose. Honor and respect what you have learned and move ahead toward the call God has given you for your family:

> **Brethren, I do not count myself to have apprehended; but one thing I do, forgetting those things which are behind and reaching forward to those things which are ahead, I press toward the goal for the prize of the upward call of God in Christ Jesus. (Phil 3:13-14)**

THE INTERNALIZED FAMILY

My wife and I are Christians and we're both in our mid-twenties. We have been married about a year and we are thinking about children soon. I grew up in an abusive home. My father hit my mother and abused my siblings and me. My mother is deceased and I stopped contact with my father two years ago. In spite of this, I still lose my temper (verbally) with my wife. Sometimes I hear myself and I am afraid I am becoming my father. I am even afraid to have children out of concern that I might hurt them. Am I destined to repeat my father's pattern?

No, you are not destined to become your father; however, you are very wise to consider the impact of his abusive actions on you. For years your brain has subconsciously recorded your father's rendition of what it means to be a man, a husband, and a father. You know, especially as a Christian, that his methods of control and anger are wrong. You know innately that there is another way. But when frustrated, hurt, or frightened, you find yourself reverting to similar techniques.

Abuse has affected you on multiple levels. First, it has created a probable sense of insecurity and anxiety. Living in an unstable environment restricted your opportunity to be nurtured and supported in a way that builds self-esteem and confidence. As a result, you may feel somewhat unprepared for situations that occur in adult life, including conflicts and challenges in your marriage.

Excessive anger is often a product of fear. It is our survivalist nature coming to the foreground whenever we feel threatened or at risk. The trouble is, when we have been abused, our perception of threat is overactive. For example, you are going to have a lower threshold of tolerance whenever you feel in danger. Growing up in an abusive home, you were forced to remain in a state of preparedness. You could not afford to let your guard down. Most likely, you have a similar response now when there is an argument or problem that becomes at all heated.

As a child you were totally without power to effect a change in your situation. A part of you now has resolved itself to never be that vulnerable again. Hence, you may become excessively focused on maintaining control of a situation, so that you are not humiliated or overtaken in some other way. This makes for a certain level of intolerance and rigidity that is unnecessary in your current home.

So many of the defenses we develop in childhood live long beyond their usefulness. In other words, you are now safe with your wife, yet you still feel a need for defense and control. You have more armor on than you need. Its like you grew up playing hockey, where pucks were flying, fights were frequent, and the need for a helmet and padding was real. But now you are in a game of croquet, so to speak, wearing the same hockey garb, just in case a fight breaks out.

It sounds ridiculous doesn't it? But for someone from your background, it makes perfect sense. A part of your psyche simply won't risk being unprotected and vulnerable. You are going to show up prepared for battle. After all, you've never played croquet before.

The struggle for an abuse victim is learning when to raise and lower the gate. When must I protect myself versus when is it safe to relax? Learning this within the context of your marriage will help you step back at times and evaluate exactly the response needed. We predict that you are usually able to do this, otherwise, you would be much more out of control than you report. Still, there may be times that you feel you're on automatic pilot, unable to stop the water from flowing over the dam.

Any recovery must have its origin in the promises of God's Word. Early in Jesus' ministry, He entered the temple and read from the book of Isaiah, defining Himself as the Messiah while outlining His purpose on earth:

"The Spirit of the Lord is upon Me,
Because He has anointed Me to preach the gospel to the
poor;
He has sent Me to heal the brokenhearted,
To proclaim liberty to the captives
And recovery of sight to the blind,
To set at liberty those who are oppressed;
To proclaim the acceptable year of the Lord."
(Luke 4:18-19)

Listen to the power of these words: "To proclaim liberty to the captives." Jesus is speaking of the captivity of sin. Remember this means liberty from your sin, and from the sins of preceding generations. By His proclamation, you are no longer enslaved by the sins of your father.

Jesus said He has come "to set at liberty those who are oppressed." Liberty is freedom, and with freedom comes choice. As a result, nothing from your past has control over your future. You are no longer predestined to act as your father acted. The oppression of that impending dread is forever removed.

Satan will work to convince you that you are not free. He will show you images of your youth and he will remind you of the times you have failed to act as you should. Since you are born-again, Satan can't have your soul, but he wants to destroy your home, your joy, and your testimony. You must rebuke his efforts in the name of Jesus and learn to recite the promises of our Lord in defense of Satan's attack. Just like Jesus did in the desert, we must resist the lie of the deceiver with God's perfect and unyielding Word **(Matt 4:1-11).**

As a free man, you must begin to make choices in advance that protect your wife and yourself from the escalation of your anger. We spoke earlier of your "psychological" armor and your readiness for a fight; learn instead to clothe yourself in the "spiritual" armor of God **(Eph 6:11).** In order to control and eventually defeat the rage that haunts you, you must learn to maintain your mind and spirit in such a way that you do not become vulnerable. It is much easier to control outbursts before they occur than it is in the middle of a crisis.

To do this, you must fill your mind and feed your spirit with Scripture each day. Absorbing the Word reminds you of who you are in Christ and helps you to maintain a godly self-esteem. Second, you must be in prayer, seeking God's peace and comfort. Emotions, questions, and confusion are best dealt with before a fight, not during. It is crucial that you and your wife learn to pray together. By doing so you offer agreement before God, empowering your effort **(Matt 18:19).** But also, you are able to hear each other make petition for your marriage and for your defeat of this destructive influence. Allow God, through prayer, to minister to the needs of your heart.

Third, honesty with your wife is crucial. It is likely that, in an effort to control and/or avoid your anger, you allow issues and problems to build up instead of discussing them with your wife. Your early recognition and communication is key to the management of emotion. The longer the build-up, the greater the risk of explosion.

The more success you have in siphoning off your anger before it grows, the more confidence you will have in expressing yourself assertively and directly. Learn also to speak of your fears and insecurities with your wife. Doing so doesn't render you weak. Instead it strengthens you and makes you more accessible to her. It will allow your wife to understand and respect you in a way that will give you a level of self-assurance that you have never yet known.

In summary, you have had to face a pain that few are confronted with. Abuse is difficult, but it doesn't have to be crippling. If you continue to have difficulty, it is not an expression of failure; rather, it is evidence that you have been badly hurt and that you may need some professional guidance. We encourage you to be open to counseling as a resource for helping you put this injury behind you once and for all.

CASE EXAMPLE

Dottie came from an impoverished background, growing up in a secluded area of the south. Her father was alcoholic and abusive physically toward Dottie's mother and all four children. He also sexually abused Dottie from the age of nine until she left home at sixteen.

After leaving home Dottie married a man fourteen years older who was also alcoholic and abusive. After four years of marriage, he nearly killed her in a drunken rage before leaving her for another woman. By the age of 21 she had two young children, no income, and no home. Eventually she moved to public housing, lived on welfare, and began to slowly piece her life together.

Soon after, she began attending a small church where the pastor and his wife led her to the Lord. This was the first time she had ever heard of a heavenly Father who loved her. The care she received from the pastor and his family was the first expression of Christian love she had ever known. Three years into her life as a Christian, she was now working in a large discount department store and had married a young Christian man from her church, and he later adopted her children. It seemed that her tragic life was finally on the mend.

After a year of marriage, she entered counseling with symptoms of severe depression, panic attacks and the beginnings of a marital problem. She was confused as she reported a life that was "better than I've ever known." Dottie couldn't understand why she wasn't happy, given her salvation, her friends, her children, and now her new husband.

In therapy we learned that Dottie was deeply afraid most of the time. She had nightmares about her father and ex-husband. She worried constantly about the safety of her children. Even though her husband was a fine man, she didn't trust him and felt it was only a matter of time before he would hurt her too. Even when she could fight off these fears for brief moments, she felt dirty and unworthy to receive the good things that had come into her life. She just couldn't make her image of herself fit into this new lifestyle.

Dottie's faith was strong and her belief in salvation sure. But she believed that she had inherited a life of pain that could only find relief upon her arrival in heaven. She had no confidence that joy could be any part of her Christian life. Dottie truly had been under intense oppression from the evil one who reminded her continually that she would never find comfort this side of paradise.

Dottie was very familiar with Scripture that related to suffering, perseverance, persecution, and endurance; but she could not relate to Scripture that spoke of her special design, her sanctified purpose, and God's desire to see her prosper. It took a long time to gain Dottie's trust and openness in counseling.

With time she was able to talk about the extreme abuse and resultant pain of her childhood. She grew up with no protection, used by another as he saw fit. It was heart wrenching to hear the humiliation she endured, facing evil day after day. As much as she had been abused by her father, she was neglected by her mother. There was no affection, no confirmation, and no hope in her early life.

As she began to express the ache of her heart, she was able to cry and express need for the first time. Prior to this time, she had been so beaten down she did not even dare vent her emotion. During counseling there were periods of suicidal thoughts, and feelings of flight and desperation, but she held steady to the process.

Dottie later confirmed that she could not have sex with her husband because doing so led to flashbacks of her father. This issue made for tension in the home and further deepened her sense of failure.

One day in therapy, I read the following scripture to Dottie to confirm to her how special she is in God's eyes:

For You formed my inward parts;
You covered me in my mother's womb.
I will praise You, for I am fearfully and wonderfully
made;
Marvelous are Your works,

And that my soul knows very well.
My frame was not hidden from You,
When I was made in secret,
And skillfully wrought in the lowest parts of the earth.
Your eyes saw my substance, being yet unformed.
And in Your book they all were written,
The days fashioned for me,
When as yet there were none of them. (Ps 139:13-16)

As soon as I was finished reading aloud, Dottie slammed her fist on the chair and shouted an expletive.

Shrink: (Looking up from the Bible surprised by her reaction) "Why are you so angry?"
Dottie: "How dare he! How dare he!"
Shrink: "What do you mean?"
Dottie: "How dare my father do what he did!"
Shrink: "Go on..." (That's what shrinks say when we are shocked and don't know what else to do).
Dottie: "He had no right to hurt a child of the Living God! Who does that *@$#&% think he is! I belonged to God before I was ever born! He planned my days! No one has the right to hurt God's child!"

Finally Dottie was getting it. She belonged to God and God would never sanction the treatment she had received. All these years Dottie couldn't get angry about the mistreatment of a lowly, unworthy girl. But when it hit her that a mere man would dare defile a creature loved and sculpted in the bowels of the earth, set apart for a special purpose by the God of all creation, she was furious.

This release signaled the beginning of her recovery and the assumption of her rightful blessing as an adopted heir to the Kingdom. From this point forward, she saw herself in a different light: the light of God's caring love. Now that she knows the love of God, she is able to know the love of her husband, her children and her friends.

How dare he...indeed!

> **But you are a chosen generation, a royal priesthood, a holy nation, His own special people, that you may proclaim the praises of Him who called you out of darkness into His marvelous light. (1 Pet 2:9)**

VALUE IN THE EXTENDED FAMILY

My parents are in their seventies, and their health is slowly deteriorating. They are strong Christians and a great source of wisdom. I want to spend as much time as I can caring for them but also soaking in the truths that are so much a part of their lives. I want my husband and children to know them and benefit in the same way. Am I being selfish in wanting this?

It seems you have great respect for your parents, and their testimony has been a powerful, positive influence in your life. It isn't selfish to crave that wisdom and to desire its transference to your children. In fact, it demonstrates honor for your parents and probably enhances their sense of personal value to you and to your family. However, do consider some key reminders.

First, boundaries and priorities are crucial. While it is important to care for your parents and to draw from them at this time, you must also honor your husband and children and see to it that your home is cared for and sustained in a proper manner. As parents age we feel an urgency to be with them as much as possible. Strive to stay in good communication with your husband, working out time, boundaries, and schedules that work for everyone. Recognize that even if your husband loves and respects your parents, his level of investment will be somewhat different than your own. Be respectful of this reality and talk frequently about how the needs of your parents are affecting him.

Second, do not assume your parents' needs are the same as yours. As with your husband, your parents will require communication and negotiation as your define your level of involvement. Be aware that independence is an important commodity as people grow older. While your parents may appreciate your availability and support, they will most likely want to maintain a high degree of autonomy nonetheless.

As these needs are defined, your parents will most likely enjoy the roles of patriarch and matriarch to your family. Older Christians feel a responsibility to add to the spiritual inheritance they will leave behind. They can become a great source of stories, testimonies, teachings, and support. In biblical times, the elders were revered for their experience and knowledge. Today seniors are too often treated as obsolete burdens who have nothing to offer beyond their middle years. This attitude has caused a "missing link" in the chain of knowledge, values, and character passed to generations today.

Your parents can be a reservoir of unlimited information that can be a blessing to your home. Giving them a platform of expression and contribution is a blessing to them, and will also give them purpose even into their later life. Work out the boundaries, maintain priority for your husband and children, respect your parents' independence, and then enjoy their contribution to your home.

CASE EXAMPLE

Our example comes from our own family experience (The Abercrombies). When our daughter Sarah was about six years old, Karen's parents moved into our home due to growing health problems. We built a small apartment for them adjacent to our house where they lived for about five years.

Having them in the home was at times a challenge. There was tremendous stress on Karen as she dealt with frequent medical crises, 911 calls, and hospitalizations, while trying to maintain her home, family, and professional life. It was hard on her parents as they struggled with the loss of their own home and, to a large degree, their autonomy. And of course my (Dr. Ab's) selfish nature was tested again and again as I struggled to share my wife, daughter, and home. The only one who seemed totally content was our daughter Sarah: she loves people, and the more the merrier!

Karen's dad has since gone to be with the Lord, and her mother is now living with Karen's brother in another city. But the five years we shared residence with each other proved to bring many blessings to our lives. Allow me to share some of them.

I saw my wife honor and care for her parents in a truly biblical way. Certainly she was tested and strained at times, but she was always mindful of the love she had been called to provide. While it was difficult for them at first, I saw her parents come to accept their new home and appreciate the love of their daughter. They came to express true gratitude and provided confirmation that this shared living situation was the right thing to do.

In the time they were in our home, our daughter saw her "Papa and Nana" everyday. She would wake up each morning and walk into their apartment, greeting them and blessing them with the energy and love that only a grandchild can deliver. Papa called her "Bug" and Nana made her banana pudding. Sarah still talks about it; she remembers how special she felt when they were around.

Our daughter saw Papa's character: he was a worker. Even when he was sick, he was always in his workshop or in the yard, fixing, cleaning, and serving our home. He was available for anyone who needed help, any time, any place. He was one of the most generous men you could ever hope to meet. Sarah was always taking broken toys, fractured dolls, and tangled fishing lines to Papa for his special remedy. When his health began to worsen, Sarah cried and said, "Papa can't die. We need him. He can fix anything!"

From Nana our daughter heard stories of her years in Europe and helped her make her special German dishes. She saw her laughter and excitement whenever family came to visit, her competitive spirit over a game of Uno or Yatzee, and experienced first hand Nana's unique love for her grandchildren. She even got some of Nana's patented scoldings from time to time.

We saw Karen's dad come to accept Christ as his Savior, led to salvation by a dear friend from our church. Then we watched as God gave him a merciful death, surrounded by his wife and all of his children and grandchildren.

Though having parents share your residence is not always the right thing to do, in our case it was ultimately a blessing to all. God favors the administration of love and honor and He blesses those who are a blessing, just as He promised to bless the inhabitants of Israel.

"For I will pour water on him who is thirsty, and floods

on the dry ground; I will pour My Spirit on your descendants, and My blessing on your offspring." (Isa 44:3)

The blessings of Papa and Nana, as designed by God, will remain with their "offspring." God has a purpose for all things.

SUMMARY

The extended family is truly a mixed bag of blessing and struggle. The power and influence of parents and grandparents extends for generations. Our task in our own family is to separate the wheat from the chaff. We must be equally diligent about maintaining the positive while rooting out the false and destructive.

If positioned with God's Word and committed to His order, we are in the proper stance to discern between the two. This chapter reminds us that our priority is to our spouse and children first. We must define our lives first within our own homes, and then work outward if appropriate. While there can be great resources available through our families of origin, there also can be points of pain and dysfunction that we cannot allow to control our home life negatively.

As with all relationships, we have shown that communication and boundaries are essential to respectful, functional interaction. Allow your heavenly Father to provide you with the peace and discernment necessary to honor your parents while fulfilling His will and plan for your marriage and children.

CHAPTER 8

WORK AND CAREER

INTRODUCTION

Today's world is busier and faster than ever before. The typical forty-hour workweek has expanded to fifty plus hours as the norm. The standard home is now supported by two paychecks, which means that both husband and wife are keeping this frantic pace. Add to this commuting time and other obligations, and you have a recipe for stress, fatigue, and diminishing family life.

When we consider the reality that more mothers are working outside the home than ever before, along with the high numbers of children being raised in single-parent homes, we can be certain that the majority of young children are spending much of their time in the care of people who are not their parents. Daycare centers are now commonly open for twelve or more hours per day. In some areas, 24-hour daycare opportunities are available, with children sometimes spending the night in facilities. Before-school and after-school daycare is a reality for many school-aged children, and many older kids are home alone during these critical hours before and after the school day.

With these "work driven" issues it is easy to see the deleterious effect in the home. In spite of the world's orientation that we can do "everything," it is clear that we cannot. When work, income, status, achievement, and survival become our primary focus, other precious and central issues of life will be sacrificed.

In this chapter we will address the importance of work and the relationships therein along with the interaction between work and home life. While it may be passé to speak of balance and priorities in this day and time, it is absolutely crucial. Work and production are necessary and can be an important part of our joy and satisfaction in life; but labor and creation of income must not become our temple of worship. All things must be done within a Christian perspective, preserving both our relations with God and with those entrusted to our care.

WORK AND MONEY

Throughout the Bible we see men and women of God engaged in labor: labor that sustains their earthly existence and labor for the good of the kingdom of God. Paul the apostle to the Gentiles was a tent maker by trade. Four of the most prominent disciples (Peter, Andrew, James, and John) were fishermen. David was a shepherd long before he was a king. And even our Lord Jesus learned and practiced the craft of His earthly father, carpentry, before answering the call of His destiny.

Yet Scripture instructs us to never forget the source of our support and the purpose of our call. Work and money can become incredible distractions, binding us to a worldly orientation and system of value. The apostle Paul wrote to Timothy:

> **Now godliness with contentment is great gain. For we brought nothing into this world, and it is certain we can carry nothing out. And having food and clothing, with these we shall be content. (1 Tim 6:6-8)**

Paul's counsel is not found in most business schools, nor is it a widely held value of our culture. The idea that "food and clothing" is sufficient for our contentment flies in the face of the American agenda. What about the "contentment" we derive from a larger house, an imported luxury car, a boat, travel, etc.? Don't I deserve to enjoy the benefits of all my hard work?

The trouble with enjoying the fruit of this production is that it never really satisfies. Paul pointed to the only true source of peace: "godliness with contentment is great gain." He is saying that the pursuit of God and godly living provides the only potential we have to be fulfilled. All of the earthly possessions we create are for our glory, not for the glory of God. Paul later warns of the danger inherent in our devotion to money rather than God:

But those who desire to be rich fall into temptation and a snare, and into many foolish and harmful lusts which drown men in destruction and perdition. For the love of money is a root of all kinds of evil, for which some have strayed from the faith in their greediness, and pierced themselves through with many sorrows. (1 Tim 6:9-10)

Notice that Paul does not say that money itself is evil. Instead he points to the capacity for lust and greed, which is natural to the flesh, as the source of our downfall. As in the case with any sin, greed and accumulation will consume us, stealing our time, energy, commitment, and worship. The more it is fed, the greater the demand. In short, earthly wealth will never, ever, be "enough."

Paul is warning us here that our preoccupation with riches leads to destruction, evil, and sorrows. Wealth, and the love of what it provides, often leads to a misplaced sense of power and independence that weakens our dependency on the sufficiency of God. We are not forbidden the creation of wealth, but we are cautioned that the management of wealth is not for the faint-hearted. The balance between the capacity to produce and our submission to God is a delicate matter.

God has gifted many people with business acumen and the skill of administration. He can and does use these individuals to do great things on behalf of His kingdom. The creation of wealth can be of great benefit to the advancement of God's purpose. For example, money builds churches, Christian schools, homeless shelters, and hospitals. Money trains pastors and missionaries and sends servants to all corners of the earth to advance the gospel. God will create and use wealth within the church, doing so through gifted individuals who support and yield to God's will.

In short, we are reminded that our wealth, spiritual and financial, is a direct result of God's hand. He gives and produces what He wants, where he wants it. When we are a faithful receiver of God's gift and a good steward of His blessing, then His kingdom will benefit and so will we. But when the wealth we hunger for is of our own creation without God's design, we are pursuing what God has not blessed. We may get some of it, but we will not have the "godliness and contentment" Paul wrote about. Instead we have built a fire that will require constant tending and feeding to continue.

NOW FOR YOUR QUESTIONS...

I work a lot of hours trying to advance my career. My goal is to make a six-figure salary within the next two years and receive a promotion that will provide even more security. My wife does not understand the importance of this effort and is constantly on my back to work less and spend more time with the kids and with her. I think my first responsibility is to provide for my family's welfare, and then we can "spend time" together. How do I help her see that?

Your question raises a lot of concerns. While we think you are sincere concerning your family's "welfare and security," you also talk a great deal about your goals and ambition. Ultimately, the answer to your question requires a thorough and true examination of your heart, aspirations, and motivation. Before you place all of your focus on the family's needs, you must be brutally honest about why this salary and promotion matter so much.

It is true that the husband has been given a specific task as leader and provider for the home. It is also true that with that role, difficult decisions must be made that often involve hard choices about work, money, time, and family obligations. In the end, your wife must be in agreement with you on these matters, giving you support for the labor and duties you face together. But, your wife will find it far easier to support God-ordained responsibilities that are grounded in scriptures that clearly describe God's requirement for the man (see Chapter 3, "The Man's Call").

For example, is the six-figure salary necessary for your family's survival, or does it generate a surplus that is well beyond what is required to adequately take care of them? Granted, six figure earnings in New York or California don't go as far as they would in states with lower costs of living, such as Alabama or Oklahoma. You must truthfully evaluate the needs of the home, the costs of your community, your long-term objectives, and yet the price your family will pay in not having you around very much as you are out earning those six figures.

Next, does the salary bring some level of security and resources that are necessary for savings and investment, or is it seen as a means to access a bigger and better lifestyle? Putting money toward savings, retirement, college, and emergencies is your obligation. Moving up to the newer car, better neighborhood, and status-clad social groups is not. Be careful not to impose your personal drive for success onto the "needs" of your family. You may find that they would appreciate more of your time, energy, and focus rather than a finer lifestyle.

Clearly, you desire a level of income and security that is less important to your wife than to yourself. It could be, as you assert, that she really does not understand what is required to adequately support and grow your family. In that case, the solution would be as simple as a round table discussion in the kitchen, looking at income, expenses, budget, etc. If there is truly a deficit and a need for more income, then your wife should be able to see it and support your efforts. If however this "need" is exaggerated, it will reveal your true incentive for working so hard and long. If your position is legitimate, then work to inform and educate your wife so she will see the necessity of what you are doing. We have found that most wives will support such situations strongly but few will truly encourage the advancement of misplaced priorities.

The Bible tells us that the man carries primary responsibility to economically care for his family. Your wife will need to understand this if the financial requirements truly dictate the building of a more lucrative career. Paul wrote:

But if anyone does not provide for his own, and especially

for those of his household, he has denied the faith and is worse than an unbeliever. (1 Tim 5:8)

As always, God is clear. The man's failure to provide for "his household" places him in direct conflict with the fundamentals of the faith, and he is "worse than an unbeliever." Yet again, provision and abundance are not necessarily the same. God here refers to the basic support and care of the family: housing, food, clothing, heat, security, etc.

Our country has the opinion that "bigger is better." We have long advanced the idea that "my kids will have it better than I did." The question though is why? Why do they need more than we grew up having? If one grew up in poverty and starvation, this might well be a correct goal to have. But most of us grew up with adequate, if not abundant circumstances. Who is benefiting from the generational redefinition of success?

In the 1950s the average family home was a little over 900 square feet. By the year 2000 it was over 2200 square feet. What happened in forty years that the American family needed more than double the space? What changed is our perception of what is adequate and necessary.

We are not suggesting you move to a 900 square foot house and take a minimum wage job that allows you to be home each day at four. But, we are suggesting that a reevaluation of the "requirements" in our lives is a good idea. We must be certain that we are placing our efforts where the benefits are eternal, not temporal. Jesus said:

"Do not lay up for yourselves treasures on earth, where moth and rust destroy and where thieves break in and steal; but lay up for yourselves treasures in heaven, where neither moth nor rust destroys and where thieves do not break in and steal. For where your treasure is, there your heart will be also." (Matt 6:19-21)

Without a heavenly focus, our earthly treasures will never suffice. The freedom we believe we will achieve rarely comes; the peace we seek is not found; the family intimacy is lacking. By demonstrating good restraint, proper planning, correct priorities, and eternal focus, we teach our children the patterns necessary for godly living and we give our wives the security and comfort they long for. Make certain you know "where your treasure is..."

Before becoming a Christian, my wife and I enjoyed a pretty full life. We both worked and made a lot of money. We bought whatever we wanted, went wherever we wished, and felt no restraint about spending. Now that we are both born-again, I am trying to recalibrate our lifestyle. I want to work less, focus more on time with my wife and kids, contribute more to the church, and scale back financially. My wife, however, does not share the same view and has continued to work, spend, and consume as we always have. How do I help her, and our entire family, change our priorities?

Let us first encourage you to continue in this movement. You have realized that the consumption of the world is not fulfilling. Activities that are entirely self-serving rarely are. Moreover, excessive devotion to the world's order not only distances us from God, it makes us His enemy. James, the brother of Jesus wrote:

Adulterers and adulteresses! Do you not know that friendship with the world is enmity with God? Whoever therefore wants to be a friend of the world makes himself an enemy of God. (Jas 4:4)

James calls us "adulterers and adulteresses" because we have betrayed the one true God with our worldly attractions. It is infidelity at the highest degree to forsake our love relationship with God for a lustful consumption of the world. Yet our love for money and the things it buys, along with the false sense of security it brings, often is the deepest struggle for many Christians to overcome. Your wife is no exception.

If your wife is born-again, then you must first rely on the Holy Spirit, through the Word of God, to convict her as you have been convicted. You cannot be the full source of her realization on this matter. Attempts to press her compliance with your changing world-view may produce resistance and hardening in her heart.

There are many biblical standards at play in your scenario. First there is the issue of leadership and authority in your home. God, not the world, must be the defining source of wisdom and direction. He then delivers that authority through the husband, to the family. Your wife must come to trust your position as a Christian husband who is now led by the Spirit of God. As such, the issue becomes adherence to God's Word and God's order, not the husband's. As long as your positions in the home line up with Scripture, you will be acting in God's will, bringing security to your wife that will help her to yield, over time, to the new goals and objectives. As you present your positions, do so with love and not animosity **(Eph 4:15, Col 3:18).**

Next is the issue of growth in the Christian life and the process of transformation that one goes through. Remember that the two of you are "new" Christians. As such, you will be discovering new information daily as you advance your walk. In prayer and Bible study you will encounter the correction, conviction, and leading of the Holy Spirit **(John 16:8)** as you are trained in the standards of godly living. Many elements of Christian life are simply unknown to the new believer, while others will be met with deeply held resistance based in our sinful nature. Frankly, we sometimes just don't want to let go of particular areas of sinful appeal.

Yet as believers, it will become harder and harder to deny and ignore the Spirit's direction. We are well on the way to transformation when we understand God's Word and learn to correctly decipher His calling. Paul wrote to the Romans:

And do not be conformed to this world, but be transformed by the renewing of your mind, that you may prove what is that good and acceptable and perfect will of God. (Rom 12:2)

The Greek word for renewing in this text is *anakainsis*, which translated means: a renovation; a complete change for the better. Renovation takes time, and married couples do not always grow in the same areas at the same pace. While your wife struggles in this area, your struggles may be more pronounced in other ways.

We encourage you to express yourself with love and understanding. Struggle and difficulty is not necessarily the same as defiance. Seek to have empathy for your wife's fear about this issue. As you discuss your position, allow your wife time to study the Scriptures and let the Spirit work with her heart. Introduce her to biblical concepts that apply to this point, but allow her to examine and pray about them.

Begin to take action on your own part, giving her notice of what you intend to do. For example, let her know you are passing up a certain business trip or forgoing working overtime in order to spend a family vacation or take a mission trip with the church. Allow your wife to see the benefit of this process in you. As she witnesses the "renewing" of your mind and the renovation of your spirit, the process may become less frightening to her. Always lead by example so that she has behavioral evidence that the change is indeed "for the better."

CASE EXAMPLE

Leo and Fran were referred to us as an "emergency case" by a chaplain at the local military base. The stress on this couple was so extreme that the chaplain feared Fran might take her life. In spite of the threat and emergency nature of their situation, neither would take off work for an appointment. To accommodate the chaplain's plea, the two were seen at 6:45 a.m. for their first session.

Leo and Fran were in their mid-forties and had been married over 20 years. They had two daughters ages 12 and 18 living at home. Both professed to be Christians yet admitted no involvement in church or spiritual growth "for years." The "crisis" between them was as follows: Fran felt trapped in the family business, working in excess of 60 hours per week, and saw no way out other than to take her own life. Leo could not understand the stress and burden she was under; would not make arrangements for her relief; and could accept nothing less than her "total" commitment to the business.

Along with these facts, she felt the children were suffering. The older daughter was finishing high school and was required to work in the business each afternoon from 3:00 to 10:00 p.m. or later, as well as on most weekends. The younger daughter basically was home alone except when she was in school. By report, both daughters were also depressed, and the younger one had become very withdrawn and overweight in her isolation. Both daughters had asked their mother to divorce their dad so they could "have their old lives back."

Fran was a teacher by training with a master's degree. She had over 15 years in the education system when Leo "insisted" she leave her job and run the three franchise restaurants he wanted to buy. He also pressured her to give up their home of 10 years and buy an "older" house that needed extensive renovation. In the middle of working 60 hours per week, Fran was also overseeing construction on the home and living in a mess of half-completed work, dirt and dust.

Leo was completing his final six months of service in the military while also working nights and weekends in the restaurants. The couple saw each other only at work, talked only about work, business, buying other franchises, remodeling, and money pressures. They saw their children rarely and attended none of their extra-curricular activities. They didn't even have meals as a family. At night they would send food to the youngest daughter, from the restaurant, through a delivery service.

The first session proceeded in this manner:

Shrink: "So Leo, tell me how you see this problem."
Leo: "There is no problem. We have had this dream for years as a family and everything is going just as planned. We just have to keep doing what we are doing, and in five years we won't have to worry about anything."
Fran: (Crying with her head down): "He doesn't get it!"
Leo: "I get it alright. We have a goal, and when it is achieved, all this will have been worth it. We just have to continue, no matter the cost."
Shrink: "Leo, you did understand that your wife wants to die? She is threatening to kill herself because she cannot cope with the pressure. Your daughters are depressed. Divorce has been a consideration. Is there no 'cost' so great as to cause this sort

of anguish."
Leo: They just have to be stronger and we will get through
this. This is no time for being weak."

Further examination found that Leo had a history of insecurity
grounded in his failure to complete college and his military career
as an enlisted man rather than an officer. He had long been intimi-
dated by his wife's education and professional career, even though
he had realized a high degree of success in the military as a master
sergeant with much responsibility.

The dream Leo referenced was not the family's dream but his
own. He admitted that he had wanted this franchise for over ten
years and that nothing would interrupt his plan for financial freedom. Interestingly, the franchise was purchased using an inheritance that had come to Fran when her mother died a year earlier.

Before the purchase of the franchise, Fran made nearly $50,000
per year, plus had full health benefits, life insurance, and retirement
funds. All of that was lost with her departure from her job. When
Leo retired from the military, they would no longer have his full
time salary ($52,000 per year plus benefits), but they would have a
regular retirement income for life of $27,000 per year, plus full
health care for the family. So even before getting a post-retirement
job or business, the family (with Fran still working as a teacher)
would have had almost $77,000 per year income plus health, dental,
life insurance and future retirement for Fran. Now with the
purchase of the franchise they had lost Fran's income and benefits,
spent her inheritance ($60,000) and assumed a debt of over
$200,000.

Leo's obsession with being a business owner (status) combined
with his urgency for wealth had created a deadly situation. Fran had
accommodated Leo's dream to support him. But now she was
making pizzas, moping floors, fixing machinery, and losing money
hand-over-fist. She wanted to return to teaching, be available for
her daughters, and hire someone to fill her space in the business. It
would be a small financial outlay to hire a minimum-wage worker
to do the work she was currently doing at the restaurant, compared
to what she could earn as a teacher. Yet Leo refused and seemed

singularly committed to keeping things as they were.

> *Shrink:* "Leo, your wife is saying she cannot cope with this situation. She is saying she is going to kill herself without relief. Do you understand the risk?"
> *Leo:* "Just five more years and we're free."
> *Fran:* "I can't make it five more days!"
> *Leo:* "Her mother was depressed too, all her life. Can you give her some medication?"
> *Shrink:* "First I am not a medical doctor, but I don't think there is a medication that can keep her going until you are rich enough and important enough to let her have some relief. She needs her husband to hear how desperate she is and help her."
> *Leo:* "Oh, I thought you could prescribe medication. That's really what we wanted. Maybe you can recommend someone that can help her get through."
> *Shrink:* "Leo, you are not hearing me."
> *Leo:* "We've got to get to work. Can you recommend a doctor before we go?"

Leo did not come back to therapy. Fran came only once more. Her family doctor gave her Prozac and something to help her sleep. As far as we know, Leo and Fran are still working on Leo's "five-year plan."

> **Then I looked on all the works that my hands had done and on the labor in which I had toiled; and indeed all was vanity and grasping for the wind. There was no profit under the sun. (Eccl 2:11)**

CAREER IDENTITY

Today so many of us define ourselves by what we do. Visit any social gathering and you will find work and career at the top of the discussion list. Meet someone new and one of the first questions will be, "What do you do for a living?" That question is much more than small talk. It is a measuring tape used to assess the other person's value and then to contrast that assessment against one's own.

As an organized nation, our work is a part of how we contribute to society. What we do vocationally is part of the working fabric of our country. We need plumbers, landscape professionals, accountants, and surgeons. Society has a role for chefs, musicians, carpenters, and even shrinks! Yet our identity ought not to rest on this piece of life. Instead, our identity is an expression of our character and it should be the same whether at work, church, vacation, or home. You see, what we do matters less than how we do it.

Ideally, our work would not define us, but rather our nature and character should define our work. As Christians we should reflect the character of Christ in all settings. Our goal should be to have an identity as a godly man or woman who, by the way, is also a fantastic realtor, teacher, woodworker, or homemaker. Again there should be no division between one's working identity and his/her identity elsewhere. Our conduct in labor or rest should reflect all of the goodness of our Lord. Paul wrote to the Philippian church: **"Only let your conduct be worthy of the gospel of Christ"** (Phil 1:27a).

If our conduct is "worthy of the gospel of Christ," then our identity is secure and solid. There is no more powerful testimony than the one that is delivered uniformly, consistently, publicly and in private. Our work is a large segment of our time. We must make certain that our Christ-like conduct, our new nature, is evident to all.

Very often, our identity and accomplishments in the workplace become a source of vanity and pride. As Christians we must be on guard against the risk of self-inflation or self-importance. Self is at the center of most sin and left untended, can provide a very constant distraction and increased vulnerability to the priorities of the world. It is wise to remember the biblical admonition:

For all that is in the world—the lust of the flesh, the lust of the eyes, and the pride of life—is not of the Father but is of the world. (1 John 2:16)

This is not to say that ambition is wrong and achievement is sin. But it is a reminder to maintain a proper accounting of one's drive and motivation. Advancement of a career, financial gain, and growth can be of benefit to the family and to God's kingdom. But all we do must be measured frequently against the standards of the Lord. Is our activity "of the Father" or is it "of the world?" We must be in prayerful consideration of this question daily as we devote our time and energy to projects, goals, titles, and earnings figures. The "pride of life" is of no value in the home nor does it generate gain for us in God's heaven.

NOW FOR YOUR QUESTIONS...

I have always wanted to be a doctor. Even as a child, it was my constant dream. Now after years of school, training, and sacrifice, I have been a family physician for almost a decade. I have enjoyed the money and frankly love being needed by my patients. I have always gone to work early and stayed late, and my patients and colleagues hold me in high regard. But outside of work I feel depressed and lost. My wife and I are distant; my children are in their own world of activities; I have no friends outside the hospital and no hobbies. It seems my dream has stolen my joy.

Your vocational dream is valuable and important. God has given you abilities and intelligence to serve this world in a unique and gifted way. He placed a calling in your life and a desire in your heart early, and He has prepared you to serve others in this special way. Thankfully you answered this call and many have been positively affected as a result. Your profession is not at fault but rather your myopic view of yourself.

Somehow you determined that medical practice is a complete, rather than partial, depiction of who you are. Many helping professions can be this way and some even create a culture whereby "total devotion" is expected. It makes for a very deceiving process wherein we make the work our idol, and in service to the idol we find self-esteem and self-importance. In other words, if you are being "doctor" you are good; if not, you are less than you should be.

Like any false idol, work will never provide true peace, worth, or satisfaction. It will always require another day, another procedure, another dollar earned to maintain a sense of personal value. In the process, your God-given abilities and earned skills are weakened in the false and selfish motivations idolatry creates.

We know that idolatry is a strong term, yet anything we place above God and our service to Him is exactly that. When anything garners that much of our energy, time, and identity, we have fallen outside of God's prescribed order and into the order of service required by our false point of worship.

By your report, you long ago stopped practicing medicine "unto the Lord." Instead your practice of medicine has been self-serving, giving you money, self-esteem, admiration, and false purpose. God gifted you for medicine so that He could be glorified through your expression of His gift. In doing so He has promised to take care of you and your family. The idolatry of work has created an order prescribed by human wisdom that requires you to place money, time, and service to patients over your communion with God, communication with your family, and even your own health and wellbeing.

God's order is perfect and it will revive you and your family. However, transitioning to God's order requires trust that you currently do not have. You have placed your trust in the activities and trends of the medical profession. To accept God's order will require you to surrender much of what you currently hold on to as your security. God requires that He alone is first in your life:

> **"You shall have no other gods before Me. You shall not make for yourself a carved image—or any likeness of anything that is in heaven above, or that is in the earth beneath, or that is in the water under the earth; you shall not bow down to them nor serve them." (Ex 20:3-5a)**

The white coat, the medical insurance forms, the ritual of hospital and office, and even the emblem of medical practice have become your "carved images." If you examine yourself closely you will find that you have bowed down and served these symbols more than God and more than your family. That order of worship and devotion of attention must reverse if you are to come into God's perfect order. Read what follows in that same passage:

"For I, the Lord your God, am a jealous God, visiting the iniquity of the fathers upon the children to the third and fourth generations of those who hate Me." (v. 5b)

This means that our idolatry will cause a ripple effect in our home and our sin will influence our children and grandchildren. It does not mean God will punish our offspring for our sin, but rather our sin and displaced order of life will hurt and limit the blessings and success of our heirs. You may feel this already as you describe distance with your wife and division with your children. Your family may respect you generally as a man and may even understand and adhere to the demands of medical practice, but without their spiritual leader, they are potentially estranged from God as well, and will recreate your lost sense of priorities.

Second to our relationship with God is our responsibility to our wife. The Bible requires us to love and care for her in a manner unlike any other earthly relationship. If we do not, we are outside God's plan **(1 Pet 3:7, Eph 5:25, Gen 2:23-24)**. It will be impossible to find the pleasure and peace one seeks in a marriage unless the man is in proper arrangement with God.

Finally, the father is central to the leadership and teaching of the children. Ask yourself, what is the example you are now giving them about godly living and family order?

Children's children are the crown of old men,
And the glory of children is their father. (Prov 17:6)

Begin to think in terms of the inheritance you are leaving for the generations to follow. Your intelligence and professional prowess are good examples, but it is the spiritual inheritance of which this proverb speaks. Work to provide the spiritual foundation that will be your crown of success. Then your children will know the peace and pleasure of an identity built in Christ, not one built in the world.

Begin your reorientation with daily prayer and Bible study. If there isn't time for this, then you really aren't ready to change the order of your life. As you begin to place God ahead of all, have a meeting with your family and confess your failings along with your desire to change.

We know of a friend who accepted Christ at the age of 40 and began to totally revamp his priorities. He sat down on the sofa in his home with his wife and two sons, sharing his decision and giving the following call to his boys: "I've always told you to do whatever I *tell* you to do. From now on, you can do whatever I *do*." He was determined to live out what he spoke. No longer did he intend to say one thing and do another. This meeting, along with a consistent Christian walk, paid great dividends in his family and in his son's future homes.

By being open with your wife and children, you create a climate of accountability that will help the whole family move toward the goal of Kingdom living. Work next to include your family in daily Bible study and prayer. Praying together creates great unity of purpose and yields a God-centered attitude.

From this genesis you can begin to evaluate your work and the need for revision. Reducing work responsibilities, on-call schedules, etc. may be a result. Or the shift may be more attitudinal. In other words, the quantity of the work may be manageable if your focus and attention on God and family are in priority positions. Let Christ be your identity and your pattern, and glory in the God of our salvation:

In God we boast all day long,
And praise Your name forever. (Ps 44:8)

I have been married 15 years to a great Christian man, and we have two children ages 13 and 8. I have a college degree and worked for a short time in journalism after marriage. When our first child came, my husband and I decided together that I should be a full-time mother and homemaker. I think that decision was a good one, but now with my youngest in second grade, I wonder if I shouldn't go back to work. My husband and kids want me to stay a homemaker, but somehow I feel I have lost my identity. What should I consider?

First, we applaud your initial decision to raise your children on a full-time basis. There is no other earthly career more crucial yet so undervalued as that of being a full-time, stay-at-home mother. The years you have devoted to your home and children will pay great dividends in the years to come. You have laid an important foundation that can never be undone, and you have taught them to value the role of parenting as a top priority rather than something done secondarily to career.

That being said, many women feel great pressure to be "more than" a wife and mother. In response to financial pressures, liberal interests, and feminist agendas, women frequently feel their contribution is limited as a stay-at-home mom. When children are school-aged, we find the pressure increases.

Clearly, your contribution is not being questioned by your spouse and children. They like having you at home and seem to value what you provide. There seems to be no financial pressure to work outside the home, and this is no small success. So often we see families who have created a box financially that they can only get out of by two paychecks. Thankfully, you and your husband have made proper provision without your financial assistance.

So what is driving you to change careers? You reference a loss of identity, yet your identity has been that of a homemaker; a role you now might abandon. It seems instead that you have lost a sense of value in your identity. Somehow, the job you found so rewarding for over 13 years has lost its significance.

As our children age, their needs change. You may have the view that they "need" you less than before. Sometimes women can even feel a loss akin to grief as children transition from one stage of dependency to another. But rest assured, while the stage has changed, the dependency has not. Most likely it will be expressed differently, with greater independence and distance, but they still need you.

Your daily presence and accessibility is a great source of security and stability for both children, even if they do not acknowledge it the way they once did. Your presence also allows your husband to focus on his work and role as provider, knowing that you are in the primary position at home.

There is no prohibition in the Bible against women working

outside the home. But, the home and its welfare is the woman's first priority. The Book of Proverbs gives the example of a godly wife, and as a homemaker; she is very much a worker. But near the end of the passage, the evaluation of her labor is found as follows:

> **Strength and honor are her clothing;**
> **She shall rejoice in time to come.**
> **She opens her mouth with wisdom,**
> **And on her tongue is the law of kindness.**
> **She watches over the ways of her household,**
> **And does not eat the bread of idleness.**
> **Her children rise up and call her blessed;**
> **Her husband also, and he praises her:**
> **Many daughters have done well,**
> **But you excel them all.**
> **Charm is deceitful and beauty is passing,**
> **But a woman who fears the Lord, she shall be praised.**
> **(Prov 31:25-30)**

She "watches over the ways of her household;" her children "call her blessed;" her husband "praises her." Yes, she works very hard, in and out of the household, but the measurement of her success comes from within. All of this work, the proverb teaches, comes through a healthy fear and reverence of the Lord, the One who is the source of her wisdom and strength.

We encourage you to let God define your worth and your task. You clearly have great fruit for your labor found in the joy and contentment of your children and husband who "bless and praise" you. Whatever decision you make, do it with clarity of mind and through much prayer. Ask God to reveal His wishes for your life. Consider your family's pleas to continue in your successful role as homemaker. Challenge the voices or deceptions that may be coming from divisive sources that place less value on the order of God and the call He has made in your life.

As a journalist, you have a lot to offer on this topic. Pray about adding some outside work to your daily routine through telecommuting. Freelance writing and other journalistic efforts are often done from home with computers, emails, faxes, etc. Approach this problem by adding a little rather than by the abandonment of a lot. You don't have to stop being who you have always been to have a career change. Consider some activities that fit into your routine rather than ones that totally rewrite it.

And let the beauty of the Lord our God be upon us,
And establish the work of our hands for us;
Yes, establish the work of our hands. (Ps 90:17)

CASE EXAMPLE

Davis loved flying jets. He had spent his whole childhood planning to be an F-16 fighter pilot in the air force. He was admitted to the U. S. Air Force Academy, graduated with honors, and then finished first in flight school. He was one of the select few with the right attributes, aptitude, physical condition, and drive to make it to jet training. When the list announcing his placement came out, he remarked: "Thank God. I would have killed myself if I had to fly a bomber or a cargo plane." All he could think about was jets.

Davis continued to advance, completed training and then achieved great success in a fighter squadron, flying many missions in wartime situations. Now after twenty-plus years and the rank of colonel, it was time for mandatory retirement in two months. He had earned medals, certificates, accommodations, and praise from the U. S. Air Force. He could name his price if he wanted to take a job with a commercial airline.

Davis' commander required him to come to therapy after he had tried to kill himself by connecting a hose to the exhaust system of his car. His teenage son had discovered him just in time, leading to a short hospitalization before coming to our office. During the first session, Davis was depressed, almost lifeless. He said that he was unable to sleep and had lost 20 pounds in four weeks. He denied that he would try to kill himself again, but indicated flatly: "There's nothing to live for."

Shrink: "Nothing to live for? How can that be?"
Davis: "If I can't be Colonel Davis Smith, jet pilot, there is

nothing else to live for."

Shrink: "What about the rest of your life that has been running parallel to your flight career?"

Davis: "What are you talking about?"

Shrink: "The hospital records tell me you have a wife of twenty-five years, four children, a master's degree, and you are a member of the First Methodist Church."

Davis: "All window dressing."

Shrink: "I don't understand. What do you mean by 'window dressing'?"

Davis: "The air force owns the jets I wanted to fly. The air force likes married pilots with children. They like community involvement and advanced education. They want curtains on the window. These things simply give you access to be who you really are."

Shrink: "And now the window is boarded up and you don't have any need of curtains?"

Davis: "You catch on pretty fast."

Shrink: "Have you ever accepted Christ as your Savior?"

Davis: "Yep. I checked that box too. But it won't put me back in the cockpit, will it?"

It was hard to tell at this point if Davis truly was so callous as he seemed, or if his depression and anger had blackened everything in his life. But clearly, his entire sense of identity and worth was found at the controls of an F-16. For whatever reason, nothing else mattered right now.

When I later met with Davis's wife and son, I was relieved to know he had been a faithful husband and involved father. They acknowledged that he was overly preoccupied with flying and with the persona of pilot, but generally he had been active and loving in the home. The wife reasoned that in spite of his success, Davis had always been insecure, and could relate to others outside the family only on professional terms. He preferred his flying buddies for company and the exchange of "war stories." Both the wife and son believed that Davis was indeed born-again and gave evidence of his spiritual leadership in the home. Yet outside the home, he was totally invested in the world of flight and the culture that surrounded it. The wife and son expected that few, if any, others would know Davis as a Christian.

In the next session, Davis asked if I had met with the family. I assured him I had met with his wife and his son.

Davis: "So what do you think now?"

Shrink: "I think they are pretty nice curtains. Too bad they have to be discarded just because you can't have your way."

Davis: "So they think I'm pretty selfish, is that it?"

Shrink: "No, they seem to love and respect you in spite of yourself. But after twenty something years of support for your dream, I can see how they could now get in the way of your true destiny."

Davis: "What in the world are you talking about? What do you know about my destiny?"

Shrink: "I know you were gifted with a very special set of abilities that few in the world can replicate. I know that you were destined to fly an aircraft that many crave but few achieve. I know you were selected to protect our country in war, did it honorably, and survived doing it. I also know God gifted you with a faithful wife and four children who respect and honor you. And by reports I have heard from your wife and son, you submitted yourself at one time to the Lord and Savior, Jesus Christ. So you were also destined to be His and to accomplish His good and perfect will. But you seem determined to override all of this evidence in order to advance your TRUE destiny, which is to be found dead in the back of a minivan from self-inflicted asphyxiation."

Davis: "I don't drive a #*&% minivan!" (Smiling).

Shrink: "No, I guess you don't. But guess what? You don't drive a jet anymore either."

Davis: "I know, I know."

Shrink: "What do you really feel about your family?"

Davis: "They are awesome. They are great. But they will never see me the same as they see me in that flight suit."

Shrink: "That's your garbage. Don't place that lie on them.

The truth is this: as much as they respect who you have been and what you have accomplished, they have looked forward to the day they don't have to worry about you and don't have to see you go away. They want you close by. They want more of you, not your career."

Davis: "Really?"

Shrink: "Really."

It took several months for Davis to recover from his depression. He had to grapple with some old teachings from his father that left him feeling insecure and impotent: teachings that left him feeling less than adequate no matter how much he achieved. He had to learn to relate to his wife and children effectively, and he came to trust their love for him. Spiritually, Davis had been under the delusion that he was in control. The change in his career status made him realize that he was not. For the first time, Davis could allow himself to feel weak and call upon Jesus to be strong. He learned to submit again to the Lord, relying on the true and ever-present power that flows from the righteousness of Christ. He learned to release the false security that came through a jet, a title, and the power of the world system.

He ended up "settling" for a six-figure income as a commercial pilot, wearing a new uniform, and with much safer flying conditions. He is more connected and involved with his family and has a more solid sense of who he is as a Christian. Not long ago he joked, "I guess flying a cargo plane isn't so bad after all."

WORK AND FAMILY

I (Dr. Ab) had a professor who years ago said: "Whatever you choose as a career will become simply a means of earning a living. Your life will be built outside of work." As a young psychology student, determined to heal the emotional ills of the world, his view seemed rather tainted. Yet over time, most of us come to see the truth in his words. That is not to say that I no longer find my work important or rewarding, but it is not the center of my universe, nor should it be for anyone. Work, no matter how gratifying, is primarily a source of financial existence. Whenever it becomes more important than our Christian development and family involvement, it is safe to say we are out of alignment with God's order.

As we have already seen in this chapter, work can take on a life and identity all its own. Wrongly, we make it into a source of self-esteem, worth, identity, and idolatry. We all know that driving an automobile that is in poor alignment will ruin the car's tires. The operation of work and family without proper balance and alignment will have a similar effect: something will suffer. Left untended, this imbalance will destroy the very fiber of one's core happiness and satisfaction with life.

As we have pointed out, work and career issues have come to take center stage in our culture. Working overtime, material acquisition, greater social status due to money, and the two-paycheck environment have all replaced home life as the central driving force in most lives. King Solomon wrote of his desperation and the absence of fulfillment that came from self-gratification and the acquisition that all his labor could provide:

> **I made my works great, I built myself houses, and planted myself vineyards. I made myself gardens and orchards, and I planted all kinds of fruit trees in them. I made myself water pools from which to water the growing trees of the grove. I acquired male and female servants, and had servants born in my house. Yes, I had greater possessions of herds and flocks than all who were in Jerusalem before me. I also gathered for myself silver and gold and the special treasures of kings and of the provinces. I acquired male and female singers, the delights of the sons of men, and musical instruments of all kinds. So I became great and excelled more than all who were before me in Jerusalem. Also my wisdom remained with me. Whatever my eyes desired I did not keep from them. I did not withhold my heart from any pleasure, for my heart rejoiced in all my labor; and this was my reward from all my labor. Then I looked on all the works that my hands had done and on the labor in which I had toiled; and indeed all was vanity and**

grasping for the wind. There was no profit under the sun. (Eccl 2:4-11)

Here, the king of greatest wealth and greatest wisdom determines that the profit of all his labor and self-gratification was "vanity and grasping for the wind." In fact, he states there was "no profit under the sun." None of us can achieve more wealth, status, or possessions than Solomon, who in the end announced a zero sum gain. The Bible gives us clear evidence that the fulfillment that comes from God, and the blessings of His perfect will, have nothing in common with this type of achievement. Under such a scenario, our heart is wrongly placed.

NOW FOR YOUR QUESTIONS...

I am a Christian man who works as an upper level executive in a national corporation. I have done well professionally and financially, and my family lives a very good life. In spite of this, I am obsessed with work and put in far more hours than even the company requires. I am preoccupied most of the time and feel chronically burdened, even though I am abundantly blessed. I am constantly fearful that we won't have enough money and that our lifestyle will have to change. Each time I reach a goal that I think will make me feel secure I just increase the requirement on myself. I know that this is wrong and that my family is suffering because of it. Still I can't seem to let go.

Thankfully you know that your approach is "wrong." Apparently, God is convicting you that something needs to change. You have placed your trust and security in the world while God wants us to lean entirely upon Him. You have already realized, as King Solomon did, that no amount of money or achievement is able to fully satisfy.

As a Christian, please recognize that you have over-evaluated your accomplishment and therefore have created a false burden to maintain it. Everything we are allowed to accomplish is a gift from God and not a product of our personal power:

As for every man to whom God has given riches and wealth, and given him power to eat of it, to receive his heritage and rejoice in his labor—this is the gift of God. (Eccl 5:19)

Clearly, God has allowed you the wealth, power, and privilege you speak of. Of course you have studied, prepared, worked, and produced, but the abundance is entirely at God's will. By giving you this gift, God has blessed your family and requires a thankful rather than a fearful, heart:

For God has not given us a spirit of fear, but of power and of love and of a sound mind. (2 Tim 1:7)

Your sin, in part, lies in the failure to acknowledge God as the source of all support in your life. If your continued production were only up to you, then your fear would be well placed. But if you will adopt a truly thankful and submissive posture with God, you will begin to feel His power and might as the source of your strength. You will realize that you are no longer alone and have no need to be obsessed with your own limitations.

God makes it clear in His Word that we are not to worry about such matters; He will provide all that we need. In spite of what the prosperity preachers teach, God does not necessarily promise success and wealth in earthly terms, but rather a provision that is more than adequate. His reasons for blessing you beyond the "basics" should have more to do with His plan for the Kingdom than simply the generation of surplus. Jesus said:

"Consider the lilies, how they grow: they neither toil nor spin; and yet I say to you, even Solomon in all his glory was not arrayed like one of these. If then God so clothes the grass, which today is in the field and tomorrow is thrown into the oven, how much more will He clothe you, O you of little faith? And do not seek what you should eat or what you should drink, nor have an anxious mind. For all these things the nations of the

world seek after, and your Father knows that you need these things. But seek the kingdom of God, and all these things shall be added to you. Do not fear, little flock, for it is your Father's good pleasure to give you the kingdom." (Luke 12:27-32)

What greater assurance can be found anywhere: "But seek the kingdom of God, and all these things shall be added to you." Again, God defines His order. First seek the His kingdom, THEN He will add all things. Jesus goes further by saying it is our Father's "good pleasure" to give us the Kingdom!

When we develop a Kingdom perspective, nothing in this world can compare to what we have already been given. We then begin to structure our day in proper order with service and focus on work that edifies the kingdom of God. This work, the Bible tells us, is all that will endure:

... each one's work will become clear; for the Day will declare it, because it will be revealed by fire; and the fire will test each one's work, of what sort it is. (1 Cor 3:13)

We encourage you to establish your transition as follows: First, redefine your abundance as a gift from God and submit to the reality that apart from Him, you can do nothing (**John 15:5**). In spite of your success, you are like a little boy in over his head in duty and responsibility. Allow yourself to develop a respectful, thankful tone with God. Let your prayer life reflect this insight, giving thanks repeatedly for the blessings you have along with the trust that God conveys by placing all of this in your hands (**Luke 12:48**). It is very difficult to experience anxiety when we are thanking God. The reality of His presence, care, and provision is very comforting.

As you are thanking God, ask for His direction regarding the abundance (**Phil 4:6**). Since He generated it, He will be faithful to use it to the good of the His kingdom. You have already stated that you work and produce more than even your employer requires. Why not seek what your heavenly Father requires and build upon that position? Remember, His order involves seeking His kingdom first.

Part of Kingdom living is the ministry to your home. You are the priest of your house and as such, you are required to be the example of godly living. Your wife and children will benefit from seeing this transition of priorities in your life. It will be important to talk to them openly about what you are doing and why. Support all you do through God's Word so that there is no confusion about your motivation. Remember that God requires attention and honor to the wife as the foundation of all we do as husbands. We must be engaged and active in this area of ministry so that our prayers are not limited in any way (**1 Pet 3:7**).

All that you have is a gift from God. You have it because He allowed you to produce it. Within that reality, find a thankful and willing heart, submitting to whatever God will have you do. In the Old Testament God required a tithe (**Lev 27:30**); in the New Testament He requires a willingness to give everything (**Matt 19:21**).

God will never require anything of you that violates His Word and His order. Therefore, whatever direction God leads you, it will be to the good of His kingdom and therefore to the good of your family.

My husband insists that I work outside the home. Even though his salary is more than adequate for our regular needs and savings, he is convinced that the "extras" matter almost as much. On his priority list are expensive vacations, dining out, a boat for the family, etc. We soon will have debt that requires me to work. I have tried to tell him our time and energy for the four children matter much more than these extravagant activities, but he remains adamant that the family "deserves" better. What can I do?

It sounds like your husband really likes vacations, eating out, and boating. It is difficult to believe that his motivation for such ventures is completely altruistic. On the other hand, many parents have very distorted views about what matters in the day-to-day happiness of a home. There are several reasons for this type of misplaced priority.

Some adults with this orientation grew up in a family where

love is shown only in gifts and special activities. For many, genuine affection, quality time, and communication are not present, and the gifts and activities serve as a substitute for closeness and interaction. As parents, these individuals are somewhat programmed to "materialize" their love.

Others come from a sparse, poor background where there was a sharp contrast between the lives they lived and the lives of those around them. When individuals grow up in poverty there develops a hunger for the "better" things in life. Partly out of anger and the frustration of always doing without, they can grow into adults who measure love and security through attainment.

In either situation, the child, and ultimately the adult, is left wanting for a true, deep involvement with his/her family. The type of intimacy and affection needed in a home is not usually found at Disney World or even on a ski boat. Activities like these can be rich and meaningful in their own way and are the basis of many nice memories. But the deepest conversations, the most spontaneous exchanges, the intimate moments, come while playing ball in the back yard, fixing dinner together, or over a game of Monopoly.

Once our (The Abercrombies) daughter was asked by her teacher to draw a picture of the "best moment" she experienced over the Thanksgiving vacation. This was a vacation that included some time at home along with a fairly expensive vacation out of town. She didn't draw the amusement park, the movie theater, or the fine restaurants. Instead she drew a picture of "Daddy and me walking our dog." The moment she most enjoyed was that walk on Thanksgiving morning, talking and spending time together, and anticipating the family coming over for the big meal.

Our world has so many options, so much abundance, that we often feel driven to taste it all. In doing so, we tend to ignore the interpersonal moments that give us real access to one another. We are convinced that the mundane elements of life are the most powerful. This is when conversation is plentiful, questions are asked and answered, and values are conveyed. These are also the times we teach our children the skills they will need in life, from cooking a meal, to mowing the grass, to relating in an intelligent and clear manner.

As therapists we see many children and teens who rarely eat dinner with the family; they don't know how to prepare a basic meal; they have no regular chores or responsibilities; and most cannot relate verbally in an intelligent and communicative way. Many are physically unfit, lethargic, and sullen. Most are a composite of experiences gleaned from television, movies, and video games. Many, unfortunately, have a powerful sense of entitlement that makes them most unattractive. That is, they believe and expect that they should have whatever they want without cost, sacrifice, consequence, or work.

We think it is important that your husband and you have a very detailed talk about your children. Rather than debate money and work per say, discuss the growth of the kids, examine how they are doing, and define your goals for them. Assuming that your children are doing well, you can build a case for full-time mothering. Help your husband see that the extravagances you have "sacrificed" as a couple have allowed you to stay home with the children, and what a tremendous difference this has made in the type of children you have raised thus far.

If your husband's concern is truly about the children, he should be able to see the benefit of your choices until now. He also should be open to your preferences as well as the children's. Presently it seems that he is the only one devoted to a "larger" lifestyle. Walk him through, step-by-step, showing the moments that have made the difference. Remind him of special times, important crises, and successful interventions that have come about because of your availability to the children.

If, however, your husband's attraction to material "goodies" is personal, he may not be willing to acknowledge the success of your current approach to parenting. In that event you have an issue that is more complicated than a difference over parenting philosophy. In a situation like this, something has stirred misdirection on your husband's part. Perhaps it is some older, unresolved matter, or it could be something in his present life that has become a crisis of self-esteem or identity. In either case, you must continue to turn to the truth of God's Word as your reference point. Presently, your husband is drawn to the world's instruction about what matters in the upbringing of children. Continue to encourage him to look into Scripture with you and let the Holy Spirit speak to him on this matter.

As a Christian man who formerly placed value in scriptural parenting and having a wife who is a work-at-home mother, the foundation is solid. Allow God's instruction to lead. A very interesting sequence of Scripture that pertains to your situation is found in Proverbs 22. While the two successive verses are not necessarily "linked," their placement and proximity relate well to your circumstance. The first verse is clear about our primary duty as parents:

Train up a child in the way he should go,
And when he is old he will not depart from it. (v. 6)

Now see what follows in the very next verse:

The rich rules over the poor,
And the borrower is servant to the lender. (v. 7)

Of course we are to be servants of God and no other. Our indebtedness threatens that bond and worship. It also threatens the fulfillment of the earlier verse because we can only "train up a child in the way he should go" if we ourselves are going in the same direction. We must at all times confront the lure of the world and return to the basics of our instruction: serve only God, and share with others that they might do the same.

CASE EXAMPLE

Joey and Mavis were in their early thirties with two preschool children. Joey works 50 hours a week as the manager of a lumber supply business. Mavis spends a minimum of 40 hours per week in a private physical therapy practice. The children are in daycare from 7:00 am until 6:00 pm each day.

The couple came to therapy on the referral of a friend. The two expressed concern that they couldn't afford therapy and could only come for a "session or two." In spite of their very high income, the family was under extensive debt. A home mortgage, car loans, credit cards, and student loans, along with the typical living expenses associated with two children, left them monthly on the brink of bankruptcy. In spite of this, the couple spent a great deal of money on recreation, frequently eating out at the best restaurants while paying for babysitters; traveling out of state to college and pro sporting events; and taking regular, upscale vacations.

We learned in the first session that there was tremendous stress and frequent fighting in the home. Joey was angry that his wife had gained so much weight and felt she should be contributing more financially. Joey pointed out that his salary was fixed, but that Mavis could earn more if she would only see more patients in her practice.

Mavis was exhausted and overwhelmed. While raising a four year-old and an infant, she was building and maintaining a private practice and handling 95 percent of the work at home. She also saw 60 percent of her earnings go toward the cost of daycare. She felt guilty that she was not available for her children. Physically and emotionally, she was absent and preoccupied. This was not the way she had planned to go through life.

Both Joey and Mavis coped with their anxiety by spending money. When overwhelmed they would escape into some place of denial, take out a new credit card, and find short-term relief in a dinner out, travel, or a new acquisition for the home. When the bills came in, reality returned, and the fighting and blaming escalated.

Shrink: "Mavis, what are you wanting from your husband?"
Mavis: "I need him to take over and get us out of this situation. I don't know what to do anymore. I am willing to submit to any solution that will relieve our burden. I'll move to a smaller house, get a cheaper car, I'll cook at home....anything!" (Crying).
Shrink: "Joey, what are you thinking?"
Joey: "I think if she would see five more patients a week we wouldn't have to change a thing. That extra $400 a week would fix our world. But she says she can't take on any more. What am I supposed to do if she won't do her part?"
Mavis: "I told you Joey, I can't let the children stay another

hour a day in daycare. I just can't do it!"

Joey: "They will be fine. It's only for a few months, then we'll be out of debt."

Shrink: "Joey, other than your home and automobiles, how much debt do you have?"

Joey: "With student loans and credit cards about $60,000."

Shrink: "So at $1,600 per month extra income, how long will it take to pay off that debt?" (hands Joey a calculator).

Joey: (Punches in the numbers). "A little over three years."

Mavis: (Crying) "I can't do it!"

Shrink: "Joey, does that number include interest?"

Joey: "No."

Shrink: "So with interest ranging from 7 to 20 percent, you are looking at six to seven years, don't you think?"

Joey: "Maybe."

Shrink: "That's a pretty high cost simply to maintain the lifestyle you have. Is it worth it?"

Mavis: "Not for me it isn't!"

Joey: "I work hard. I deserve some recreation and fun. I don't see a problem with working hard and playing hard."

Shrink: "The problem, Joey, is that this philosophy only works for you. Everyone else in the family is suffering. As the leader, it's your responsibility to find a solution that places less stress, not more, on Mavis and the children."

It may be hard to believe, but Joey took on the challenge. They came to therapy only a few times but they aggressively began to confront the issues at hand. They signed up with a reputable, non-profit, credit-counseling firm. They restructured their debt and made some hard decisions about lifestyle. They even decided to accept a transfer with Joey's company to another state noted for a lower cost of living. There they bought a less expensive home, learned to grill chicken on the barbeque, and to enjoy Mavis' part-time contract with a local hospital. They found that by giving up four dinners a month in fine restaurants; the elimination of one elaborate vacation to Mexico per year; and watching the big game with friends on TV was more than enough to speed up the elimination of their debt.

We recently got a letter saying that after three years, they were debt free except for the house and one car payment. In those three years Mavis never worked over 20 hours a week and the children were with her most of the time. Joey was coaching his son's soccer team and he had become quite a good cook, preparing a lot of the fine meals they used to go out for on Friday nights. Joey wrote: "Life is good."

Joey and Mavis were held captive by the world that created a debt that could never be satisfied. Only when Joey's heart changed could the family begin to receive God's fullest blessing that rescued them from their captivity, just as Judah was freed from the control of Babylon:

> **For I know the thoughts that I think toward you, says the Lord, thoughts of peace and not of evil, to give you a future and a hope. Then you will call upon Me and go and pray to Me, and I will listen to you. And you will seek Me and find Me, when you search for Me with all your heart. I will be found by you, says the Lord, and I will bring you back from your captivity. (Jer 29:11-14a)**

SUMMARY

In this day of climbing salaries, climbing debt, and climbing the corporate ladder, we often place our spiritual life in the position of lowest priority. As a result, the patterns and expectations of money and status begin to define our worth and success rather than the goal of godly character.

In this chapter we have offered evidence that work is important, income necessary, and earthly production required. Yet we have stressed the need for God's order to prevail, just as it should in all areas. The perspective and teachings of our Lord guide us to have a system that is balanced through imbalance. That is, we can only stand steady if the preponderance of our emphasis is with God over the world.

When our spouses and children are our first ministry; when building the Kingdom is primary to building a worldly system; and when our identity is in Christ and His character, not in business or corporate life; then we are walking in a manner that protects and blesses our movement. God will provide all things needed when our lives are submitted examples of trust and faith, relying only on Him and His infinite goodness.

CHAPTER 9

FRIENDSHIP AND FELLOWSHIP

INTRODUCTION

In discussing friendship and fellowship, we step outside the context of the family and address ourselves to those relationships with neighbors and fellow Christians around us. The Bible gives us much counsel concerning these associations and provides examples of outreach, charity, support, and love for us to follow.

He who loves purity of heart
And has grace on his lips,
The king will be his friend. (Prov 22:11)

Purity and grace are high standards of conduct, but they are the character of the King, Christ Jesus. As believers, we want to be known as the King's *friend*, a term given to Abraham **(2 Chron 20:7)**, Moses **(Ex 33:11)**, and the Disciples **(John 15:14).** The qualifications for His friendship are belief, faith and obedience; the benefits are eternal. In this association with Christ, we absorb His character, and in so doing we become by our actions what we are called to be in word: friend.

As born-again Christians, we are called to certain relationships with other Christians and also with unbelievers. Our burden, our responsibility for the fellow Christian is unique and separate from our dealings with the rest of the world. It is important to understand the distinction and to set our lives according to the directions given in Scripture. Keep in mind that all relationships flow out of our bond with Christ. We must be obedient friends to Him if we are to be powerful in our love and testimony to others.

BRETHREN AND NEIGHBORS: DIFFERENT OBLIGATIONS

Repeatedly in Scripture, Jesus teaches us the true meaning of friendship through His expression and example. Jesus came as an outreach from Heaven, offering friendship, fellowship, and salvation to anyone who would answer. But as we know, there became a sharp division between those who believed and those who did not. It is not unlike the split that is evident in our society today. We must discern who is a friend of the Lord versus who has yet to accept His truth.

Jesus spoke of this gulf that would be created by His presence. He knew that there would be no gray areas, no partial belief: **"Do not think that I came to bring peace on earth. I did not come to bring peace but a sword" (Matt 10:34).**

Throughout His ministry on earth, Jesus reached out to the sick, the sinful, the corrupt, and the self-righteous. Everyone exposed to Christ had the same opportunity to believe and to follow. As the Scripture states above, the rift between believers and unbelievers was dramatic and cutting, like a sword. Jesus grieved for the lost, but He sacrificed Himself on the cross for His friends:

> **"Greater love has no one than this, than to lay down one's life for his friends. You are My friends if you do whatever I command you. No longer do I call you servants, for a servant does not know what his master is doing; but I have called you friends, for all things that I heard from My Father I have made known to you. You did not choose Me, but I chose you and appointed you that you should go and bear fruit, and that your fruit should remain, that whatever you ask the Father in My name He may give you. These things I command you,**

that you love one another." (John 15:13-17)

As our Creator, Jesus knew full well who would follow and who would deny. He knew who would defend Him and who would persecute Him. And He knew who would see the kingdom of God and who would not. Yet He made sure that everyone who encountered Him had the opportunity to see, hear, and believe. Even beyond His death and resurrection, Jesus laid the groundwork for the future world to hear and choose between friendship and enmity.

By establishing His disciples to carry the gospel throughout the nations **(Matt 28:19)** and through the call of the Apostle Paul to minister to the Gentiles **(Rom 11:13),** Christ provided the continuing opportunity to join His fellowship. We as believers are a part of that call, and we share the obligation of reaching the lost through whatever means. But outreach and evangelism differ from fellowship and friendship. As we go forward, this distinction will be critical for charting our course in the relational world.

Our brothers and sisters in Christ are our first responsibility. We are called to unity, peace, and love within the body of Christ and we should strive to eliminate all division **(Ps 133:1)**. Our neighbors are those around us in the world who either don't know Christ as their personal Lord and Savior or who have rejected Him. We are not called to unity with the world, but instead must be separate and distinct in all we do. Yes, share the gospel. Yes, minister to the physical and spiritual needs of the lost. But we must be very cautious regarding "friendship" and attachment to individuals and situations that are not of God.

NOW FOR YOUR QUESTIONS...

I have been a Christian for about two years, but all my friends are unsaved. My pastor suggested that maybe I should make some relationships within the church with other believers, and that I should consider putting some "space" between myself and my "worldly" friends. Jesus loved everybody, and He associated with the dregs of society. Why can't I enjoy my friends? Maybe they will get saved if we continue to hang out.

Jesus does love us all, and He hungers for us to come to Him. And, as you say, Jesus came for the sinner (which means all of us), and He did reach out to the "untouchables" of His day. But, reaching out and hanging out are not the same. Jesus didn't dine with the tax collectors to have fun and enjoy godly fellowship. He was there with a single purpose: to call them into the kingdom of God:

> **Now it happened, as Jesus sat at the table in the house, that behold, many tax collectors and sinners came and sat down with Him and His disciples. And when the Pharisees saw it, they said to His disciples, "Why does your Teacher eat with tax collectors and sinners?" When Jesus heard that, He said to them, "Those who are well have no need of a physician, but those who are sick. But go and learn what this means: 'I desire mercy and not sacrifice.' For I did not come to call the righteous, but sinners, to repentance." (Matt 9:10-13)**

You must determine your true motives for continuing your association with unbelieving friends. Are you there out of concern for their souls, or because you wish to hold on to a piece of the world? Very often we try to live a divided life: standing on salvation while reaching back into the mire of our former lives.

For example, if you have been living a godly testimony for the past two years, then your unbelieving friends would by now most likely be saved or gone. The world does not like nor does it find peace in proximity to Christian living. Either they become convicted of their own sin and are drawn to Christ, or they resist and avoid the association. The fact that you are all still comfortable with each other probably means that nothing much has changed about your lifestyle that would either convict or repel your friends.

During Jesus' day, individuals were either compelled to believe in Him or provoked to hate Him. The Pharisees, clothed in the sin of their rituals and self-righteousness, could not bear association with the purity and truth of Christ. So hardened were their hearts that they demanded the Lord's life (**Luke 23:21**). Notice there was not a climate of "you do your thing and I'll do mine." The idea that such diverse positions can coexist peaceably is simply unfounded.

We encourage you to pray and seek God's revelation on this matter. Ask Him to strengthen your conviction to share the gospel lovingly but boldly with your unsaved friends. Seek His strength, and know that by establishing your obedient walk, you will lose some if not all of those around you. Petition the Father to bring another believer into your life as a partner and friend. We all need the fellowship of another brother or sister who is walking as an alien in this land. Remember the words of Jesus:

"If you were of the world, the world would love its own. Yet because you are not of the world, but I chose you out of the world, therefore the world hates you." (John 15:19)

My wife nags me about my buddies, and I don't get it. I am a good Christian man, saved at 20. I go to church, serve on committees, and read my Bible. But sometimes I need a break from the "church stuff." Everybody needs a night to blow off steam, have a few beers, and catch a game. I don't think I am going to hell because I have some fun once a week with the guys!

If you are born-again, as you say, then hell is not in your future. But we encourage you to examine your willful determination to break the boundaries of a Christian lifestyle on the grounds that you deserve some fun **(Heb 10:26-31)**. By your report, your joy and fulfillment are not found in the things of God. Instead you describe your Christian life as duty and obligation only. You seem to be marking off squares of Christian activity, saving them up like trading stamps, and cashing them in for some worldly excitement.

Christian life is in part duty and obligation. We owe more to the Savior than we can ever repay. In that debt there is a call for activity that serves the Kingdom. But we are also called to share in the joy of the Lord and to have His peace over our lives. Very often, Christians view obedience as restriction rather than liberty. As a result, we can view ourselves as bridled or restrained, forbidden the customary "pleasures" of the world.

The Bible tells us that this is an incorrect perception. Jesus taught that our joy is made full in obedience:

"If you keep My commandments, you will abide in My love, just as I have kept My Father's commandments and abide in His love. These things I have spoken to you, that My joy may remain in you, and that your joy may be full." (John 15:10-11)

Your issue may have something to do with your heart. When our hearts are open and tender **(2 Kgs 22:19)**, then the presence of God and the abiding love of Christ is our fulfillment. We must be consistent in our submission if we are to be blessed by His hand.

As for your activities with your "buddies," you be the judge. Do these activities honor and advance your relationship with Christ? Do your activities influence others positively (toward Christ) or negatively (away from Christ)? Are your activities under your control, or are you under the control of the activity? The Apostle Paul wrote:

All things are lawful for me, but all things are not helpful. All things are lawful for me, but I will not be brought under the power of any. (1 Cor 6:12)

By your report, your choices at the very least: expose you to questionable conduct; divide you from your Christian walk; and create conflict in your marriage. Challenge yourself to examine the authority in your life. The only power we should come under is the power of Jesus moving, filling, convicting, and directing us.

As a Christian family, what is the best way to reach out and associate with unchurched families around us? We are careful about not joining in activities that threaten our Christian walk, but want to be a lighthouse for our neighborhood. Any suggestions?

Our responsibility to the non-Christian is significant. We are to be the "light and salt," acquainting others with the reality of Christ

(Matt 5:14, Col 4:5-6). You are wise however to avoid activities that would compromise your testimony. We understand that while no Christian will be perfect, we must truly strive to set ourselves apart for the work we've been given **(2 Cor 6:17)**. This doesn't mean adopting a superior attitude, but it does mean that we cannot expose ourselves or our children to the patterns of the world.

As part of our ministry, we have focused on "area evangelism," centralizing our prayer and activity to a specific city, neighborhood, or street. An excellent resource for consideration is *That None Should Perish* by Pastor Ed Silvoso.[5] In working with other families, we have found it very effective, leading to a form of "relational evangelism" as our efforts connect us to specific individuals and families in the process. Jesus set the pattern for this activity when He sent out the seventy, two-by-two:

> **"But whatever house you enter, first say, 'Peace to this house.' And if a son of peace is there, your peace will rest on it; if not, it will return to you. And remain in the same house, eating and drinking such things as they give, for the laborer is worthy of his wages. Do not go from house to house. Whatever city you enter, and they receive you, eat such things as are set before you. And heal the sick there, and say to them, 'The kingdom of God has come near to you.'" (Luke 10:5-9)**

Listen to Jesus' instruction: "first say, 'Peace to this house.'" This means that we are to seek the Father's blessing and guidance regarding which house to enter. All evangelism must be bathed in prayer and preparation. Praying for the home or homes in question allows the Holy Spirit to pave our way and to ready the hearts of the individuals to receive the gospel. But also notice that Jesus tells the disciples that everyone will not receive the peace and blessing of the Lord. When they reject it, let that peace return to you and seek God's direction for proceeding.

Next, Jesus encourages relationship with the unbeliever: "And remain in the same house, eating and drinking such things as they give." In other words, spend time, share a meal, and get to know the people. This Scripture does not mean we should attend a keg party, "eating and drinking such things as they give" for the sake of the gospel! You do not lead someone to Christ by joining in activities that defile your testimony in any way. Instead, have dinner with them, invite them to a barbeque with other Christian friends, etc. Unbelievers shouldn't be criticized or "put down" for the nature of their activities, but they should see a marked difference in our lifestyle. When someone is in quicksand, you extend a branch and pull them out, you don't dive in after them!

Jesus then tells us to "heal the sick." This means we sometimes address physical needs along with, or ahead of, spiritual needs. For example, as you build some association with a family, you may come to learn of marital problems, health issues, or financial struggles. An important part of our outreach then becomes care and support of these needs, as much as possible. Remember though, that your ultimate goal is their salvation.

When you know a family or individual needs healing, pray for them regularly, asking God to provide an answer to their dilemma. Offer to pray with the family and let them know you are making intercession to God on their behalf. Even families who don't pray or don't believe in prayer are sometimes comforted by our efforts to intervene. As we pray with them, and as God answers our petition, the unsaved person may feel His presence strongly for the first time. This prayerful Christian effort can be key to creating an environment where the gospel can be received.

Finally, Jesus teaches us to announce, "The kingdom of God has come near to you." Notice the order of "relational evangelism:" prayer and preparation; seeking God's peace on a home; association and fellowship; building connections; meeting physical needs through intercessory prayer and direct support when possible; and finally, sharing the gospel of Christ.

This process was powerful in biblical times and it is powerful today. As we have established throughout this book, humans are relational by design of the Master. When we approach the unbeliever from that perspective, we give him/her evidence of God's work in our lives and the love of Christ that is available to all. There is nothing wrong with making "cold contacts" and door-to-door evangelism. But in relationships a bridge is built that allows others to see Christ in our hearts and in our actions.

But do remember that we are not called to stay "forever" when the truth of Christ is rejected. Jesus told His witnesses:

"But whatever city you enter, and they do not receive you, go out into its streets and say, 'The very dust of your city which clings to us we wipe off against you. Nevertheless know this, that the kingdom of God has come near you.' " (Luke 10:10-11)

Our duty is the delivery of prayer, the offer of intercession, and the conveyance of the truth. If that truth is rejected, we are not bound to a deep, ongoing relationship. Jesus tells us basically to "move on." Be careful not to become entangled in their lifestyle beyond their rejection of the gospel. You may not be the one who sees the full fruit of your witness. You have planted a seed; God will bring the increase **(1 Cor 3:6).**

Finally, we are compelled to offer some advice that should be fairly obvious, but often becomes a real problem under the banner of evangelism. When reaching out to the unsaved, make sure your efforts are male to male, female to female, or couple to couple. It is unwise and ultimately inappropriate for any Christian to build a relationship across gender lines for evangelism. The potential for boundary breaches and distorted objectives is too great.

Certainly, there will be times when the man of the house meets a female neighbor at the grocery store, or the woman of the house is introduced to a male neighbor at a soccer game. These beginnings are fine but must not become exclusive of spouses. Instead, when you see a potential for evangelism, link the person of the opposite sex to your spouse as quickly as possible. Statements like: "You need to meet my husband" or; "I suspect you have a lot in common with my wife," create clear positions right from the start.

Since your evangelical efforts will be to reach out to people who don't know Christ, it is likely that their lives may be in turmoil. Marital and other problems are not uncommon. The potential for "wrong" interpretations of our interest and care is too great. Make certain everything is clear, appropriate, and honest from the beginning.

This goes for unmarried individuals too. Efforts of outreach across gender lines are often misread as "romantic interest." When doing God's work, it is crucial that we tend only to the task of saving a soul, not making a date. Have Christian friends of the opposite sex whom you can use as a resource for the unchurched singles you encounter.

FRIENDSHIPS WITH CHRISTIANS

As with all topics, the Bible gives us plenty of direction for being a friend. Our deepest and most urgent responsibility is to the Church, our fellow believers. Again, this does not negate our love for the unsaved nor does it ignore the reality that we may have dear relations and family that are lost. But unity can only be found with those of like minds.

Personally, we believe the time is coming when Christians will be forced to draw strength from one another to a greater degree, as the division between God's children and the world becomes more pronounced. Jesus told us that this division would invade even our homes and families:

"For I have come to 'set a man against his father, a daughter against her mother, and a daughter-in-law against her mother-in-law'; and 'a man's enemies will be those of his own household.'" (Matt 10:35-36)

If we examine the church in places like Korea, China, and parts of Africa, this statement of Christ is already fulfilled. In settings like these where the church is largely underground and deeply persecuted, individuals commonly will turn over family members to authorities for the practice of the Christian faith and evangelism.

Christians in this country will face increased pressure from those who seek to quiet biblical truth and who long to make our country exclusively secular. Our Christian relations will be critical if we are to hold firm to the truth that we have been given.

**A friend loves at all times,
And a brother is born for adversity. (Prov 17:17)**

Accordingly, Christian fellowship must be a central element of our support and perseverance. But fellowship with Christians is also a tremendous source of joy and satisfaction. The bond that is found in the love of the Lord is superior to any other. Paul spoke of this to the Roman believers:

Let love be without hypocrisy. Abhor what is evil. Cling to what is good. Be kindly affectionate to one another with brotherly love, in honor giving preference to one another; not lagging in diligence, fervent in spirit, serving the Lord; rejoicing in hope, patient in tribulation, continuing steadfastly in prayer; distributing to the needs of the saints, given to hospitality. Bless those who persecute you; bless and do not curse. Rejoice with those who rejoice, and weep with those who weep. Be of the same mind toward one another. Do not set your mind on high things, but associate with the humble. Do not be wise in your own opinion. Repay no one evil for evil. Have regard for good things in the sight of all men. If it is possible, as much as depends on you, live peaceably with all men. (Rom 12:9-18)

NOW FOR YOUR QUESTIONS...

What are the key features of Christian friendship?

Christian relationship, by design, must begin with ***unconditional love***. Jesus was clear about how His followers would be recognized:

"A new commandment I give to you, that you love one another; as I have loved you, that you also love one another. By this all will know that you are My disciples, if you have love for one another." (John 13:34-35)

As our example, Jesus displayed love in all He did. It did not matter what pressure He was under, what persecution He received, or what conflict He confronted; Jesus demonstrated consistent, unconditional love. Notice however that unconditional love does not mean unconditional acceptance. Jesus did not accept or condone everything His followers did. He certainly did not endorse the actions of His persecutors. But even as He spoke truth, confronted lies, and chastised sin, Jesus conveyed a supernatural love for all who would receive it.

Within our Christian relationships we must remember that we are heirs together of the grace of life; we are brothers and sisters. As such, we carry the same responsibility for loving, serving, and sacrificing ourselves for one another. Like Jesus, we must be "action oriented" in our expression of affection for our fellow Christian brothers and sisters. Jesus didn't simply profess His love; He reached out behaviorally to demonstrate the depth of His feelings for others.

Regrettably, Christian relationships can sometimes be long on talk and short on action. There is a tendency to express connection superficially without truly developing a deeper involvement in each other's lives. While we cannot create this level of intimacy with all Christians, it is important to cultivate two or three associations that have the potential for true depth, transparency, and trust. Even Jesus chose only twelve disciples, and only three of those (James, John, and Peter) became His most intimate friends. In these close friendships we have the opportunity to reduce our defense, to demonstrate our vulnerability, and to serve one another biblically.

Other important features of Christian friendship include **support and encouragement**. Living amongst the unsaved can make us feel isolated and out of place. In our human state, isolation can create feelings of despair and vulnerability. Because we are relational, we can be drawn toward ungodly associations simply out of loneliness and fear.

Christian fellowship helps us to feel bonded and sustained. Through the sharing of God's Spirit, we are connected in a way that is unlike any other relationship on earth. This affiliation helps us to remain mindful of God's order and plan for our lives, while pushing us forward toward the goal He has established.

In the Old Testament, Moses was denied entrance to the Promised Land, but was told to "encourage and strengthen" his successor Joshua, as he would take on the challenges of claiming God's territories.

But command Joshua, and encourage him and strengthen him; for he shall go over before this people, and he shall cause them to inherit the land which you will see. (Deut 3:28)

In the New Testament, Jesus sent out His disciples in pairs, knowing that He was sending them out in the midst of a resistant and hostile land.

After these things the Lord appointed seventy others also, and sent them two by two before His face into every city and place where He Himself was about to go. Then He said to them, "The harvest truly is great, but the laborers are few; therefore pray the Lord of the harvest to send out laborers into His harvest. Go your way; behold, I send you out as lambs among wolves." (Luke 10:1-3)

The writer of Hebrews warns of the deceitfulness of sin that must be combated with daily exhortation:

Beware, brethren, lest there be in any of you an evil heart of unbelief in departing from the living God; but exhort one another daily, while it is called "Today," lest any of you be hardened through the deceitfulness of sin. (Heb 3:12-13)

As Christians we must remain aware of Satan's intent to shake our faith and weaken our belief. Regular contact and support from a fellow believer brings the promises of God's truth to remembrance while providing a source of edification and perseverance.

After support and encouragement, the feature of ***accountability*** is central to Christian friendship. A true Christian friend is willing to speak the truth to his brother or sister in Christ, and the truth is measured against God's standard, not the standards of the world. Often, worldly relations are lacking in accountability because of the absence of moral absolutes. The world provides great latitude for sinful conduct. As believers, we must be strong enough in our love for one another that repetitive sin finds no comfort.

King David enjoyed a close and intimate relationship with God's prophet, Nathan. Nathan had been an advisor and encourager for the king throughout years of leadership. Yet when David committed the sins of adultery and murder, Nathan, under God's leading, confronted his friend as soundly and firmly as possible:

> **Then Nathan said to David, "You are the man! Thus says the Lord God of Israel: 'I anointed you king over Israel, and I delivered you from the hand of Saul. I gave you your master's house and your master's wives into your keeping, and gave you the house of Israel and Judah. And if that had been too little, I also would have given you much more! Why have you despised the commandment of the Lord, to do evil in His sight? You have killed Uriah the Hittite with the sword; you have taken his wife to be your wife, and have killed him with the sword of the people of Ammon.'" (2 Sam 12:7-9)**

Granted, we do not speak directly for God as His prophet Nathan did, but as Christians we do have God's Word as our guide for righteous living. It is important that we address departures from that code whenever we see a brother or sister in sin. To avoid the need for correction is to avoid a God-given responsibility.

The key essentials in Christian friendship are: unconditional love, support, encouragement, and accountability. Remember, these factors must be active rather than passive. We must show our love, express our support, and show up for the confrontations. In love we rejoice in success, exhort in defeat, and go to battle when rebellion strikes. Like Christ we are called to go beyond what is expected for our friends. Jesus said: **"And whoever compels you to go one mile, go with him two" (Matt 5:41).**

CASE EXAMPLE

I (Dr. Ab) met Bruce Edwards several years ago when he led a men's retreat at our church. He is an evangelist and pastor from Mansfield, Texas. We are both "big" guys (not fat, just big boned!), enthusiastic about the Lord and committed to service. But Bruce was the mature, seminary-trained, worldwide evangelist who for years had laid it all on the line for Christ. I loved him instantly as my brother and my mentor. For some reason, he attached himself to me as well.

Since that time our wives and children have bonded and we have become very much like family to each other. Bruce is on the board of our ministry and has been here several times to preach and teach for our organization. He and his wife Cindy have invited Karen and me to their church in Texas to lead marriage retreats and teach.

Bruce is my greatest "real life" example of unconditional love. He calls me, emails me, and sends me letters. When we're together we're like two overgrown adolescents, pushing, shoving, joking and laughing. He is my counsel, listening to me for hours over the years as I ramble in my ignorance about spiritual issues. He endures my complaints and whining with love and patience. Many have been the times Bruce has listened to my petty struggles when he has just returned from the Philippines or Cambodia where he slept in an unairconditioned hut with no running water, ate only rice, and preached the gospel eight to twelve times a day in the public school system.

As much as I respect and admire Bruce, as much as he is my teacher, I will never match his capacity for encouragement and support. Each time I leave him, he puts his arm around me and tells me, "You're my hero, man." Me? I'm Bruce's hero? I know so little, and he knows so much. I do so little, and he does it all. Yet he never elevates himself; never discounts my meager efforts; but instead encourages me to grow and serve and honor my Lord.

Believe me when I tell you, I am not a hero in the Christian faith. But when I've been in Bruce's company, I feel I could be. I feel hopeful, determined, and committed to go to the next level. Bruce always leaves me feeling that I've gotten one step closer to who I am becoming in Christ.

But Bruce is more than laughter and encouraging words. He can be deadly serious, direct, and firm. He knows and loves God's Word, and he addresses everything we are as friends within that context. As casual and open as we can be together, Bruce never forgets his responsibility as the "senior" member of our team to train and instruct me in the truth.

Bruce has a way of cutting to the core of an issue. Once when I was grappling with two choices and my fear of making a wrong selection, Bruce knew the issue really was one of commitment. He knew I was holding back and ultimately was not giving myself totally to God's service. I still wanted it both ways. Spoken with the love that only a brother can give, he said: "Before I get off the phone, I want to give you a Scripture to look up. Read it and pray about it and see what God will have you to do." He gave me a verse from the Old Testament and we said good-bye.

I was eager to look up the scripture, expecting a verse of encouragement that would make me feel better. But my old buddy, in love, had thrown me a curve ball of accountability. The verse read:

He did right in the sight of the LORD, yet not with a whole heart. (2 Chron 25:2 NASB)

Ouch! My brother saw through me and called me to task. Bruce, through Scripture, challenged me to get in God's will "all the way." I wasn't sure I liked this part of Christian friendship! My friend knew that encouragement must eventually lead to decision, and he loved me enough to bust me right in the chops.

Bruce doesn't shake me often, but when he does it is meaningful. His capacity to confront me is grounded in his love for me. I can receive the confrontation (usually) because I know he cares for me without obligation. He doesn't hold me accountable in anger; he doesn't challenge me out of superiority. He intervenes because he loves me and because he loves Christ. He wants me to be all that I can be for the kingdom of God. That is Christian friendship.

One of my best friends from church is now having an affair and has separated from his wife and kids. He wants things to go on as "usual" between us and expects me to understand this extramarital romance and his planned divorce. I don't want to abandon him, but I cannot endorse his behavior. How do I help him?

Let's apply the features of Christian friendship described in the previous section. First, to love your friend unconditionally does not mean to accept his behavior without condition. You are correct that you cannot endorse his choices, but neither can you remain in fellowship with him if he refuses to repent and reverse field.

Support and encouragement are still appropriate activities, however. Sometimes when we have fallen, we can become trapped in sin out of guilt, shame, and fear. By verbalizing your love for him, you can offer the encouragement he needs in order to recover. Satan is telling your friend all kinds of lies right now, including the lie that "all is lost." Well, if all is lost, why turn around? Assure your friend that there is a method of recovery and that you will help him get there. But as long as he remains involved with the other woman, there is no amount of love or encouragement that will save him from his own destruction. If he is determined to stay on that path, he will have to deal with God's discipline alone.

As Christians, we bear a responsibility for our brothers and sisters. Scripture tells us that we have the duty to restore one who is fallen, in as much as it is possible to do so.

> **Brethren, if a man is overtaken in any trespass, you who are spiritual restore such a one in a spirit of gentleness, considering yourself lest you also be tempted. Bear one another's burdens, and so fulfill the law of Christ. (Gal 6:1-2)**

Paul instructs the reader: "consider yourself lest you also be tempted." We are to know that we have no spiritual superiority, only spiritual duty. Every one of us is vulnerable to temptation, and we must respond to our brethren with full knowledge of our humanness. Thus, with a gentle spirit, you are to pursue the correction and recovery of your friend. But the Bible also tell us that should a brother refuse to turn from his sin, we are to adopt a different pattern:

> **But as for you, brethren, do not grow weary in doing good. And if anyone does not obey our word in this epistle, note that person and do not keep company with him, that he may be ashamed. Yet do not count him as an enemy, but admonish him as a brother. (2 Thess 3:13-15)**

We as Christians are to withdraw our company from believers if they refuse to cease sinful activity. When in sin, the heart is hardened. Paul tells us here that our withdrawal may provoke the person to feel ashamed. Our admonishment will help cut through the hardness so that they will respond with godly remorse that renders change.

Paul further tells us in Scripture that it is our obligation to judge the behaviors of our fellow Christians and to break association when necessary. Unbelievers will be judged by God:

> **But now I have written to you not to keep company with anyone named a brother, who is sexually immoral, or covetous, or an idolater, or a reviler, or a drunkard, or an extortioner—not even to eat with such a person. For what have I to do with judging those also who are outside? Do you not judge those who are inside? But those who are outside God judges. Therefore "put away from yourselves the evil person." (1 Cor 5:11-13)**

Love always, but do not always endorse. Encourage and support movement away from sin, but withdraw from its willful continuance. Isolate the sinner so that he might become ashamed and awaken his deadened heart. In the end, we are to judge the conduct of our brethren and break association ("not even eat with such a person") if they refuse to be restored. If and when he returns to his senses, receive him and return your affection and care to his life. This is "tough love" God's way.

CHURCH RELATIONSHIPS

While the Body of Christ is spiritual and not restricted to a physical church congregation, the local church is our single greatest source of Christian relations. Churches come with their own culture, cliques, and hierarchy. Some organizations are true to biblical structure, while others are riddled with the organizational elements of human design. Generally speaking, church bodies, like other collections of human beings, are imperfect and challenged.

Relationships within a church system run the full gamut from close personal friendships to pastor/layperson relations and everything in between. In a church you may be both a student and teacher, senior and junior in spiritual maturity. But whatever the size of your church, whatever your role, the biblical guidelines are the same. The primary element stressed throughout the New Testament is the call for unity. Paul wrote to the church at Corinth:

Now I plead with you, brethren, by the name of our Lord Jesus Christ, that you all speak the same thing, and that there be no divisions among you, but that you be perfectly joined together in the same mind and in the same judgment. (1 Cor 1:10)

This instruction is amazingly difficult: no divisions, perfectly joined, with the same mind and judgment. In fact, within the human capacity, it is impossible. Only when a church is filled and directed by the Holy Spirit can this type of unity exist. When human agendas reign, there is little common purpose. Where God's order provides the authority for the church, then there is an established set of absolutes. A singular set of guidelines produces clarity that, when followed, should eliminate debate.

As a member of a local congregation, your role is to follow this order of authority. In God's order, He has given certain organizational and spiritual authority to pastors, teachers, administrators, deacons, and elders. As a church member you have a hand in the selection of many of these leaders by voting or by serving on committees. But once the leadership is established, you must strive to honor and serve as God leads through them.

The leadership (the elders) of a church is called to serve and shepherd the flock while being examples to all. The leadership is encouraged to guide the church with a willing spirit of eagerness and accountability. The younger (spiritually) members of the church are called to humility and growth. Their humble submission will honor God, and they will be advanced (exalted) in due time. Peter, the leader of the early church wrote:

The elders who are among you I exhort, I who am a fellow elder and a witness of the sufferings of Christ, and also a partaker of the glory that will be revealed: Shepherd the flock of God which is among you, serving as overseers, not by compulsion but willingly, not for dishonest gain but eagerly; nor as being lords over those entrusted to you, but being examples to the flock; and when the Chief Shepherd appears, you will receive the crown of glory that does not fade away. Likewise you younger people, submit yourselves to your elders. Yes, all of you be submissive to one another, and be clothed with humility, for "God resists the proud, but gives grace to the humble." Therefore humble yourselves under the mighty hand of God, that He may exalt you in due time. (1 Pet 5:1-6)

Certainly the Bible contains much more regarding the order, purpose, and roles within a church body. But as a beginning, the fulfillment of unity, leadership, service, shepherding, humility and grace will serve us well. Leadership that serves and a membership that submits is a great start within God's order.

NOW FOR YOUR QUESTIONS...

My pastor seems like a nice man, but he isn't very accessible. Our church only has about 300 members, yet I find it hard to build a relationship with him. Shouldn't he make time to know me on a personal level?

Indeed our pastors are very important figures in our lives. Most of us long for some personal connection with our spiritual teacher and mentor. But do keep in mind that 300 members is not a small number. By the time a church reaches this size, it generally requires other staff members and lay leaders who share in the responsibilities of ministry. Research tells us that a pastor can personally minister to a congregation of about 100. Beyond that number, layers of staffing and delegation of duties becomes a priority if people are to be served correctly.

Within the biblical structure, the pastor best correlates with the position of teacher. Jesus is called "Teacher" throughout the Gospels by his disciples and others. The Greek word for teacher, *didaskalos,* refers to one who teaches concerning the things of God and the duties of man. To bear this title is an awesome responsibility for the pastor, as he must study and pray, seeking the discernment of the Holy Spirit so that God's Word is advanced as He intended.

To judge your pastor on the basis of his accessibility may be unfair. His first and primary role is to teach "the things of God and the duties of man." In that role, you need him to be focused, studious, prayerful, and correct. His second responsibility is spiritual leadership for the church staff and members. That does not necessarily mean having a personal relationship with all 300 in the pews. Instead, he must create methods of service and ministry that he oversees.

Often this means having an associate or administrative pastor who is responsible for certain aspects of personal ministry, outreach, education and/or organizational management. Sometimes there are ministers to students, youth, and/or families who counsel and train segments of the church. Deacons and elders, Sunday school teachers, and other lay leaders also carry responsibilities for relationships and ministry within the church. As the leader, your pastor cannot do it all. Rather, he has the task of orchestrating the unity, purpose, and direction of the ministry. This simply can't be done on a one-to-one basis.

Recognize that your pastor probably already works more than 50 hours a week (this is the norm). When he is with church members, he is always the pastor. He can't just be John or Bob…He is Brother John or Pastor Bob. Imagine, after working a 50-hour week, if you had to plan all your "free" time with your boss or subordinates from work, so that over dinner or bowling you had to be Plumber Jim or Accountant Sam.

Living in the fish bowl of the pastorate is difficult for the preacher and for his family. It is not an easy call to answer. We recommend that you consider how you can bless your pastor through some form of service that honors him without requiring his time. Send him a letter of encouragement and let him know you are praying for his family. Buy some tickets to a play or ballgame for him and his family (no one else). Offer to serve in an area of need at the church. This may mean taking on a task nobody wants. Imagine the burden you might remove from his shoulders.

Far too often, we consider our church a place where we go to receive what we need. We go for teaching, fellowship, youth programs, etc. But the purest and most rewarding part of church involvement is service. Consider serving the servant: your teacher. We know you would both benefit.

I am a deacon in a Baptist church with about 250 members. We have a recurrent problem with one of our associate pastors who fails to keep good boundaries with female church members. He is single, but has dated socially within the church, creating significant conflict. It has now been reported that he is "sexually involved" with a college-aged woman in the congregation. We have addressed this as a deacon board and with the senior pastor. No one has been willing to confront the young man and address the problem. To me it is a moral failing that must not be brushed away. Am I right?

If one of your pastors is sexually active outside of marriage, then you most certainly are right. You have a moral and spiritual obligation to see that this issue is addressed, for the good of the church and for this young man. Chances are that biblical intervention may restore this minister and preserve the integrity of the church. It may also protect this young woman from further harm.

Ignoring the problem ignores scriptural responsibility.

The best way to confront the passivity of a deacon board and pastor is with God's Word. But before you press them, challenge yourself to the rigors of Scripture:

Do not receive an accusation against an elder except from two or three witnesses. (1 Tim 5:19)

As a staff member, the associate pastor is an elder (leader) of the church. Be very certain that you are acting with correct, substantiated information. It would be tragic indeed to affect or end a servant's career based on rumor that is false. Once you have established the viability of the claim against him, God has provided a structure for confrontation and restoration. Jesus said:

"Moreover if your brother sins against you, go and tell him his fault between you and him alone. If he hears you, you have gained your brother. But if he will not hear, take with you one or two more, that 'by the mouth of two or three witnesses every word may be established.' And if he refuses to hear them, tell it to the church. But if he refuses even to hear the church, let him be to you like a heathen and a tax collector." (Matt 18:15-17)

Once you have established a credible report against this church leader, then perhaps you should begin as Jesus advised: "...go and tell him his fault between you and him alone." If the deacon body and the pastor have not confronted the issue, the brother might respect you and be open to a private consideration of the matter. He needs to hear that you are coming to him in love, but with a serious report and concern about his conduct. Allow him an opportunity to confess and repent. Perhaps he will then submit to a process of restoration on his own.

But should he resist and refuse to hear the credibility of your concern, go to him again with "one or two more." This is not to create embarrassment, but rather reality. Often it is difficult to reject the testimony and concern of two or three friends. Again, there is the opportunity for a change in direction, appropriate submission to church discipline, and the prospect for restoration. If he again rejects your effort, you have the witness of others to support your position to the church leadership.

At that point, you should again take the issue before the board and pastor, along with your witnesses. Share the biblical process you have initiated and the result. With the validation of your witnesses, require the church leadership to take the next step and take the issue before the church. Most likely the board and pastor will accept the scriptural process you have followed and agree to the next effort of reclaiming this young man. If the minister is unwilling to accept the call of the church for repentance, then, as Jesus tells us, it is time to end the association with him. At this point he is handed over to the discipline of God, as the church has completed its responsibility.

Ultimately, even the young pastor's final release from service is done lovingly. Without discipline and consequence, he will not recover. Hopefully, your love and concern for him will help him to turn from his sin early. It is a blessed thing when a brother is retained. But if you begin this process, you must be willing to complete it. God's order and plan is perfect, but our execution of His directives must be absolute.

CASE EXAMPLE

There was a rumor going around church that Arnie, one of the Sunday school teachers, had a gambling problem. If so, the issue was not obvious. He was a respected professional in the community and seemed to have a good family life. He had served the church faithfully for years. Still, no one in church leadership was really very close to Arnie; not much was known beyond what was visible of his actions within the church setting.

When the rumor reached Sam, one of the church elders, he confronted the one spreading the gossip. Through that person he learned that Arnie's daughter had spoken of the problem within the youth group and had asked for prayer. Sam admonished the gossip-monger for spreading potentially hurtful information throughout the church and cautioned him to subdue his tongue. He then went to the pastor and the youth minister and found that indeed, there had been concern offered by the family and others in the church. Arnie was reportedly in significant debt and was missing work to gamble in Gulfport, MS, about two hours away.

Sam asked his pastor's permission to deal with Arnie biblically and was given latitude to do so. Sam met with Arnie privately and expressed his concern, telling him what others had observed. Arnie minimized the issue and said it had been "greatly overblown." He acknowledged that he had been to the casinos "a few times," but had repented and stopped going long ago. He denied having an ongoing problem, debt problems, or family conflicts related to the gambling. Sam prayed with Arnie and asked permission to give a report to the pastor, which he did. Arnie was left in leadership for the time being.

Rumors persisted, however. Eventually, Arnie left his law firm stating, "I needed a change." It later turned out he had been released from his employment there. One Tuesday, Sam went by Arnie's house to see him and found he was not home. His wife confessed that she was afraid Arnie was at a specific casino he frequented. She was terrified of the unpaid bills piling up, including the mortgage payment. She said Arnie had been going to gamble every day since losing his job.

Sam left the house and drove directly to the casino, two hours away. He found Arnie sitting at a gambling table. Quietly, Sam walked up behind Arnie and put his arm on his shoulder. Sam said: "I am here for you, my brother. I think we need to talk." Arnie seemed to melt right there on the spot, the tension overwhelming him. Arnie and Sam left the casino and found a place to talk. Arnie broke down and confessed the whole saga of his fall into gambling, the devastation it had wrought, along with the depth of the financial threat. Arnie was contemplating committing suicide. Sam told him he would stay with him, and that God would see him through. They prayed, then drove home together.

Sam helped Arnie meet with his wife and children, and he helped them formulate some short-term plans for survival. Again he asked for permission to inform the pastor only, and the pastor became involved as well. There was no need to involve the rest of the church. Arnie agreed to step down from teaching and to get emotional and spiritual help for restoration.

Sam helped Arnie find a Christian therapist and accompanied him to the first session. With the advice of the therapist, Sam helped Arnie find a support group for gambling problems and again, attended the first meeting with him. Arnie met weekly with the pastor and Sam for prayer and support and agreed to use them as points of accountability.

It took some time, but Arnie has reclaimed his life, started a new law practice, revived his family, and renewed his spiritual walk. He struggles with impulses to return to his addiction, but he surrounds himself with prayer, study, and godly counsel. Arnie is being restored because a brother saw not only a failing, but a need. Sam walked Arnie through God's structure for recovery, and as usual, the structure God gave was all that was needed.

A man who has friends must himself be friendly, but there is a friend who sticks closer than a brother. (Prov 18:24)

I have grown increasingly unhappy with my church. I've been a member there for five years, but I don't like the direction the church is taking. They seem to be too focused on raising funds and building buildings. The pastor's sermons are too long. The church is filled with hypocrites. How do you know when it's time to leave?

As a member for five years, you have a responsibility to participate in the direction and vision of your church. Too often church members believe they are "helpless" responders in the church organization, staying quiet, growing angry, and then leaving because they feel powerless to make a change.

Your anger with the church and its leadership is obvious. Are you really so angry because of the building plans or the length of a sermon? We encourage you to evaluate your own heart, the status of your spiritual life, before making a rash decision about your church.

Very often our own personal situation blinds or distorts our perception of the church. Jesus taught:

"And why do you look at the speck in your brother's eye, but do not consider the plank in your own eye? Or how can you say to your brother, 'Let me remove the speck from your eye'; and look, a plank is in your own eye? Hypocrite! First remove the plank from your own eye, and then you will see clearly to remove the speck from your brother's eye." (Matt 7:3-5)

Please do not misunderstand: we are not suggesting that you are a "hypocrite." But as Jesus instructed, our first inspection for spiritual order must be internal, not external. Whenever we're overcome with intense feelings that are negative and judgmental, we should evaluate our own heart, motives, and behavior first. In doing so, it is important to spend time in prayer, seek godly counsel, and engulf yourself in Scripture.

Remember what you are asking God for: you are asking for self-revelation and discernment. Be careful not to seek out counsel that is in agreement with you about all the things that are wrong in your church. Don't search purposely for Scripture that exposes the sins of your brethren. Instead, search for answers with a humble spirit, asking God to reveal your sin, your error.

It is true that churches can lose their proper course, and it's equally true that you should be able to judge and discern church activities that are biblically incorrect. But you must do so with a pure, open heart, not one that is filled with misdirected anger that may distort what you see.

We should choose our church because its doctrine is biblically sound; its preaching and teaching are scriptural; and its organization and accountability is in keeping with proper New Testament church order. In short, its belief system, teaching, and management are consistent with God's Word. So far there is no evidence that the church is violating biblical order.

Raising funds and building programs are consistent with church authority as described in the Bible. It is scriptural to support the church financially and to have proper facilities to advance the work of the church. However, if you believe the church has a moral issue with money and has misused or misrepresented the funds thereto entrusted, that is another matter.

In the case of mismanagement or misrepresentation, you are responsible for intervention. It is not your province to simply walk away mad. As a member, you have a voice, a vote, and an obligation to confront wrongdoing. Our hunch is that you have not expressed your views to the pastor or leadership and have remained silent regarding such matters.

If there is sinful management of money, you must speak honestly and directly to them about this issue. But if there is no sin, simply disagreement of opinion, the issue changes. As long as the church expenditures and building program are honest and do not violate biblical standards, your obligation and authority end with an opinion and a vote.

As for the long sermons and hypocritical membership, we think you should simply challenge your heart and evaluate your anger. In fact, if the church is filled with hypocrites, longer sermons might be needed!

In the end, this is your church family. Do you leave your physical family over a disagreement or disappointment? Do you leave them over the issue of sin without trying to restore them and help them? Probably not. It should be no different in the church.

However, if you do leave the church, for whatever reason, do so peaceably and respectfully. Express you concerns, vote your heart, state your convictions. If there is sin, confront it through the proper channels. But when your efforts have reached a natural end, leave without incident and do not create strife or division in the membership. Let the congregation make their own judgment about these matters. If the leadership is in sin, God will address Himself there. Do not be a purveyor of evil.

SUMMARY

Relationship outside the family is an important and viable part of life. Friendship and fellowship are essential to the Christian life, giving us opportunity for affection, support, encouragement, and accountability. With our brothers and sisters we find the bond of the Holy Spirit, and we gain a Kingdom perspective which protects and shields us from the ungodly elements of the world.

Relationship with the unbeliever allows us to fulfill our biblical obligation to spread the Gospel. Relational outreach, intercessory prayer, and evangelism should be at the core of every Christian's service. We should take a godly pride in activities that honor God through the building of His kingdom. We must not ignore the responsibility and the blessing that come through this important relational quest.

As part of the body of Christ, we also have a duty to serve in a local church congregation, using our talents and gifts as God calls. Working and relating within such an organization can be challenging. Yet we must seek to honor God through our service. Look for opportunities to contribute to the local church, support its leadership, and edify its teachers and pastors. Let God's hierarchical structure be your guide for peaceful church existence.

CHAPTER 10

UNHOLY ALLIANCES

INTRODUCTION

The United States of America has been recognized historically by its adherence to Judeo-Christian values and biblical order. The centrality of the marital home, the procreation of children, and the integrity of the family unit were the standard norms when our nation was founded.

We structure our work and career, church involvement, fellowship, and recreation around the family as the central pillar of importance. To state it differently, we work for the preservation of our home; our church is the unifying focus of the week, bringing our families together in worship; fellowship and recreation is primarily shared with the family unit. In short, most of our life begins and ends with the home, just as God ordained in the beginning.

While it has been stated elsewhere in this book, God's instruction to the family (marital unit) is a crucial grounding point that bears repeating. In Genesis 1 we note God's order as He blesses and instructs the first husband and wife:

Then God blessed them, and God said to them, "Be fruitful and multiply; fill the earth and subdue it; have dominion over the fish of the sea, over the birds of the

**air, and over every living thing that moves on the earth."
(v. 28)**

Here it is clear that the family is to "fill the earth and *subdue* it" while having *"dominion"* over "every living thing that moves on the earth." That is a powerful instruction that is so often overlooked today. Subdue, according to the dictionary, means to "conquer and bring into subjection." All other creatures, structures, and wills of the earth then are to be in subjection to the family unit as defined by God (man, woman, children).

The word dominion means "supreme authority." Yet we see that the marriage and family has lost its authority in our world. Instead, we are becoming a nation that seeks to "equalize" all people, all systems, all preferences, and all relationships, without regard to its conduct, morality, or contribution (negative or positive). However, God's Word does not convey the same message of authority to all. Rather it is very clear that there is a preference and a sanctioning of the family unit to act with "supreme authority" as subjected proponents of His will. God has defined what works, not what humans believe to be fair.

Slowly but surely we are defiling this most basic instruction through the normalization and empowerment of aberrant relationships and alliances that express the selfish desires of individuals over the order and will of God. Unions such as pre-marital sex, cohabitation, multiple remarriages, polygamy, and homosexuality are gaining such recognition and generally have become accepted as "typical and normal" in our society's structure.

As a result of the weakening of the prescribed family unit, we have seen selfish motivation and free expression take over in business, career, and other relational areas. There is quickly becoming no centralizing unit that bonds individuals to proper, godly conduct. It is literally a situation of everyone for him/herself.

This chapter will explore the inherent dangers that come through alliances that lack the sanction of God. The risks of these associations go far beyond the immediate impact, and when the long view is taken, these risks promise to affect the very core of our existence and means of operation as a relational country. Throughout this chapter we present a clear and ever-present call to God's original plan, perfect and complete in all manners.

HOMOSEXUALITY, BISEXUALITY, ETC...

A powerful political voice has developed within the ranks of an extremely small minority of citizens. The homosexuals, bisexuals, and transgendered persons have proven to be a force to be reckoned with. Representing perhaps one to two percent of the population, this group of vocal and determined advocates have found great influence in the court systems of this country, the congress, the entertainment and news media, and unfortunately, the church.

Their long-term plan has been to normalize an abnormal sexual and relational life, while winning the sympathy and support of Americans through the promotion of themselves as a disenfranchised minority. Now the airways are literally flooded with sitcoms, news reports, and documentaries that hammer out a very consistent message: "we are a legitimate expression of love and relationship and deserve not only equal treatment, but preferential treatment."

Hence this organized group is seeking the right to marry (already granted in Massachusetts), the right to adopt children (accepted by several states), the right to spousal and family benefits provided through employers (common in many companies), along with "special" considerations "due" them because of their "minority" status.

For example, they are having some success in promoting hate crime legislation that makes the injury or murder of someone from this class of people a more serious crime with greater punishment. They also are pursuing hate crime legislation that could eventually restrict free speech and even the reading of God's Word by punishing anyone (including a pastor) who speaks against the practice of homosexuality or associated activities.

Pockets of society are very supportive of this movement. Thankfully, we are seeing an awakening among evangelical Christians that is responding appropriately to the threat this movement promises. Many states are now passing amendments to their state constitutions that define marriage as a union between one man and one woman. These amendments are passing by large margins. Many representatives in the congress, along with the President, are determined to generate an amendment to the U. S. Constitution that defines marriage in the same way.

Still, it is amazing that we are in the position of having to "reclaim" what has been a defining feature of civilization throughout history. Unfortunately, we are very close to lowering the gates to the degree that everything anyone dreams about can be legislated and adjudicated into the normal fabric of relational life.

NOW FOR YOUR QUESTIONS...

I am a Christian man, and a homosexual. I attend a church with a lesbian pastor, where ALL of God's people are accepted and loved. We have a community of gay, bisexual, and transgendered individuals along with open-minded heterosexuals. I want to marry a man I have been living with for three years. It is not a sin to love and honor someone. Why shouldn't I be allowed to marry just like anyone else?

As Christian believers we are bound to the Word of God as our source of truth and instruction. As a consequence, we can only sanction and bring validation to relationships and behaviors that are recognized as acceptable by the Scriptures. Homosexual sex (**Lev 20:13, Rom 1:26-27, 1 Cor 6:9**), fornication (**Eph 5:3, Col 3:5, 1 Cor 6:9**) and sodomy (**1 Tim 1:8-11, 1 Cor 6:9**) are all forbidden unions and activities according to God's Word.

Additionally, there is no provision in Scripture for the creation of a marriage between two people of the same sex. God cannot sanction nor bless a union that blatantly violates His Word and instruction. A homosexual marriage does exactly that.

Many liberal theologians look at the scriptures noted above and suggest that other explanations are in order. How is another "explanation" possible in the following passage?

If a man lies with a male as he lies with a woman, both of them have committed an abomination. They shall surely

be put to death. Their blood shall be upon them. (Lev 20:13)

They claim that the Old Testament prohibition no longer applies and suggest that it was a product of the archaic Hebrew culture. But God's instruction contains a constant relativism. In other words, *everything* that applies then, applies today, because: **"Jesus Christ is the same yesterday, today, and forever" (Heb 13:8).**

The next argument some people try to make is that Jesus Himself never spoke directly to the issue of homosexuality; therefore, He must not have disapproved of its expression, they reason. According to this argument, only the words in red, denoting the spoken words of Christ, should be used as our reference. It is a common distortion of the Bible to select and use segments that seem to give permission for our craved activities while ignoring the entire Word, the complete context of the Bible.

In this case, the proponents of homosexuality attempt to find sanction in the *absence* of comment. That is like a child saying to his parents: "You mentioned the dangers of drugs generally, but you didn't say anything negative about cocaine specifically; therefore I assumed you didn't object to its use."

The whole Bible is from God, and we are expected to apply every word thereof. Jesus frequently quoted Moses, David and the prophets; passages that now are canonized as part of the Old Testament (**Mark 7:6-7, Matt 13:14, Luke 4:17-19, 4:4**). The apostles also quoted Moses and the prophets and referenced the Old Testament scrolls repeatedly. Still Jesus brings the greatest validation to the entire Word, including the laws of God in the following:

"Do not think that I came to destroy the Law or the Prophets. I did not come to destroy but to fulfill. For assuredly, I say to you, till heaven and earth pass away, one jot or one tittle will by no means pass from the law till all is fulfilled." (Matt 5:17-18)

Subsequently, the teachings of the Old Testament, along with the expansion of the New Testament, still apply. There is no undoing of the Word for modern application. There are no suitable adjustments to account for a changing culture.

Other liberal theologians and homosexual proponents also argue that New Testament comments about homosexual behavior are "misunderstood." They rightfully state that homosexuality is often listed along with other expressions of sin. They argue: "Why then is homosexuality singled out as "worse than" other sins listed?" Consider the following:

Do you not know that the unrighteous will not inherit the kingdom of God? Do not be deceived. Neither fornicators, nor idolaters, nor adulterers, nor homosexuals, nor sodomites, nor thieves, nor covetous, nor drunkards, nor revilers, nor extortioners will inherit the kingdom of God. (1 Cor 6:9-10)

First of all, homosexuality is not singled out as "worse than" other sins. The issue is this: no group of organized fornicators, thieves, idolaters, or drunkards is seeking special privileges, nor are they seeking to have their sin acknowledged as "normal, acceptable, and godly." Drunkards and thieves are not pushing, as a "special minority group," to become pastors and bishops.

It is the homosexual movement that has singled out this biblical notation of sin and claimed its uniqueness. Their claim is to the right for ongoing, willful sin to be excluded from the list and given accepted status within the church and society. God's Word simply does not allow this. Continuing in Chapter 6 of 1 Corinthians we see this clearly:

And such were some of you. But you were washed, but you were sanctified, but you were justified in the name of the Lord Jesus and by the Spirit of our God. (v. 11)

"And such *were* some of you...." Is there any question about what Paul means here? The behaviors that are listed as sin are *former* actions that are no longer present in our justified state. When we are "washed, sanctified, and justified" in the name of the Lord

Jesus Christ, we are to diligently seek the expulsion of sin from our lives, making previous willful conduct an element of our past. To claim that one can remain boldly and happily homosexual, while pursuing the kingdom of God, completely denies His teachings.

You say that you are a believer in Christ. There is no doubt one can be saved yet still struggle with sexual sin. It is possible to have Jesus in your heart and fall into the sin of homosexual behavior. But it is not possible to do so without the conviction of the Holy Spirit that will make you acutely aware of your sin and the need for change. If you have accepted a gospel that affirms homosexuality while encouraging the denial of God's Word, you have accepted a false gospel. This is a lie that may not only keep you in a painful and abnormal lifestyle, but it may in fact keep you from spending an eternity with God. Evidence of our salvation comes not only in our profession of faith, but in our submission and surrender to Christ.

This submission and surrender to Christ is certainly not always immediate, nor is it perfect. But acceptance of Christ requires the confession of sin and the request that Christ take control of your life and change your areas of challenge. If you have come before Jesus, claiming Him as Savior yet refusing to acknowledge the sins of homosexuality, sodomy, and fornication, then your salvation is in question. How can I be saved from my sins if I am unwilling to see the totality of that sin?

Unfortunately, you are under the counsel of others who have a distorted orientation to Scripture. Please consider the following principles and seek godly counsel from someone outside your current church association.

First, the Bible is either true or it is not true. You cannot have it both ways. It must be taken in its entirety; it must be taken literally; and it must be given reverence as God's final Word on all issues addressed therein. God has addressed homosexuality as sin that must be removed from our lives. He doesn't call for perfection, but He does insist on the confession and acknowledgement of sin. His Word is not a buffet table from which we pick and choose truth. We are called to address everything in our lives that He defines as unacceptable.

Salvation is free but obedience is work. We cannot win salvation, but in salvation we are to show love, humility, submission, and honor to the One who saved us. You cannot do this in the company of those who tell you otherwise; who suggest that you can have eternity with God while purposely denying His Word and instruction.

Blessed is the man
Who walks not in the counsel of the ungodly,
Nor stands in the path of sinners,
Nor sits in the seat of the scornful. (Ps 1:1)

There are many false teachers who will lead you astray. Paul cautions his student Timothy:

For the time will come when they will not endure sound doctrine, but according to their own desires, because they have itching ears, they will heap up for themselves teachers; and they will turn their ears away from the truth, and be turned aside to fables. (2 Tim 4:3-4)

All of us are gullible to swallowing teachings that are easy to digest. Most, to some degree, hope for a doctrine that is "according to their own desires." Getting back to the original question posed here, your pastor is teaching a doctrine that supports her desire and the desires of her congregation. She is telling you that a practicing homosexual can have Christ and live in disobedience to His Word. It would be easier for us all if we could have heaven and never be convicted of sin, but this is not how God works. Read your Bible and accept it literally. Find fellowship with believers who accept you and are willing to go to war for you, helping you battle the sin and vulnerability of homosexuality.

CASE EXAMPLE

Trey and Ramona have been married 20 years and have two adopted children. Ramona is a teacher at a Christian school; Trey is an educational minister with a local church. Trey has struggled with feeling attracted to other men throughout his adult life. Ramona has known of the temptation and has been a constant support and prayer partner. According to Trey, he has never acted on the impulse to have sex with another man.

For nearly seven years Trey has felt victory over such feelings and the two have enjoyed a better marriage and a stronger ministry. Two weeks ago, much to Ramona's surprise, Trey moved out of the home and will not tell her where he is living. She convinces him to come for a consultation.

Over the course of a few sessions, Trey confesses that he has a renewed interest in homosexual sex and is closer than ever to acting on it. We were curious about how this issue had reopened after a long period of peace concerning this issue.

Shrink: "What happened that stirred your interest in homosexual sex? It seems you were at peace with this issue for a long time."

Trey: "I was; or so I thought. Then I began talking to some people on the Internet and I learned that these feelings really never go away."

Shrink: "According to who?"

Trey: "According to researchers, ministers, and other Christians who are also homosexual."

Shrink: "So your feelings had stopped, but these others told you that was not possible, so you accepted their word and began to have these feelings again?"

Trey: "It turns out I was simply in denial. Since I thought you couldn't be a Christian and homosexual, I felt I had to extinguish this very real part of myself."

Shrink: (Somewhat dazed by the psychobabble...) "So now you have come out of your denial, reclaimed this true self, and have accepted that the Christian life and the homosexual life have potential to live in harmony?"

Trey: "Exactly!" (He was really excited that we understood.)

Shrink: "You are an education minister at a Bible-teaching church. How do you reconcile this position with Scripture?"

Trey: "It's like balancing a checkbook. If you are off a few pennies you can obsess and make yourself miserable, or you can simply write in the amount you want it to be. So I simply have accepted that on some points, I will be unbalanced (laughs). Grace is given because we cannot live up to the Bible's instruction perfectly. Besides, the more I learn from my mentors, the more I question the absolute prohibitions against the gay lifestyle."

The more Trey spoke, the greater the sense of his delusion. While he had struggled and prayed for years, achieving a season of victory and joy, he had fallen prey to the ungodly teaching and distortions put forth by a misguided few. He had traded the grace and mercy of God for the ignorance advanced by this demonic force.

...because, although they knew God, they did not glorify Him as God, nor were thankful, but became futile in their thoughts, and their foolish hearts were darkened. Professing to be wise, they became fools, and changed the glory of the incorruptible God into an image made like corruptible man—and birds and four-footed animals and creeping things. Therefore God also gave them up to uncleanness, in the lusts of their hearts, to dishonor their bodies among themselves, who exchanged the truth of God for the lie, and worshiped and served the creature rather than the Creator, who is blessed forever. Amen. (Rom 1:21-25)

Trey knew God, but failed to glorify and thank Him for the deliverance from homosexual thoughts that freed him for nearly seven years. He, as the passage says, became "futile" in his thoughts and his "foolish heart was darkened." Hardened by lust, emboldened by the lie of Satan, Trey went on to abandon the incorruptible God he had known for his entire adult life and worshipped and served the creature rather than the Creator.

Regrettably, therapy ended soon and unsuccessfully. Some would argue that Trey did not change because it was "natural" for him to act out his homosexuality. Others would say that shrinks have no right to tamper with human biology. But no amount of false science or political manipulation can change the literal instruction of God. To willingly violate the truth of God's Word, once you know it, will bring God's discipline. As it says in the passage above: "Therefore God also gave them up to uncleanness, in the lusts of their hearts, to dishonor their bodies among themselves..."

This was the case for Trey, who refused to examine his plight any further. He refused to restrain himself, come under instruction, or receive counsel. He was determined to follow through with his impulses, resting upon the deadly intelligence of his ungodly teachers.

We believe that Trey was a true believer in Christ; that he was saved. Evidence of this is found in God's chastening of Trey as he advanced his homosexual lifestyle. The Word tells us:

Likewise also the men, leaving the natural use of the woman, burned in their lust for one another, men with men committing what is shameful, and receiving in themselves the penalty of their error which was due. (Rom 1:27)

For whom the Lord loves He chastens, And scourges every son whom He receives. (Heb 12:6)

God will discipline his children, even unto death. Trey lost his ministry. His wife divorced him. His children rejected him and refused to see him. He filed for bankruptcy. He vanished into the homosexual community. Five years later, Trey died of AIDS.

CASE EXAMPLE

Roland's attorney referred him to us for treatment. He had been suspended from his job with the State of Florida for wearing female clothing and make-up to work. While working on a project outdoors, Roland had removed his outer shirt due to the heat. To the astonishment of all, he was wearing feminine underwear and false breasts. His appearance led to comments from co-workers; a fist-fight broke out, and then he was suspended.

Roland arrived for therapy wearing full make-up, earrings, shorts, and a halter-top. He asked to be called "Rhonda" and said he should be referenced using only female pronouns (she). He wanted to make sure that the therapist he was seeing understood transgender issues, and he came with the mindset that he would be counseled to transition to a full-time feminine identity.

I (Dr. Ab) explained that I am a Christian therapist and could only give counsel that is consistent with God's Word. Roland indicated that was fine with this because he was a Christian, and he knew that God loved him whether he was male or female.

Roland reported that he had been married for 30 years and had three children ages 15 to 27. He said he had been dressing in women's clothing since returning from Vietnam in the late sixties, and that his wearing of feminine underwear had always been a part of his sex life with his wife. He denied homosexual feelings or behavior. Roland was adamant that he preferred sex with women and was proud to report that he had been monogamous throughout his marriage. Roland said that the use of women's clothing and underwear had always been a "private matter" between him and his wife. He only began to wear make-up and women's apparel in public during the past two years.

Shrink: "Why do you think you have become bolder about wearing women's attire?"

Roland: "Because I am tired of restraining who I really am. The fact is, I was born a female in a man's body. I have tried to deny it and cope with it the best I can. But now I am 50 years old and there are laws to protect my rights. Now I am going to live the way God intended for me to live."

Shrink: "God intended for you to be a woman?"

Roland: "Of course."

Shrink: "Why then do you have a male organ and male chromosomes, and why did you live productively as a male until you came home from Vietnam?"

Roland: "Look, God made some mistakes with the male apparatus. It happens. God has given us medical and scientific methods for correcting this little problem. As for my life before Viet Nam, you know nothing! You have no idea what my life was like or how productive it was!"

Shrink: "You're right. Maybe I assumed too much. Tell

me about it."

Roland: "Well, do I start with the sadistic stepfather who called me a fairy and a wimp, or do you want me to tell you about my passive, cold mother who did nothing to protect me from his crap? I can't tell you how many times I was humiliated, called a sissy, told I would never amount to anything! So after high school I joined the Marines. Not too many wimps and fairies in the Marines! I was deployed to Vietnam where I fought like a maniac and killed a lot of people. Got the medals to prove it! But when I came home I realized I was becoming just as cold, cruel, and hostile as my stepfather. That's when I decided God had made a mistake. The world didn't need another jerk like him. So I rejected that side of myself. I soon realized that I didn't even like being male. When I first put on women's underwear, I was free from all that garbage. I knew I had found my true self. It just took a while for the world to come around. Now I have friends, we have rights, and the courts will help us get what we are due: the right to be female!"

Roland was a very angry and frightened man. Mostly he was frightened to find any remnant of his stepfather within himself. When he saw traces of that same hostility in war, he psychologically rejected himself entirely. To do this he had to either commit suicide or create a totally different persona: that of a female.

Roland had suffered for years with a mixture of confused feelings and impulses. He was still filled with rage and unresolved pain. His attachment to women's clothing was now complicated by the creation of a sexual fetish. Now he was emboldened by the gay/transgender political movement that validated his feelings and inclinations by telling him he was born a "female in a male's body." This group's radical stance and hyper-endorsement of abnormal conduct, if unabated, would lead to the permanent loss of Roland's career, the loss of his wife and children, and surgery to remove his God-given male organs.

It took a long time for Roland to accept that his attraction to the feminine persona was grounded in anxiety, depression, and anger, and that it was not a result of some tragic heavenly error. It took even longer for him to abandon his association with other confused individuals that would have him take drastic measures, such as surgery and hormone treatment, in order to bolster their viewpoint and advance their cause.

I never did call Roland "Rhonda" as he requested. I refused to refer to him as "she" (although it made him furious). Instead I promised him that God made no error and that, with time, he would be able to receive and accept God's affection and plan for the man He had created. Eventually Roland ceased his involvement with the Metropolitan Church of Christ, a homosexual/transgender community with a false doctrine and misguided social norms. He and his family started attending a Bible teaching church, and he began to learn of the perfection of God's design and order.

Roland came to accept the truth of the Bible's teachings on homosexuality and related issues, including the biblical prohibition against cross-dressing:

A woman shall not wear anything that pertains to a man, nor shall a man put on a woman's garment, for all who do so are an abomination to the Lord your God. (Deut 22:5)

But greater than God's prohibition against certain activities is His promise of perfect, unrestrained love. Roland spent a great deal of time reading the promises of God. He learned that God uses all things to the benefit of His good and perfect will. Roland came to accept that God had planned and created him, designed him with a purpose, and knew him before the foundation of the world.

These are reassuring realities for a man who once believed he needed to eradicate everything God had created in him because he thought he was an error, a fluke, and a freak. Since accepting Christ as his Savior, Roland has come to know the peace and assurance that comes only through an identity based upon the King of kings. His family is intact; he has a new job; and he has found security in a male sexuality that is strong but lacking in the hostility and abuse of a very distant stepfather.

OPEN MARRIAGES AND SEXUAL RELATIONSHIPS

During the 1970s, psychologists and sociologists began to change the landscape of sexual relations. Fueled by the distorted research of Kinsey and the sexual revolution of the 1960s, social scientists came to the conclusion that the human animal is not designed for monogamy. Monogamy, they argued, is paramount to repression of the natural desires and needs of the individual. Long revered values of chastity and monogamy were traded in for sexual exploration, multiple sexual partners, and open relationships that allowed a base level of commitment while permitting sexual involvement with others.

Sex was quickly reduced to a physical expression of pleasure and not necessarily related to love, investment, exclusivity, or longevity. Individuals and couples were encouraged to partake of the forbidden and create new adventures, sexually and relationally.

This excessive focus on sex in relationships has defiled and weakened the special meaning of intimacy in marital life. The shift to physical emphasis over spiritual and emotional connection has been very destructive, adding to marital confusion, infidelity, and divorce.

We have already demonstrated God's emphasis on monogamous relationships in the previous chapters on "The Single Life" and "Marriage God's Way." In this section we will reveal the degree to which this "open" sexual orientation has permeated the American home, and even the Christian family, as an accepted way of life.

NOW FOR YOUR QUESTIONS...

My wife and I are very committed to each other and have been sexually monogamous for five years. We attend church, work hard, and have high standards of moral conduct. We both have an interest in sex outside of marriage. We have talked about it and done quite a bit of research. It seems harmless as long as we are committed to each other, practice safe-sex responsibly, and never let anyone else come between us. I see no sin if we are both willing and no one is hurt by the arrangement.

Thankfully the two of you have not ventured down this path...yet. We are relieved to know you have been monogamous to this point because that is the ONLY way God intended marriage and sexual expression to be. Let's take each point individually:

First you say you "attend church" and have "high moral standards." That's excellent, but it is not the same thing as having a relationship with Jesus. Only through Christ can we access the Holy Spirit who will then confront our foolish imaginings with His truth. In our opinion, anyone can fall prey to sexual sin, the Christian or the unbeliever. But we do not believe that a disciple of Christ can willfully and repeatedly pursue sexual relations with multiple partners and feel comfortable doing so. The attraction of sin is universal and understandable, but the "comfort" you claim about proceeding is troubling.

The two of you need to have a very honest and detailed discussion about your faith and evaluate your status with God. If you have not received Christ as your Savior, please do so. The final chapter of this book, "Final Thoughts," provides information about salvation and the steps one must take to be born-again. You will have an innate resistance right now because of the pull and attraction you are feeling in this sexual area of your life. That is why it is crucial that you do not act on this desire in any form. Once you go over the line, it will be much harder to come back. Sometimes when our heart is hardened, the first and only thing we can do is "freeze." Stay still and examine the Scriptures to find the meaning of a true born-again relationship with Christ.

Next, you and your spouse must examine the factors that are stimulating this interest in an unhealthy lifestyle. For example, are you involved in pornography? Do you have friends that share this orientation who are encouraging you to explore and participate? Is there an attraction one or both of you feel to specific people that drives your interest in extramarital sex? Is there a history of sexual promiscuity in your past single life? Has there been a history of abuse? You must not yield to the idea that these inclinations are normal and deserve expression: they are not and do not.

In our 25 years of experience with couples, we have not seen one positive outcome of extramarital sex. Not one. There are, however, hundreds of catastrophes we could report, some of which began in the same manner you are describing. Curiosity, flirtation, research, and the slow breaking of boundaries have led many to marital, psychological, and spiritual demise.

We have found that ideas of "open" relationships generally begin in the mind of one partner. The other partner, acting in fear, will acquiesce. This of course makes for a cycle of pain that is beyond explanation.

One example involves a particular couple we treated. The wife had entertained fantasies of outside sexual partners for years. She talked about it frequently, prodding her husband to consider it. Finally, after 15 years of marriage, there was the right party, the right amount of alcohol, the final measure of pressure applied, and the husband consented. The two had sex with another couple, all four in the same room.

It was everything the wife had hoped. For the husband it was the realization of his greatest fears, and the beginning of a tragic nightmare. He saw actions, emotions, and excitement in his wife that was very different from what he had known in their private sexual relationship. He was heartbroken, knowing that he would never really have her as his own again.

She continued in this promiscuous lifestyle while her husband became depressed and withdrawn. Within two years they were divorced. Five years later, he is still broken; she is still acting out sexually. Their two children are also the victims, living between two very injured homes.

We predict that your desire for an open relationship far exceeds your wife's. She may be swept along by the idea, but she is probably driven more by fear than a true sense of interest and acceptance. You say there is "no sin" if "no one is hurt." The trouble is; someone is ALWAYS hurt.

Of all the reasons Christ might have granted the right to divorce, he gave only one: sexual immorality **(Matt 19:9)**. Our Lord didn't cite irreconcilable differences, poor communication, or even abuse. Possibly the sheer pain of sexual unfaithfulness was the driving realty. When "two become one flesh" **(Gen 2:24)** there can be no other partners without a division of that covenant. To divide flesh is of course a very painful thing. Our Savior knew that the pain of sexual sin was potentially too great to bear.

Your effort to justify the moral acceptability of your plan is futile. God's Word is unyielding in its treatment of sexual iniquity. There is no margin of acceptance given in Scripture. Avoid the lie; hold to the truth; pray for strength; and for the assurance of your salvation with God.

CASE EXAMPLE

Micah and Jocelyn were in their mid-forties when they entered therapy. They had two adolescent daughters, successful jobs, membership in a Baptist church, and separate homes. They had been living apart for over a year because Micah had refused to accept the ultimatum he had been given by his wife.

Jocelyn explained that the couple had been troubled with an "inadequate" sex life throughout their 15-year marriage. Micah looked depressed, speechless, and humiliated as his wife described in detail his "failings" in the bedroom.

> *Jocelyn:* "I think he is gay or something. I have done every-thing I know to do but he just doesn't satisfy me. I don't think he likes sex with women."
>
> *Micah:* "That's not true. I find you very attractive and I want to please you. But you put so much pressure on me that I am afraid."
>
> *Jocelyn:* "See what I mean? I want him to take control, not be afraid. I don't see any hope."
>
> *Shrink:* "What have you tried before coming to therapy?"
>
> *Micah:* "Her proposed solution is "swinging." She wants to live together but have sex with whomever she wishes. She wants me to have sex with other people too so that I can supposedly learn to be more aggressive and more confident in bed."
>
> *Shrink:* "I see…" (Classic stall tactic when shrink is speech-less!)
>
> *Jocelyn:* "We tried it a few times. I think it worked out great. I would stay with him if he would agree to continue in this

vein. He is a good friend, a great parent, a solid provider; but I require good, frequent sex to be happy. In that regard, he is a flop."

Micah: (Crying openly) I can't do that anymore. One time she brought home this bisexual man and insisted we both have sex with him. She is so convinced that I am gay! She thought that if I had homosexual sex then I would be happy and fulfilled and she could continue in her madness. (Crying harder) I actually went through with it. I had sex with that man!"

Jocelyn: "And I think you liked it!"

Micah: (Angry) "I HATED IT!! She knows I was abused as a child by an uncle. That's why she thinks I am gay! I don't want a man. I don't want some other woman. I want my wife and my family! When I refused to continue this type of activity, she moved out. She won't come home unless I submit to her demands."

Admittedly, this is an extreme case with multiple dynamics and problems. The couple was divided into individual therapy with separate therapists. In the course of therapy it was learned that Jocelyn too had been a victim of sexual abuse as a child and that this was a driving factor in her sexual obsession and acting out. Unfortunately, she did not remain in treatment, stating she had found her "remedy." She actually was deeply involved in a sado-masochistic sex club where she acted out not only her sexual preoccupation but her rage as well. She was ultimately unwilling to be married if her husband would not participate in this ring of evil.

Micah continued in therapy and ultimately they divorced. He had accepted Christ as his Savior as a teen and now recommitted his life to purity and growth. Micah had a tremendous amount of shame, anger, fear, and confusion to address in therapy. With time, he was able to heal many of his wounds while maintaining a functional life. At present Micah has not remarried and plans to remain alone for the time being. His daughters live with him and are doing well. The girls rarely see their mother, who is lost in another world of sex and violence.

This case provides clear evidence that the breakdown of marital boundaries leads to destruction. It also provides a glimpse into the patterns and experiences that generate this type of aberrant sexual pursuit. Extreme as it is, the case demonstrates that "open sexuality" is not of God. Instead it grows out of injury; it grows out of satanic lies; and it deepens, rather than heals, pain and suffering.

The insanity displayed by this couple cannot compare with the peace and security found in a contained, exclusive sexual life. So as thoughts enter our minds, images entice, and temptations come, we must be willing to seek God's cover and boundary in order to survive. In His cover we can examine the forces, spiritual and emotional, that promote and advance wrongdoing. In unity with Christ we find unity with our spouse, a very wonderful place to be.

The body is not for sexual immorality, but for the Lord, and the Lord for the body. (1 Cor 6:13b)

BUSINESS AND POLITICS

We have already seen that compromise in one part of life weakens the structure in all. The breakdown of the family, the surrender of its "dominion," and the failing boundaries of our culture have given way to a selective view of morality. Moral absolutes have surrendered to a perpetual "gray area" where everything is open for review and consideration. Nowhere is this more evident than in business and politics.

We have noted throughout the book that identity with Christ is an all-encompassing merger. We are called to be the same publicly and privately, at work and play, with friends, strangers, and family. It is especially dangerous when Christians begin to divide the various pockets of our world, making concessions in some, holding firm in others. Like the rest of the world, we often yield to decisions that best serve our immediate need rather than allowing God to provide His care and support as promised.

Too many times we hear of "Christian" businessmen and women who handle financial matters unethically. More than once I have heard of corrupt business deals and financial injury between "brethren." Often we learn of believers who trusted someone from their church, only to then be taken advantage of. There are countless stories of shady business associations and alignments between Christians and non-Christians, justified under the claim of necessity or making provision for the family's welfare.

The world of politics is no different. All kinds of the most bizarre partnerships occur in government positions. Trades and deals are abundant within all levels of the legislature: "I won't challenge gay marriage if you will support our bill on affirmative action;" "I'll stay quiet on the debate concerning abortion if you don't interfere with our proposal for corporate tax relief." But the believer is taught: **"Let this mind be in you which was also in Christ Jesus" (Phil 2:5).**

Could you imagine Christ negotiating a deal with the Pharisees that would save His life and allow Him to operate His earthly ministry without interference? Would Jesus sacrifice a portion of His plan in one area to gain success in another? Of course not! The truth is always true and the totality of purpose is in God's hands, not ours.

We then must insert the mind (attitude) of Christ into decisions we make, no matter the area of reference. We must make a living as a consistent Christian with proper Christian associations. We must vote for and support politicians who advance a consistent and whole record of voting in accordance with God's directives. And should we be honored to serve in public office, we must keep God's measurement as our yardstick, not the patterns and procedures of the system.

NOW FOR YOUR QUESTIONS...

I have a great opportunity to make some money with a local real estate investor. As a deacon in our church, I have been cautioned about my potential partner, many citing problems with his ethics and integrity. I know he has cut a few corners and that he has taken advantage of others in the past. Still, don't I have the responsibility to provide for my home the very best way I can? We are talking about a great deal of income over the next five years.

You write as if you already know the answer...but would rather not know it. As a deacon you know very well the importance of living a blameless life.

> **Likewise deacons must be reverent, not double-tongued, not given to much wine, not greedy for money; holding the mystery of the faith with a pure conscience. But let these also first be tested; then let them serve as deacons, being found blameless. Likewise, their wives must be reverent, not slanderers, temperate, faithful in all things. Let deacons be the husbands of one wife, ruling their children and their own houses well. For those who have served well as deacon obtain for themselves a good standing and great boldness in the faith which is in Christ Jesus. (1 Tim 3:8-13)**

Much of your answer lies in the first sentence of Paul's charge. The deacon must not be "double tongued." As a church leader you cannot profess one code of conduct and live another. We are called to a consistent, faithful application of the truth. This business relationship will force you to lead a double life of compromise and concession. It will not advance God's kingdom, only your bank account (if indeed this man of low integrity breaks with his former pattern and decides to honor his commitment to you).

The last part of the first sentence above gives the rest of your answer: A deacon must not be "greedy of filthy lucre." Lucre is an Old English term meaning monetary gain or profit. Greed is what makes the gain "filthy." Your willingness to compromise your integrity and your calling as a church leader to realize profit is the exact definition of greed. The money has become more important to you than blameless, godly living.

By the way, you are also rejecting godly counsel that has come to your from other church leaders. By refusing to heed God's Word and the counsel of His servants, we drive ourselves headlong into destruction. Stop looking for validation outside of the Bible and Christian counsel. If you look long enough, someone will eventually tell you what your itching ears want to hear.

I am a Christian Democrat who votes the Democratic ticket religiously. I know that in general their platform supports ideas I am opposed to, like abortion, but I feel I have to make a balanced decision. Isn't it acceptable to concede certain political issues in favor of an overall package you find favorable?

We can't tell you not to be a Democrat, Republican, or an Independent. What we can tell you is that you will be held accountable for supporting government leaders who repeatedly act in violation of God's Word. You raised the issue of abortion as an example, so let's pursue this issue. When we support a candidate of any political party who endorses the killing of babies in the womb, then we have participated in that killing. Judges and politicians who sanction laws that allow abortion have been responsible for literally millions of deaths over the past decades. When we know their positions in advance, yet then give them power to place that position in action, we are culpable. James wrote:

For whoever shall keep the whole law, and yet stumble in one point, he is guilty of all. (Jas 2:10)

Simply stated, this means that we cannot violate one commandment and be found blameless in the other nine. If we endorse sin, we compromise the *entire* teachings of the Bible.

As Christians we must be very cautious about an alignment with any "party" or "organization" that has an inconsistent agenda. We are members of the Body of Christ, and this affiliation should be our only focus of allegiance. In supporting and voting for political candidates and judges, we must discern the truth of the individual, not his/her party affiliation. Don't be seduced by the world's representation that deals must be made to advance the overall ideal. There is no deal, no agenda worth the conciliation of God's Word.

SUMMARY

The Bible is loaded with examples of unholy alliances; relationships and unions forged in disobedience to God's command. In every case, the concession generated a reliance on man and a rejection of

God. When we make agreements that we think will protect us, we are counting on our wisdom and the wisdom of others to see us through. When we allow our fears and our desires to dictate our bonds, then we have detached ourselves from the one True Source of protection, joy, and stability. Jesus said:

> **"And do not fear those who kill the body but cannot kill the soul. But rather fear Him who is able to destroy both soul and body in hell. Are not two sparrows sold for a copper coin? And not one of them falls to the ground apart from your Father's will. But the very hairs of your head are all numbered. Do not fear therefore; you are of more value than many sparrows. Therefore whoever confesses Me before men, him I will also confess before My Father who is in heaven. But whoever denies Me before men, him I will also deny before My Father who is in heaven." (Matt 10:28-33)**

We are called to have reverence (fear) of our Heavenly Father and His ordinances. We are also called to trust His sovereignty and His overwhelming love and value for us. Only God has true eternal power over our lives and our eternity. Everything that happens on earth, He permits. Each time we endorse and pursue an ungodly association, we deny Christ and His truth. Trust that God's Word is your all-sufficient guide.

CHAPTER 11

RELATIONAL BY DESIGN

INTRODUCTION

Our Creator is a relational God. That means that He is close, available, and connected to believers in a way that is different from all other proclaimed deities. Rather than being distant and unattainable, our God has chosen to reveal Himself to the world in an accessible and personal way. Evidence of this is found throughout Scripture as God draws us repeatedly toward intimacy, communication, and fellowship with Him.

God's relational nature is also present in the order He defines for Christian living. Within the Bible are multiple instructions that convey the importance of marriage, parent-child relationships, the genealogy of the family, fellowship and friendship, work, and unity of the body of Christ. God also warns us of relational positions that compromise His plans for us by undermining His order of correct and natural affiliations.

To understand God we must be in His constant company. We can only do this through His Son Jesus Christ, who paid for our access to the Father through His sacrifice on the cross. Through Christ's atonement we are given full privilege as adopted children of the Kingdom. Without relationship with Christ, there can be no association with the Father.

The beauty of God's love is depicted fully in this sacrificial act. Knowing that we could not climb up to Him, He came down to us:

And the Word became flesh and dwelt among us, and we beheld His glory, the glory as of the only begotten of the Father, full of grace and truth. (John 1:14)

To leave heaven and all its glory, to assume the flesh and existence of a human for the salvation of the world, is the epitome of relational love. No other religion can claim a God of love that would do as much for its people. This is relationship according to God's standard, and it is very different indeed from the relational agenda of the human species. Humans have come to place a much higher value on independence, freedom, and self-fulfillment. As a result, we see a world of selfish motivation that is in direct opposition to the faithful, sacrificial love of our Creator and Savior.

Most of us learn about relationship through our families. By living in a home environment, absorbing the character and patterns of our parents, we evolve into adults who often perpetuate what we have observed as children. As Christians we are to apply the same principles of observation to our heavenly Father. By doing so, we begin to absorb and convey His patterns, character, and principles. That being said, let's examine God's expression of relationship in Scripture, and then let's seek to understand its relevance to our spiritual and earthly associations.

IN THE BEGINNING

Then God said, "Let Us make man in Our image, according to Our likeness; let them have dominion over the fish of the sea, over the birds of the air, and over the cattle, over all the earth and over every creeping thing that creeps on the earth." (Gen 1:26)

On the sixth day of creation, God created man in His own image. Just as we plan and prepare for our children, God planned and created a setting for His special creation. When we (The

Abercrombies) were expecting the arrival of our daughter Sarah, we created an environment that would welcome her, support her, and provide her the best opportunity in which to excel.

We bought a house, decorated the nursery, filled the pantry with all the essentials, and waited with anticipation. We wondered whom she would resemble. Would she have blonde hair like her mother or brown like her dad? Would she have green eyes or hazel? Would she have her mother's tall, slender frame or would she be more "filled out" like her father? When she came we were thrilled to see a mixture of characteristics that made her exclusively ours. Thankfully, her mother's physical features have "won out" over time and she is a beautiful girl. God is merciful!

In a similar manner God built a world for His creation: He decorated a garden paradise, and He stocked the land with plants and animals that were sufficient in all ways for man to thrive. And just as we anticipated a child who would be like ourselves, God forged man in His likeness. God must have felt a similar pride when He spoke with Adam and showed him all that had been provided for his good.

God's association with man was superior and different from all other created things. This is evident in God's communication and teachings that were delivered directly from His mouth to Adam's ear. Like a proud father, God gave Adam dominion (control) over the entire garden with the unlimited instruction to manage the earth **(Gen 1:28)**.

Relationship is grounded in this expression of value that God conveys for His creation. It is found in the demonstration of trust, the transference of freedom, the direct communication, and the respectful tone of authority. Adam is given responsibility, resources, and training to avoid what is harmful and threatening **(Gen 2:16-17)**.

God spoke to Adam as a father lovingly educates and cares for his son. The Bible records the interactions between Adam and his Creator. God addressed Adam numerous ways: "God said" **(Gen 1:26-28, 2:18)**; "God blessed" **(Gen 1:28)**; "God brought" **(Gen 2:19)**; "God commanded" **(Gen 2:16)** and; God called" **(Gen 3:9)**. These acts of communication were personal and poignant. They express God's intent to maintain connection with His child.

But in disobedience Adam and Eve broke fellowship with God by trusting the voice of the deceiver. This betrayal of God's spoken word led to yet another communicational act: "God sent" and "He drove out" **(Gen 3:23-24)**. Adam and Eve were exiled from the Garden and from God's association.

In this discourse, God was faithful to His Word but the created ones were not. God gave them everything, including a caution that death would be the consequence of breaking union with Him. God fulfilled every proclamation, up to and including the punishment for disobedience.

This pattern of relating is central to understanding God's most basic objective for mankind. We were made for His pleasure and for His glory. We can fulfill neither if we fail to maintain relationship with Him. Without relationship we have no hope and no eternity. Therefore, God places relationship, communion, and faithfulness in high regard. If these features are central to our relations with Him, they are central to all relationships we will experience in life.

COVENANT-BASED INTIMACY

The intimacy of God's involvement with man has been recorded throughout the Scriptures. It is evident that God is active and engaged with mankind. During biblical times His involvement was close and personal, speaking directly to humankind in various forms. With Adam, Abraham, and Moses God spoke unswervingly and audibly.

Later in Scripture He spoke through prophets and prophetesses, through dreams and visions, through angels and other messengers. Finally, He spoke personally, embodied in the human frame of His only begotten Son, Jesus Christ. Today He speaks through the Holy Spirit who was sent as our Helper and Comforter, and through His inerrant Word, the canon of the Bible.

The Bible demonstrates that God had a special relationship with Abram (Abraham), calling him to be the Father of the Hebrew nation. God tested and strengthened Abram, then blessed him as the chosen patriarch:

Now the Lord had said to Abram: "Get out of your

country, from your family and from your father's house, to a land that I will show you. I will make you a great nation; I will bless you and make your name great; and you shall be a blessing. I will bless those who bless you, and I will curse him who curses you; and in you all the families of the earth shall be blessed." (Gen 12:1-3)

In this passage, God gives Abram a specific plan to follow, and with that plan, a promise of blessing and protection. Abram is called to trust God relationally and to obey His Word so that the plan of His kingdom could be advanced. In the next verse, we see Abram's response:

So Abram departed as the Lord had spoken to him, and Lot went with him. And Abram was seventy-five years old when he departed from Haran. (v. 4)

There was no questioning of God, only the answer of movement. Abram acted with faith and confidence, giving authority to God's objective over his own. In this we see that our relationship to God is one of submission. We are not mightier than the Lord of Hosts, nor can we be wiser or more discerning. Obedience is a central feature of knowing and receiving God's perfect plan, protection, and blessing.

Later in Genesis we see God speak to Abram over and over again, rewarding obedience, ratifying promises made, correcting disobedience, and expanding the vision of God's objective.

When Abram was ninety-nine years old, the Lord appeared to Abram and said to him, "I am Almighty God; walk before Me and be blameless. And I will make My covenant between Me and you, and will multiply you exceedingly." Then Abram fell on his face, and God talked with him, saying: "As for Me, behold, My covenant is with you, and you shall be a father of many nations. No longer shall your name be called Abram, but your name shall be Abraham; for I have made you a

father of many nations. I will make you exceedingly fruitful; and I will make nations of you, and kings shall come from you. And I will establish My covenant between Me and you and your descendants after you in their generations, for an everlasting covenant, to be God to you and your descendants after you. Also I give to you and your descendants after you the land in which you are a stranger, all the land of Canaan, as an everlasting possession; and I will be their God." (Gen 17: 1-8)

Notice the expansive nature of God's speech. He addresses not only the blessing of Abraham but establishes a covenant that is "everlasting." Again God's emphasis on permanence and faithfulness is demonstrated. God addresses the "generations" to follow and the inheritance that will translate from one age to the next.

It would be amazing for humans to adopt the same commitment to life, family, and relationship. If, like our Father, we could see beyond ourselves, beyond the current moment, and into the succeeding generations, we would generate a very different view concerning our roles and responsibilities to one another. Everything we do today has a profound and perpetual effect on our loved ones and will define much of what they do in the future.

By reading the Scriptures we know that God is a faithful keeper of promises made. We know He cannot lie and that His behavior toward us is consistent and purposeful. Because of these facts, we can submit, follow, and learn His ways, placing them into action in our own lives. Our spouses and children need and deserve a similar faithful devotion that provides a bedrock foundation of security and confidence. Family harmony is closely tied to this sense of security.

Intimacy and trust in God is possible because He is always the same. Human trust and reliance is similar and depends upon the unfailing expression of integrity, honesty, and character. By examining the covenant nature of God, we can learn a great deal about the potential of genuine truth. We must remain mindful of the promises and responsibilities inherent in each of our relationships and work daily to assure that we are meeting our commitments.

In biblical times there was great emphasis on inheritance. The focus was not so much on the transference of material wealth, but rather the wealth of character and spirituality. Great attention was given to the lineage of the family and the passing down of blessings and promises. Hebrew children were raised to have a connection to the past and to the future. By assuming a similar perspective, we can create a base of honor for our elders and ancestors and responsibility to our spouse and children. We know that this is God's orientation because the Bible takes great care to record the history of families presented there. Also, God defines Himself as a "generational" God:

Moreover He said, "I am the God of your father—the God of Abraham, the God of Isaac, and the God of Jacob." (Ex 3:6a)

God deals in decades, centuries, and generations. He is not a God of immediacy. His promises are powerful enough to endure and create life from one era to the next. This unending, unyielding, covenant-based devotion is the very character of God, and it is the pattern for our faithfulness to Him and to those in our lives.

In our counseling practice we have seen the influence of generational curses and covenants. So often our clients are either burdened or blessed by the history that precedes them. Themes of illness, abuse, alcoholism, divorce, etc. are often the roots of a family tree. These patterns are not predestined or certain to reappear generation after generation, yet they are very influential. Often it seems there is no choice but to do what we have always known.

As born-again Christians we are extracted from this ancestry and given freedom as adopted children of the Kingdom. But sometimes extinguishing the memory and the effect of this experience can be daunting. We have known believers who struggle every day to quiet the voices of the past, trying to live within the new agreement found in salvation. Certainly Satan is present to remind us of our past and to generate doubt concerning our capacity to free ourselves. You may have heard the deceiver's voice whenever you find yourself acting as your parents acted, or whenever you are tempted to follow old family practices that are detrimental to your spiritual and emotional health.

But remember that Jesus became our sin (**2 Cor 5:21**) and He assumed our curse (**Gal 3:13**). Under the new covenant, we are joint heirs of the Kingdom, partakers of the promise that frees us from bondage to sin and failure. This process of adoption gives us equal access to the inheritance God promised His children. And as we see through Abraham and the generations that follow, God is true to all that He guarantees.

LONG-TERM RELATIONSHIPS

Relationship with God is shaped for eternity. Yet even within the confines of our earthly life, we see God work out His long-term objectives over many years. As we explored in the previous section, God is always focused on the greater picture, the plan and time-frame we cannot see:

> **But, beloved, do not forget this one thing, that with the Lord one day is as a thousand years, and a thousand years as one day. (2 Pet 3:8)**

Humans panic; God does not. His Word reflects a patient, long-suffering God who knows every twist and turn of the story before it occurs. He simply calls upon His servants to trust, to hear, to communicate, and to obey. There is a reason for every call, every instruction, and every trial. If we adopt His nature and yield to His will, we will be cared for, protected, and ultimately blessed.

Moses' life is a prime example of a long-term plan that required a long-term relationship in order to be realized. Moses, who was destined as a baby to be murdered under an Egyptian plan to control the population of its Israelite slaves, is miraculously saved and adopted by the family of Pharaoh. Rather than suffer death as an infant, he is afforded influence, education, and privilege. As a young adult, Moses is stirred to anger for the mistreatment of his people and murders an Egyptian guard. Moses' crime makes him a fugitive who takes refuge in the wilderness for years, hiding in obscurity (**Ex 2 and 3**).

But God had saved Moses from death as an infant, and God had provided the protection and benefit of the Egyptian home. God had a plan to release His people from bondage, and Moses was His chosen vessel:

And the Lord said: "I have surely seen the oppression of My people who are in Egypt, and have heard their cry because of their taskmasters, for I know their sorrows." (Ex 3:7)

"Come now, therefore, and I will send you to Pharaoh that you may bring My people, the children of Israel, out of Egypt." (Ex 3:10)

From the time of infancy onward, we see God's hand on Moses. At the time God calls him to service, Moses is far removed from the privilege God had afforded him in the Egyptian palace. Now Moses is broken, living the consequence of his sin in exile. He is tending the flock of his father-in-law when God confronts him with the "big picture," complete with a burning bush **(Ex 3)**.

One has to wonder what went through Moses' mind. Did he suddenly realize he had been spared death as an infant so that he could complete a great work for God? Did he grasp the importance of his preparation as an adopted Egyptian? Could he now understand the anger that burned in his heart when he saw his Hebrew "brethren" beaten? Did the sin of his murderous act and his subsequent flight serve to "break" him and generate the humility that would allow him to serve the Lord without question?

The Bible suggests that Moses had none of these revelations. Like most of us, he saw only the momentary absurdity of his God-given task, as he questioned the Almighty:

But Moses said to God, "Who am I that I should go to Pharaoh, and that I should bring the children of Israel out of Egypt?" (Ex 3:11)

In our relationship with God, we may not find His plan evident in the events of our lives. Instead, we may feel carried along by circumstances, wondering when God will intervene. But with Moses we find a great example of God's pervasive care and intent for each of us. It teaches us the importance of having a Kingdom viewpoint, seeing beyond the moment, and seeking always the route God has chosen.

Of course Moses yielded to God's call and did indeed bring God's people "out of Egypt." But God's long-term goal for Moses required him to remain in leadership for many years to come, enduring the struggles and grumblings of the Israelites throughout their forty-year trek through the wilderness. God put Moses in this position of authority and great responsibility. He was the portal through which God communicated with the others.

Over time, Moses was entrusted with many tasks and enjoyed a special rapport with his Creator. Through Moses, God delivered the Ten Commandments **(Ex 20)**, ordered the building of the tabernacle **(Ex 38)**, and eventually fulfilled the covenant made with Abraham by bringing the Israelites into the Promised Land of Canaan (although Moses was not allowed to cross the Jordan into Canaan) **(Ex 6:8, Josh 1:2)**.

The Bible tells us that Moses' relationship with God was unique and exclusive. The relationship between Moses and the Lord was like no other described in Scripture:

So the Lord spoke to Moses face to face, as a man speaks to his friend. (Ex 33:11a)

Yet as we read the account of Moses' life from his birth until death, we see his humanness, even in the presence of the almighty God. In his life we see Moses resist God **(Ex 3:11-13, 4:10)**; we see him angry with God **(Ex 5:22, Num 11:11)**; and we read how he disappoints God **(Num 20:12)**.

Like the rest of us, even Moses could not always see the overall mission, the long-term objective of his connection with God. But God was always moving Moses and the Israelites toward the fulfillment of His covenant with Abraham. God could not be deterred from the execution of His promise.

In the end, Moses did not see the Promised Land, nor did the

Hebrews that he led out of bondage. God kept them in the wilderness until their children could receive the inheritance. While there was a consequence for disobedience and the failure of faith, the promise, the fulfillment of the greater plan, was not withdrawn.

Our relational lives are similar, in that we must be cognizant of the covenant, even when we have failures and disappointments. For example, a marriage will have periods of anger, resistance, and distress, just as God experienced with Moses, but the covenant and responsibility to the union must prevail along with the responsibility to the offspring, building a relational and spiritual future.

Relationships can provoke "wilderness experiences" wherein we feel lost, frustrated, forgotten, and hopeless. In spite of this, there must be attention given to the greater good, the ultimate gain. A covenant, whether it be marital, parental or something else, must be honored, even in the heat of relational challenge.

The Promised Land for the family is the realization of a rich spiritual life, free of idolatry, focused on God's leadership. It is fidelity, loyalty, and faith in the face of adversity. The ancient "land of milk and honey" is equated to living in the fruit of the Spirit (**Gal 5:22**), which is evident in our speech to one another, our actions, and our peace. It is a restful senior life, with godly adult children, passing on the lessons of covenant intimacy to our grandchildren. It is leaving an inheritance that is of the Kingdom not the world.

Like our Father, we must adopt a vision that extends beyond our lifetime. We must attend to every decision and every action with respect to its effect on this and future generations. By doing so we disavow the character of the world with its focus on instant gratification, and we assume the character of our Lord which is purposeful, patient, and responsible. This attaches us to His family lineage and divides us from the limitations of our own.

HUMAN RELATIONSHIPS

As a full member of God's family, we are to act in accordance with His family order. We have seen already that His order is covenant-based and permanent in its foundation. We have seen that it is long-term in its orientation, building a legacy from one generation to the next. Through biblical examples we see the importance of communication and association with God through His Son along with the need for trust, faith, and submission to His sovereign authority.

From this basis we can establish a framework for our earthly relations. Can you imagine the influence of such a foundation on our marriages, our parenting, our friendships, and our business? Promises would be kept. Integrity would reign. Each action taken would be considered within a long-term context. Inheritance would be defined in relational and spiritual terms. Responsibility and accountability would be ordinary. Relationships would be conducted with godly reverence and submission to His plan and objective, with focus on the greater work of the Kingdom. As the song says, "What a wonderful world it would be...."

As believers we have access to a perfect order of life and relationship that is alien to those who are without Christ. As Christians we first have the Holy Spirit to guide and convict us, to comfort and lead us, and to make intercession on our behalf. Building relationship with the Spirit allows us to be more finely attuned to the direction and leading of God.

Secondly we have the capacity to read and grasp the meaning of Scripture in a way that is not fully available to the average reader. God's Word is complete in its instruction on all matters of relational life. There is no situation and no crisis that God failed to address in Scripture. There is an answer for every relational dilemma.

Be aware that the Word of God often flies in direct opposition to the "wisdom" of conventional thought. To live in God's order we must be separate from the patterns and teachings of the world (**2 Cor 6:17**). Remember that perfect is a measure that is without compromise. If we desire His perfect order, His perfect peace, there is no substitute for His perfect instruction. True, we are not perfect in our current state, but our Father has provided for our every need. We encourage you to use no other reference when determining your path.

CHAPTER 12

CLOSING THOUGHTS

By now you know that the title of this book is somewhat over-stated. We are certain that in spite of our sincere effort, these Christian shrinks did not answer ALL your questions. However, we have laid a foundation for anyone who truly wants to know what God has to say about effective relational life. Clearly, God's Word is the one sufficient source of answers for all our questions. Thankfully, His Book fulfilled every promise.

Our problem as human beings comes not in the absence of information, but rather in our struggle to learn and submit to the truth of God's perfect order. This has much to do with the great proliferation of written material coming from psychology, sociology, philosophy, and others. We do not always like the information God gives us. Instead we are drawn to the weakened renditions of "truth" that flow from the mouth of man. Our effort here has hopefully redirected your focus away from the world and directly toward God and His unchanging Word.

It is a troubling time when television shrinks and Hollywood personalities are quoted with authority over the words of Jesus; when medication is taken daily while the Bible is read rarely; where the idolatry and worship of the self is glorified while Christ is ignored. This is exactly why any remedy that does not incorporate the very Word of God is doomed for failure. Everything of this world is temporal. It lasts only until the next idea, the next trend, or the next thrill. God's Word endures; it never changes; it never lies. Where in our market can you find such a guarantee?

Certainly God uses people as ministers, counselors, doctors, and aides at multiple levels. Often situations are simply too extreme or too painful to manage without professional help. In those circumstances the need for godly, Bible-centered counsel cannot be overemphasized.

There are many dynamics that require us to seek help. Sometimes we simply do not know where or how to find the biblical answers we need. There is, in short, a deficit of information. At other times the crisis itself is so upsetting that we are overwhelmed and confused about where to turn and how to proceed. Depression, anxiety, grief, and other issues can be so severe that we become practically incapacitated and frozen, unable to find solutions we would ordinarily employ.

When these or other impediments block your recovery, and when the nature of the crisis or pain endures beyond a reasonable time (a few weeks), help will be needed. Our final advice centers on this point as we seek to clarify when, and how, to find the right Christian shrink. Because of your pain, you may need the help of a pastor, relative, doctor, or friend in making this choice.

How do I select a "shrink"?

In spite of the referenced danger, good, biblical mental health providers do exist. They are identified by the markings noted above. When selecting a counselor, find out about his/her training, background and licensure, but also discern his/her orientation to answers. All counsel should be grounded in Scripture, as there is no other source of correct guidance. The first time a principle is given that violates God's Word, run, don't walk, out of the office!

When we are in crisis, discernment is more difficult. When selecting a counselor, do so with the help of a pastor or trusted Christian friend. But do not be afraid to ask some very important questions. Any Christian therapist worth consulting should be open to your inquiry into the following areas:

- *Education:* Find out what type of training the counselor has had: secular or seminary based. If trained in a secular program, determine how he/she augmented that education with biblical instruction. The best of all worlds would be a seminary-trained counselor with a strong biblical foundation, followed by training in counseling and therapeutic methods. In addition to his/her formal education, ask about any advanced or post-graduate training the counselor has had. For example, many pursue advanced certificates in marriage and family therapy beyond their graduate education.

- *Years of Experience:* Although there are exceptions, professionals with less than five years of experience should be avoided. There are some things that simply cannot be learned in training or internship. Experience completes the preparation and should be given a high priority.

- *Licensure:* Licensure gives assurance that the minimum standards for practice have been met and usually includes an examination and internship. However, licensure can give you no information about the counselor's competency in the Bible. Most states do not license the title "Christian Counselor." Instead you will find licensed psychologists, professional counselors, social workers, family therapists, etc. Licensure only means they are certified as having the typical secular training and experience. To know where they stand as Christians, you will have to ask some pointed questions.

- *Personal Testimony:* Every Christian should be ready to give an accounting of hope and a personal testimony of Christ. Your counselor should be no different. He/She should be able to discuss openly his/her relationship with Christ and the point in time when he/she accepted Him as personal Lord and Savior. Listen for evidence of a changed life and the fruit of salvation. Be careful of testimonies like: "I've always known God" or, "I was confirmed in the church when I was 12." It is impossible to have "always" known God personally, and confirmation is not necessarily the same as salvation.

- *Use of Scripture:* Ask the counselor directly if and how

he/she uses God's Word as part of the counseling. Vague or indirect answers should be a point of concern. Also determine if Bible study is part of the process. If the therapist says that Scripture is best explored with someone else, like your pastor, then he/she may not know God's Word well enough to give you wise counsel.

- *Use of Prayer:* Prayer must be a part of any healing process. Find out if the potential therapist prays with his/her clients as part of the therapy. Failure to pray in session is often a refusal to submit to God's authority in the counseling.

- *Authority of Scripture:* Determine if the counselor views Scripture as a literal, inerrant, authoritative truth, or as a "guideline" or "philosophy" of living. Biblical counseling should present the Word fully, in proper context, and as final in its authority and application. To use it as a "guideline" permits modification and digression that will not be in your best interest. Often when confronted with a difficult truth, these counselors will abandon Scripture and offer their "wisdom and experience" instead. You often hear these professionals say things like: "Yes, God hates divorce, but He doesn't want us to be unhappy either." When you have a counselor speaking for God rather than showing you His clear Word, as it is written, move on.

- *Church and Pastor:* It is important that the counselor is a part of a church fellowship and has a good reputation with his/her pastor. Most counselors should be happy to use their pastor as a reference. The issue of one's denomination may also be a factor. If the denominational affiliation of the counselor teaches a doctrine that differs from your own, or one that is liberal in philosophy, you should reconsider your selection. For example, some Mormon counselors refer to themselves as "Christian Counselors," yet their doctrine would differ significantly from the teachings that evangelical Christians know to be truth.

- *Specific Orientation:* Depending on your reasons for seeing a therapist, it may be important to ask his/her orientation about a specific issue. For example, if your teen-age son is struggling with questions about homosexuality, you will want to know what the counselor believes about the Bible's instruction in this area. When asking specific questions, you may be amazed with the answers given by professing, biblical counselors. One "Christian" counselor we know of actually told a client that the "new translations" of the Bible no longer forbid homosexuality and that "earlier versions" only did so due to "cultural" reasons.

While certain crises require quick, urgent decisions, pray that God will lead you to make the correct choice. The Holy Spirit will help you discern the truth about the need for counseling and the choosing of a professional.

Shouldn't my faith be enough?

A sense of failure is one of the primary roadblocks to seeking help. For the Christian, there is often the belief that the need for professional help reflects a failure in faith. While it is true that our faith can be challenged, even weakened at times, pursuing godly counsel does not indicate failure in our spiritual life.

In acquiring biblical instruction, we actually reaffirm our belief in God, His Word, and His authority. When we see a counselor or pastor who is known to utilize the wisdom and teachings of a sovereign God, we ratify our faith and advance our trust. If we give up on Scripture and turn to secular methods alone, then our faith can come under attack and we can be left vulnerable to the lie and deception of the world.

Often it is difficult to know the reason for a trial, especially when we are in the middle of it. Waiting on God's clarity and answer can be challenging. This is when the "world's wisdom" seems so appealing because it provides an "answer" right now. Sometimes emotional pain can be so great that any solution seems better than the ongoing state of confusion and inactivity.

Acting impulsively and emotionally with our pain does indeed demonstrate a failure in faith, especially when we know that the proposed action violates God's teaching. Good biblical counsel will not necessarily provide quick relief. Instead, the Word may reveal the need for perseverance, waiting, and trust. Remember, God is healing the spiritual first and the physical second.

Faith in man is a misplaced faith. Total trust and confidence are submitted states reserved for God alone. However, if the counselor is committed to God's Word as a guide for everything said, planned, and acted upon in therapy, then he/she has a foundation that respects God's authority and will. The foundation of Scripture is always worthy of our faith and hope.

Now faith is the substance of things hoped for, the evidence of things not seen. (Heb 11:1)

In our faith, we find hope that God will do all He promised to do through Christ Jesus, even when the outcome of that work is yet "not seen." As believers, we have faith that transcends all the confusion of the world, because the answers we seek are outside the world's format. Adherence to our faith means that we wait expectantly on the Lord to provide exactly what we need spiritually. A productive spiritual life is the center of all blessing **(3 John 1:2)**.

God has an order of physical health and prosperity that flows through the health of the soul. Thus, the health of our soul enriches us in all things. Our faithful pursuit of spiritual attention provides the proper framework for God to bless us physically and emotionally. How often did we see Jesus refer to "faith" as the source of one's healing?

And He said to her, "Daughter, your faith has made you well. Go in peace, and be healed of your affliction." (Mark 5:34)

Living out our faith does not require us to retreat and wait for God to act. In fact, we can have movement and activity that is productive *because* we have faith in God's providential hand. The danger only comes when we attempt action based on emotional or physical need alone, and fail to contemplate God's Word and direction. In this case, godly counsel can be a strong act of faith, provided it helps you stay grounded and focused in the spiritual elements of the crisis. By doing so, we are less vulnerable to take an incorrect action simply to find short-term relief.

In summary, faith is "enough." But faith and counsel are not necessarily in conflict. Any action taken to fortify the soul, grow the spirit, and strengthen obedience is by definition an act of faith. It is an action grounded in the firm assurances of God that He will meet our every need. Pray that God will define your path, and ask for discernment about, if and how, a counselor may be used along the way.

The TRUE source of wisdom...

"For the wisdom of this world is foolishness with God" (**1 Cor 3:19a**). Where are you getting your information?

This chapter has made clear this simple, biblical truth; unless God is at the center of any counsel you receive, you are receiving "foolishness." God can and does use individuals as vessels to deliver His Word. If He used a donkey to speak wisdom, He can even use a shrink! (**Num 22**). But whether you listen to a donkey or listen to a therapist, make certain he/she is listening to God!

Apart from a relationship with Christ, we are hopelessly lost. God's Word demonstrates that life change, growth, and harmony come through the spiritual realm first and then flow to the natural realm. This does not mean that with salvation comes an ongoing flood of blessings and prosperity. In fact, we are promised trial, temptation, and even persecution (**1 Pet 4:12-13, Heb 2:18, 2 Tim 3:12**).

The only real peace is the peace that comes through the assurance of eternity with God, honored through our gratitude for the gift and our obedience to His commands. Jesus said: **"Peace I leave with you, My peace I give to you; not as the world gives do I give to you. Let not your heart be troubled, neither let it be afraid"** (**John 14:27**).

The promise of the Christian life is the reduced dependence upon the peace "as the world gives." The world's peace is fleeting and carnal. It cannot nourish us and complete us; it can only sustain us minimally. We can work and strive for the world's version of fulfillment, only to be left hungry again and again. But Jesus told His disciples: **"I have food to eat of which you do not know"** **(John 4:32b).**

Reading this book may be part of your search for peace. Answers with substance are hard to find, but in God's Word there is the hope for life eternal. When accepted totally, Scripture alters our worldview, redefines our focus and priorities, and takes us out of the superficial, temporal order of the world. A redeemed life should be a changed life.

God sent His Son to save us from eternal death. Jesus did not come promising us a happy marriage, cooperative children, or a healthy emotional life. He came so that we might have "spiritual life" and hope beyond this earthly existence.

Be assured that life looks different when there is hope. Christians have marital problems, even divorces. Christians face infidelity, abuse, loss, and pain, just like everyone else. But for the believer, life is a vapor **(Jas 4:13-14)** and paradise **(Luke 23:42-43)** is the final destination. Paul wrote:

> **For I consider that the sufferings of this present time are not worthy to be compared with the glory which shall be revealed in us. (Rom 8:18)**

Do you know Jesus?

Before finishing this book, take a measurement of your hope. If you have never accepted Christ as your Lord and Savior, the peace of God's Word and instruction may seem difficult to grasp and even harder to follow. But upon your confession of sin and submission to our Lord and Savior Jesus Christ, you are freely given the same hope, the same orientation that exists in all true followers of Christ. At that point, Jesus sends His Holy Spirit so that you have a permanent Counselor and Guide that is forever a part of you.

> **"And I will pray the Father, and He will give you another Helper, that He may abide with you forever— the Spirit of truth, whom the world cannot receive,**

because it neither sees Him nor knows Him; but you know Him, for He dwells with you and will be in you." (John 14:16-17)

With the "Spirit of truth" living within us, God's Word is illuminated. All of the instructions, encouragements, promises, and plans of the written Scripture come to life within you. Suddenly, and more so as you grow, you are empowered with a truth that only believers can fully access; a Truth "whom the world cannot receive."

A similar dilemma exists for the believer who has abandoned his/her walk with the Savior and is feeding on the world's wisdom rather than holding to the truth available through a fully accessed relationship with Christ. Even as a born-again believer, sin and disobedience separates us from God **(Isa 59:1-2).** Take this opportunity to search your heart and evaluate your standing before Him. We do not lose our salvation, but we can create a gulf of division that injures our communication and unity with God. In our rebellious state, we can become hardened and worldly, just as if we never had a salvation experience.

Spend time in prayer before reading further. Ask God to reveal your needs. Ask Him to show you what you cannot see about your situation and about your spiritual condition. If you are in sin, ask His forgiveness. Let God begin to demonstrate His power through your pain and weakness.

And He said to me, 'My grace is sufficient for you, for My strength is made perfect in weakness.' Therefore most gladly I will rather boast in my infirmities, that the power of Christ may rest upon me. (2 Cor 12:9)

If you have never accepted Christ, begin your new life with this prayer:

*Father, I am a sinner (**Rom 3:23**) worthy of eternal death (**Rom 6:23**). I know that I am lost and cannot save myself. I must be born-again (**John 3:3**). I believe that Jesus Christ came to earth to save me and to give me eternal life (**John***

*14:6). I believe He died on the cross for me as the total, complete sacrifice for my sins and for the sins of the world. He died on my behalf, and then He rose again to life on the third day to conquer death and to reveal that He is the Messiah, the Savior. (**Rom 10:9-11**).*

*Jesus, please come into my heart and save me from my sin (**Rev. 3:20**). I submit myself to you and ask you to take control of my life, my family, my work, and all other areas of my existence. Thank You for loving me and saving me. I ask You to show me Your way and help me to walk in a manner that honors You (**2 Cor 5:15**). Thank you. In the precious name of Jesus, Amen."*

If you prayed to accept Christ, you have taken the first step toward the hope that comes through a redeemed existence. If you have recommitted your life, you also have reconfirmed your hope and faith. In either case, you should now seek out a Bible-teaching pastor for counsel and support in the initiation of your new walk. Do not rest on this prayer alone, as it is just the beginning. You need spiritual guidance, direction, and discipleship, and you need help to understand just what a Christian life should look like.

As you begin to study God's Word as a new believer, or as one who is newly rededicated, you will find many opportunities for change and struggle. But God is a transforming Creator who wants us to be close to Him, to learn His ways, and to adopt His manner. As you grow in your study of Scripture, God will faithfully raise you up into a mature, contributing member of His kingdom. God bless you as you discover the riches of His glory and the plans He has for you and for the relationships in your life.

Therefore, if anyone is in Christ, he is a new creation; old things have passed away; behold, all things have become new. (2 Cor 5:17)

NOTES

INTODUCTION
1. The United States Census Bureau website: www.census.gov
2. The Barna Research Group website: www.barna.org

CHAPTER 5
3. Elisabeth Kübler-Ross, *On Death and Dying* (New York, NY: Touchstone, 1969).

CHAPTER 6
4. James Dobson, *Love Must Be Tough: New Hope For Families In Crisis* (Dallas, TX: Word Publishing, 1983, 1996).

CHAPTER 9
5. Ed Silvoso, *That None Should Perish: How To Reach Entire Cities For Christ Through Prayer Evangelism* (Ventura, CA: Regal Books, 1994).

CPSIA information can be obtained at www.ICGtesting.com

233113LV00001B/99/A

9 781597 813853